Advance praise for *Oh She Glows for Dinner*

———

"Angela's newest cookbook might just be my favorite yet. Not only did she ingeniously think to include fun menus, but each and every recipe is also full of time-saving tips for a busy lifestyle. And, of course, each recipe is colorful, healthy, and delicious. I can't wait to cook from this book weekly. It's going to be a staple in my kitchen."

—TIEGHAN GERARD, bestselling author of *Half Baked Harvest Cookbook* and *Half Baked Harvest Super Simple*

"Earlier last year I completely removed eating meat from my diet. I had the hardest time finding food that kept me full because of the lack of protein. Angela's recipes in *Oh She Glows for Dinner* have so much flavor and are the perfect plant-based options! Sometimes cooking for a family of five can get exhausting, and these recipes are quick and easy and my entire family loves them! Our favorite is the Glow Green 30-Minute Pesto Pasta!"

—MOLLY SIMS, bestselling author of *The Everyday Supermodel* and *Everyday Chic*

"I have been such a big fan of Angela's cookbooks, which are filled with recipes that are extremely family-friendly, plant-based, and nutritious. I am so excited about Angela's new cookbook, *Oh She Glows for Dinner*. I love that she's integrated meal plans into this book, as I am always looking for help and suggestions for dinner. If you have kids, you know that dinnertime sneaks up on you fast! This book is so beautiful, and I can't wait to cook some of these drool-worthy recipes for my family."

—JILLIAN HARRIS, bestselling coauthor of *Fraiche Food, Full Hearts*

"*Oh She Glows for Dinner* proves just how simple, delicious, and joyful eating a plant-based diet can be. Filled with Angela's vibrant recipes and thoughtful tips, it will make you excited to cook dinner, even when life gets busy."

—JEANINE DONOFRIO, author of *Love and Lemons Every Day*

oh she glows
FOR DINNER

oh she glows
FOR DINNER

Nourishing Plant-Based Meals
to Keep You Glowing

ANGELA LIDDON

AVERY
an imprint of Penguin Random House
New York

AVERY

an imprint of Penguin Random House LLC
penguinrandomhouse.com

Copyright © 2020 by Glo Bakery Corporation
Food photography and styling by Angela Liddon.
Cover photo and photos on pages 6, 8, 14, 16, 17, 20, 43
by Sandy Nicholson.
Photo on page 5 by Sarah Martin.
Cover prop styling by Catherine Doherty.
Cover food styling by Claudia Bianchi.

Most Avery books are available at special quantity discounts for bulk purchase
for sales promotions, premiums, fund-raising, and educational needs.
Special books or book excerpts also can be created to fit specific needs.
For details, write SpecialMarkets@penguinrandomhouse.com.

Library of Congress Cataloging-in-Publication Data
Names: Liddon, Angela, author.
Title: Oh she glows for dinner : nourishing plant-based meals to keep you
glowing / Angela Liddon.
Description: New York : Avery, Penguin Random House LLC, 2020. |
Includes index.
Identifiers: LCCN 2020008785 (print) | LCCN 2020008786 (ebook) | ISBN
9780593083673 (hardcover) | ISBN 9780593083680 (ebook)
Subjects: LCSH: Vegetarian cooking. | LCGFT: Cookbooks.
Classification: LCC TX837 .L4784 2020 (print) | LCC TX837 (ebook) | DDC
641.5/636—dc23
LC record available at https://lccn.loc.gov/2020008785
LC ebook record available at https://lccn.loc.gov/2020008786
p.   cm.

Printed in China
3 5 7 9 10 8 6 4 2

Book design by Ashley Tucker

The recipes contained in this book are to be followed exactly as written.
The publisher and author are not responsible for your specific health or allergy
needs that may require medical supervision. The publisher and author are not
responsible for any adverse reactions to the recipes contained in this book.

For Arlo and Adriana: Seeing the world
through your eyes has been the most magical
experience of my life. As Arlo likes to say,
"I love you . . . you're my whole entire world!"

For my mom: I'm endlessly grateful for all the love,
encouragement, advice, and support you've given me
over the years. Thank you for being my biggest fan and
for being such a bright light in this world! I love you.

CONTENTS

ABOUT THIS BOOK

I recently read a quote and found it quite amusing and relatable: "Who knew the most taxing part of being an adult is figuring out what to cook for dinner every single night for the rest of your life until you die." After reading it and laughing, I thought, *Yes! I'm not alone*. I have a feeling this idea resonates with many of you, too, because one of my most frequent recipe requests is for more plant-based main course meals. I hear you, I really do. And that's exactly why I created this cookbook—to inspire you to cook these nourishing plant-based meals and to help solve your "What the heck is for dinner?" dilemma, as well as provide oodles of tips and time-saving tricks to make the process as streamlined as possible.

It's safe to say that life is getting busier and moving at a faster pace for all of us, and the time we have available to cook seems to be diminishing. In my own life, I've found that I really need to make cooking a priority and deliberately carve out time for it in my day, or else it just doesn't seem to happen. As much as I wish it would, a magic cooking fairy isn't going to appear in my kitchen and do all the work for me (that is, until I teach my kids how to cook?). As a busy parent, I know how hard it is to try to juggle it all, which is why I love to provide as many helpful tips and tricks in my cookbooks as I can. I want my recipes to work for you.

I write my recipes as if you were here in my kitchen with me and I was walking you through each one, showing you exactly how I cook them. That's why they are so rich with detail. I, along with my incredible group of recipe testers, test everything we can think of to help make these recipes practical for "real life." I share tips for things like how long a recipe can be stored in the fridge or freezer, directions for reheating (I'm on #teamleftovers, especially when their flavors get better the next day), how to make a recipe allergy-friendly, how to transform a dish's flavor profile, how to make a meal kid-friendly, what to serve with a dish to make it into a heartier meal, or whether something is a reliable "on the glow" packable lunch or travel option. I've also added a new section called "Up the Glow" in some recipes. Up the Glow appears whenever I have a fun way to amp up the recipe (whether it's adding ingredients for a flavor boost or a suggested recipe pairing). Because I like to keep my ingredient lists concise, these Up the Glow suggestions are not essential—rest assured that if you skip them, the recipe will still pack a flavorful punch!

For *Oh She Glows for Dinner*, I've created over one hundred practical, crowd-pleasing, and helpful recipes that are streamlined as much as possible without sacrificing one bit of flavor or texture. Inside, you'll find a nice mix of weeknight-friendly recipes, as well as weekend and special occasion recipes. I share my go-to speedy weeknight dinners like Fast Family Fajitas (page 53), Glow Green 30-Minute Pesto Pasta (page 55), Pumpkin Spice and Everything Nice Salad (page 191), and Weeknight Tex-Mex Quinoa with Cashew Sour Cream (page 75). And, when time is a bit more plentiful, try recipes like my Ultimate Creamy Salt-and-Vinegar Scalloped Potatoes (page 147), Cheesy Lentil Bolognese Casserole (page 59), and O Canada! Spiced Maple Cream Torte with Warm and Gooey Apple Pie Compote (page 233).

I also include meal plans and menus in this cookbook. I can't tell you how many times I've been asked by my readers, family, and friends for strategies to help speed through meal prep on the weekend or suggestions for which recipes to serve for a special occasion. I know from personal experience that the hardest part is often figuring out *which* recipes to combine or how to get started with meal prep. I knew that I had to create these helpful guides for this book. You'll find more info on my meal plans and menus on page 20!

It's not an understatement to say that the plant-based movement has been absolutely booming in recent years. When I started experimenting with and sharing vegan recipes in 2008, there wasn't nearly as much acceptance of this way of eating as there is today, and I never anticipated how much growth would happen in just a decade. In 2019 alone, the US saw a whopping 600 percent increase in the number of people identifying as vegan, and the UK saw a 350 percent increase, according to Ipsos and Globaldata.com. Canada is seeing a lot of growth, too, with about 10 percent of Canadians reporting in 2018 that they follow a vegetarian or vegan diet, and the updated Canada's Food Guide has shifted to a largely plant-based focus. It's been truly exciting to see such immense change happening due to so many passionate people and organizations all over the world. It seems like every single day I hear about a new athlete, celebrity, CEO, or eighty-two-year-old grandpa talking about how much a plant-based diet has changed their life for the better. I can often relate to these stories, because forgoing animal products and embracing a plant-based diet has been one of the best commitments I've made in my life. When I eat a balanced plant-based diet, it gives me loads of energy and a sense of well-being. Not only do I feel in tune with my body's needs by eating this way, but I feel so grateful to have the platform to share my journey and my favorite recipes with my family, friends, and this incredible community. It's one thing to try out this way of eating and enjoy the delicious food, but to see so many people around me get hooked, too, is just the best feeling, especially being able to help the environment, animals, and hopefully our health in the process. It's truly an exciting time for plant-based-curious home cooks and professional chefs alike. Plant-based cooking is endlessly inspiring once you really dig in and start experimenting with ingredients and flavors.

When I first tried plant-based eating over a decade ago, I started at ground zero—I had no cooking experience to speak of (unless being a pro at baking a boxed cake mix counts?) and had to teach myself all the things I now do with ease in the kitchen. I'm so pleased I didn't give up, and glad I gave those veggies a fighting chance! After years of daily practice creating and writing recipes, playing with plant-based ingredients and flavors, and learning as much as I could, cooking now feels downright intuitive to me (well, most days). Now I have so much confidence when I create dishes on a whim . . . and I can tell you that this culinary passion has been one of the biggest surprises of my life (if not *the* biggest). If you aren't there yet, please don't get discouraged. I didn't even know how to roast a pan of veggies when I started out. I truly started from scratch. If you are new to plant-based eating, take it slowly if you need to, one day at a time. Try one or two new *Oh She Glows* dishes a week (a lazy weekend afternoon when you aren't in a hurry is a great time to try out a new dish!) and keep it simple until your confidence grows. You will get there! I want to make this journey as delicious and fun as possible for you.

Oh She Glows for Dinner is going to provide you with tools, tips, and tricks to help you get more plant-based meals on the table, and in the process, you'll hopefully fall in love with so many vibrant, balanced, and downright irresistible recipes. I can't even tell you how excited I am about this collection of recipes, which has been years in the making—it's the true culmination of everything I've learned through creating *Oh She Glows* over the past decade.

Here is a sneak peek of all the exciting, delicious, and helpful things you'll find inside this cookbook.

More savory mains, sides, soups, salads, and sauces, pretty please!

As I mentioned earlier, I've been asked by you, my dear readers, for even more main course recipes, so that's exactly what I've given you in this cookbook. Savory dishes are the star. These are the recipes you're going to want to make for weeknight dinners, portable "on the glow" lunches, and weekend and special occasion meals. There are oodles of crave-worthy entrées, mix-and-match sides, hearty soups and salads, special occasion dishes (with make-ahead tips), and tons of unique sauces, pestos, dips, "parmesans," and dressings that will transform basic ingredients into flavor-packed, fresh meals. And, of course, I also included a tempting Treats and Drinks chapter because I couldn't keep my new fave sweets from you. Who doesn't like a little something sweet after a nice meal?

It's all about flavor

If I could choose just one word to describe my newest collection of plant-based, whole-food recipes, it would be *flavor*. Oh yeah! I've worked tirelessly to ensure that this cookbook has *layers upon layers* of different flavors and textures, all working in unison to build seriously mouth-watering plant-based dishes. These recipes have an exceptional balance of the sweet, salty, acidic, and umami flavors that our taste buds are all consciously (or subconsciously) looking for when we bite into food. The dishes are bold, vibrant, and bursting with flavors and textures. These are the kinds of recipes that you won't be able to stop talking about! We sure haven't . . .

Glow Getters: Meal Planning and Prep

Glow Getters: Meal Planning and Prep provides four weeks of meal plans to help you prepare recipes in advance without taking up your whole weekend. They were created with busy people and families in mind and can be prepped in 1 hour to 1 hour 30 minutes. How's that for doable? Realistic, not overwhelming . . . that's what I'm all about. I can't wait to hear which plans are your favorites!

Menus to Get Your Glow On

I love hosting family and friends and sharing my favorite recipes, so I created twelve delicious menus for popular occasions for this book. This section contains a variety of menus (each with at least one gluten-free, nut-free, and make-ahead option) for special occasions and holidays like Mother's Day, Holiday Get-Togethers, Girls' Night, Oh She Glows Cookbook Club, Date Night In, and more. Having preplanned menus has saved me time (it's so nice to take the guesswork out of meal planning) and sanity, and I hope you'll find them to be a great reference tool.

Clear and detailed whole-food recipes packed with pro tips

I know firsthand that it's not much fun when a recipe is vague and poorly written, or when it simply doesn't turn out. I love to provide you with as much information as I can because I know a well-written recipe makes all the difference. I prefer to be a bit "wordy" in my directions to ensure that I fully explain my process to you and walk you through the recipe, rather than try to create recipes with the world's shortest word count. So please don't get discouraged if some directions appear a bit long—that's simply me giving you as much helpful info as I can to ensure you have success and really get a feel for the recipe like I have. I've also included more personal tips and tricks in the "Tips for Cooking" section of the Oh She Glows Kitchen chapter. You'll find everything there from the basics (how to read a recipe correctly) to the OSG-specific (how to understand my custom allergy and preparation labels, how I measure flour, and how I have calculated the timing in the recipes for you). To help you customize your eating for your own needs, I have also included a section called Helpful Recipe Lists (page 340), where you can search for recipes by category, including by allergy label. It's a quick, at-your-fingertips guide to which recipes in the book are gluten- and/or nut-free, freezer- and/or kid-friendly, and "on the glow" portable! Because of that handy list, I can tell you that there are more than seventy-five gluten-free or gluten-free-option recipes (not including sauces and dressings) in this cookbook! Not too shabby!

Storage

Whenever I can, I like to make recipes and freeze them for future meals, so in this book I've included handy storage, freezing, and reheating instructions to save you time and guesswork.

MY STORY

The support and encouragement that I've had for all things *Oh She Glows* has been the most incredible journey—one I never expected in a million years and didn't know was even a possibility for my life. I used to think that aligning one's passion with a career and having success with it only happened to the special unicorns of the world . . . not to people like me.

Since I was very young, I've battled low self-esteem. The reasons for it are beyond the scope of this book, but I've fought internal battles of disordered eating, anxiety, and depression over the years; at times, it felt like I'd never make progress. I thought if I tried to make everything perfect—including myself—I'd have a better chance of overcoming my relentless negative inner dialogue. But chasing perfectionism is one of the scariest journeys you can be on because nothing is ever good enough. For a long time, I really didn't know if I would find my true purpose in this world.

So no, I certainly did not expect the community that would emerge through the creation of *Oh She Glows*, the success of my blog, two bestselling cookbooks, and an award-winning recipe app. I definitely didn't anticipate being able to inspire others to make positive changes in their lives, and to be supported in such a way that has changed my entire life. When I think about how grateful I am for this community's support, I can't help but feel emotional. I can't thank you, my readers, enough for believing in me. Your encouragement has been so motivating, and it's fueled me to keep learning, growing, and pushing myself—not just in the culinary world but on a personal level, too. It's been refreshing to be able to channel my struggles into something so positive.

Parenthood and Finding Inspiration

After taking a break from book writing (and welcoming our second baby, Arlo!), I knew the timing would have to be right if I was going to dive into another cookbook. As a mom of two, I feel like I've been in "survival mode" ever since we became parents. In interviews,

I'm often asked to share my secrets for finding balance as a busy mom and business owner. *Oh shoot, they think I have things in balance!!!* I always think, highly amused. Meanwhile, I'm over here feeling like *I'm* the one needing secrets! As I always share, the honest truth is that I haven't found the perfect balance. Good grief, not even close. Pieces of my business, relationships, well-being, and mental and physical health have all suffered to some degree at one time or another. There were phases when some of those things felt like they wouldn't ever recover. Heck, there are many parts of my life that are *still* highly out of balance (and probably always will be). That's just my reality. Some months have been easier than others, but at times, I feel like this elusive "balance" is a four-letter word. What I prefer to call *unbalanced acceptance* has been much easier to embrace than trying to force all areas of my life to be in sync. It's been a refreshing concept, and I'm learning to trust the process, as chaotic as it can be at times.

Despite the unpredictability of my life as a parent, I've felt more gratitude and love than I knew possible in this new chapter of my life. It's cliché but true that the hardest things in life are the most rewarding. I may not know whether I'm coming or going most days or what my five- or ten-year plan is, but I have a lot of love in my life, and that's the most important thing. The rest will work out on its own! I hope that if any of you reading this are struggling with a life stage that feels chaotic or confusing, you'll give yourself patience, understanding, love, and permission to take time for the pieces of the puzzle to fit together. Know that it will work out in the end, even if you can't see it yet.

During my early days of motherhood, I assumed I'd be able to avoid picky eaters if I just gave the little ankle biters enough variety when they were babies and toddlers. I can't even say that without laughing now, about six years into parenting, because sometimes, no matter how hard you try, kids are just kids. Indeed, *I was wrong* (I've found myself saying that a lot during my parenthood journey) about that whole variety thing because despite my best efforts, both of my kids have gone through picky phases. I would love to be able to report that we have picture-perfect meals every night and my kids devour everything I make for them, but that would be a lie (and you might hate me, anyway). If I ever figure it all out, you'll be the first to know!

Now that Adriana (also known as "Annie") and Arlo are getting a bit more adventurous with food (depending on the hour, of course), it's been fun to share these new meals with the fam and let them discover new flavors, cuisines, and textures. I even assigned the kids each a role as an Official Cookbook Recipe Tester, to help them feel included and excited. Sometimes, you have to get creative . . .

One day when my youngest, Arlo, was about a year old, I was hit with a wave of inspiration for this cookbook. I could not get my ideas down fast enough. I was inspired to write, create, photograph, and share. The creative process tends to come in waves, and I've learned over the years that the periods when I feel burnt out are fleeting, even though they can be so distressing to go through when you work in a creative field. I've also learned that these uninspired times are a *necessary* part of the process for growth and recharging your energy. If you are stuck in a phase of life in which you feel unmotivated or just blah, trust that your creativity and your joic de vivrc will come back! They really will, and when they do—oh, watch out, world—you're a force to be reckoned with.

My Journey to Health: Postpartum

As a new parent, your focus tends to be entirely on the baby's well-being, for obvious reasons (gotta keep that tiny human alive!!), but it can also mean that many of your own health issues go overlooked. I fell into the trap of not paying much attention to my own health postpartum—I simply trudged ahead each day, chalking up most health issues to being sleep deprived. Talking about how much we were up in the night and how much coffee we'd plan on drinking that day became a bit of a running joke with my fellow mom friends. I let my health concerns linger way too long without trying to find answers.

Since when is it acceptable to feel this awful? I asked myself one day, feeling like a mere shadow of my former self. I was experiencing cyclical allergic reactions, a huge uptick in anxiety (to the point where some days, I didn't want to leave the house), low mood, inflammation, food sensitivities galore, foggy thinking, and a whole host of other symptoms. Once I finally made the time to dive deeper with my health professionals, I was quite surprised to find out how much a woman's health can change after she's had kids. After doing a monthlong in-depth hormone test, not only did I find out that my hormones were hugely imbalanced (some of my hormones were nearly off the charts . . . good grief, no wonder I felt bad), but my thyroid levels and adrenals were imbalanced, too. Despite feeling overwhelmed by how many things were out of sync, I felt empowered with the information and determined to feel like myself again. Finally, with a great deal of trial and error, I was able to address the issues and start to feel better. And, oh boy, did it ever take a long time to start feeling better.

The silver lining is that my postpartum health challenges have taught me invaluable lessons. One big lesson is that progress isn't always linear, and that getting to the bottom of things can require a huge amount of persistence, patience, and self-compassion. It's taught me to be patient, take care of myself, value my health even more than I ever have, ask questions, and never give up when trying to find a solution. I had to be my own advocate and trust myself when something felt very off. More than ever, I've felt so much gratitude for having access to healthcare, which, unfortunately, many people do not.

My postpartum health challenges have also reminded me just how important it is to make time for a nourishing plant-based diet. I really feel my best when I take the time to ensure that my meals have enough protein, healthy fats, vegetables, fruit, whole grains, and an array of vitamins and minerals. From experience, I know that a plant-based diet works well for me, but, like anything in life, it benefits from some planning and preparation. When I was in the thick of new motherhood with two little ones, while also juggling my business, I started to rely on processed plant-based foods way too much. I have nothing against store-bought energy bars, popcorn, and crackers, but when they start to take the place of nourishing home-cooked meals, I simply don't get all the nutrients I need. Two pregnancies and extended breastfeeding back-to-back, combined with not making time for consistent well-rounded meals, eventually took a huge toll on me. It was a vicious cycle—I was run down, and due to feeling run down, I wasn't eating very healthy or balanced, and that only made me feel worse. Repeat, repeat, repeat. I even stopped taking my vitamins once I was finished nursing (why, I'm not sure . . . this plant-based mama still needs vitamins!), and I simply ran on autopilot for too long.

There is always a bright side, though: The various health issues I went through were impossible to ignore and served as a reminder that I'm not invincible. I needed a huge flashing "STOP" sign to force me to pause and take time for myself and my health, and to try to off-load some things from my plate so I could heal myself and get my glow back. And that's exactly what I did (albeit slowly and stubbornly . . . hey, I'm a Taurus, after all). Creating this cookbook gave me even more inspiration to get myself back on a healthier path; to create balanced plant-based recipes full of protein, healthy fats, and nutrients; to make time for nutritious meals as much as possible; and to remind myself just how good my family and I feel when we eat well. The proof is in the vegan pudding. We can all get offtrack in life—you might have "off" months (or years), but if you can turn it into a learning experience, you are well on your way to coming out stronger than you were before.

I have no doubt that there are still many challenges ahead, but the past few years have taught me an invaluable lesson: I must make time for my own health on a consistent basis (I have to walk the walk), I must carve out time each day for healthy, balanced, plant-based meals (or they just won't happen!), and I need to remember to navigate life's ups and downs with self-compassion and patience. I hope sharing my story inspires you to make time for your own needs, to make time in your day to nourish your body with these feel-good meals, and, if you are struggling, lets you know you aren't alone in this. My readers have always lifted me up and helped me get my glow back whenever I needed it, and I will never stop trying to repay the favor. I truly hope these recipes help you glow from the inside out, and give you time to pause during life's busy seasons.

Keep on glowing,

Angela
xo

GLOW GETTERS:
MEAL PLANNING AND PREP

Over the years, I've been asked countless times to create meal plans, and I knew I wanted to include some in this cookbook. I've attempted ambitious three-hour meal preps in the past, but they felt overwhelming and impossible to squeeze into our busy schedule. Often, they made so much food that we had a hard time using it all up before it spoiled.

As a solution to my meal-planning dilemma, I came up with these user-friendly, advance-prep plans. My Glow Getter plans take only 60 to 90 minutes (working at a brisk pace!), plus a little cleanup time (10 to 20 minutes) tacked on at the end of each plan. (Note that the total times don't account for soaking nuts or seeds, so it helps to check ahead for those.) Each plan includes three hearty recipes to simplify and reduce meal prep during your busy week. Plans 2 and 3 are great ones to start with if you are a beginner cook because they don't involve recipes that are cooked simultaneously and, as a result, are less intense. Since we are storing these recipes in the fridge, it helps to start with very fresh veggies to ensure that the recipes store for as long as possible.

I encourage you to read the meal plan in full (and check out each recipe in the plan) ahead of time to understand the prep that is involved. It also helps to make the individual recipes on their own first to get a feel for them before making them in the plans. Once you make the plans a few times, they'll go a bit faster as you become more familiar with them. Real talk: The kitchen tends to be a hot mess by the end of meal prep, but keep in mind you'll be saving on cleanup time later in the week so it's still a big win, if you ask me!

It helps to try to gather many of your ingredients, containers, and tools before beginning—this helps with flow, and it means you won't be spending five minutes looking for a spice or peeler when you're in the middle of a recipe (or is that just me?). If you have a dishwasher, it's helpful to have it empty (and ready to be filled!) before you begin the meal plan. I'll let you know at the top of each plan a lot of the equipment you'll be using (note that the equipment sections do not list every single thing, such as everyday items like measuring cups or small bowls). It's also helpful to label the containers with the recipe names so you don't forget what's inside as well as the date you made it. I use green painter's tape for labeling my containers since it's effortless to remove! Be sure to see my Kitchen Tools and Appliances chapter (page 332) for my most-used items, including the handy glass containers I use to store everything.

Many of the recipes in these plans are only partially prepped (such as chopping and storing raw veggies and making a sauce) and are then refrigerated until ready to cook and serve. If a recipe is partially prepped, there will be a tip at the bottom of that meal plan letting you know how long the recipe can be stored before cooking and serving (for example, the raw florets in my Creamy Buffalo Cauli Tacos [page 67] can be refrigerated for up to 3 days before you cook and complete the recipe). It's helpful to make a few notes in your calendar indicating when you plan to serve the recipes. Some recipes in these plans, like my Smoky Black Bean and Brown Rice Veggie Burgers (page 131), are cooked *in full* during the meal prep. If the recipe is cooked in full during the meal plan, please refer to that recipe's Storage tip (found at the end of the directions) for how long it can be stored in the fridge. At the end of each plan, I'll suggest two additional weeknight-friendly recipes, in case you're looking for more inspiration later in the week and are motivated to tack on a couple more recipes!

Here's a quick guide to the container sizes I use in the plans that follow: large: 7 to 8 cups (1.75 to 2 L), medium: 3 cups (750 mL), small: 1 cup (250 mL). However, by all means, use whatever containers you have on hand. Lastly, if you'd like to download and print the meal plan instructions (it's so handy to have them printed on the counter while you prep), please visit ohsheglows.com/ohsheglowsfordinner to access them.

Glow Getter Meal Plan I

Undercover Roasted Veggie Tomato Pasta (page 93)
Instant Pot Potato and Cauliflower Red Thai Curry (with Stovetop Option!) (page 65)
Mediterranean Smashed Chickpea Salad with Tzatziki Aioli (page 119)

Total time: 1 hour 10 minutes, plus cleanup

MAIN EQUIPMENT:
- extra-large rimmed baking sheet
- chef's knife/paring knife/cutting board/peeler
- Instant Pot or large pot
- citrus juicer/reamer
- box grater
- colander
- large bowl
- potato masher
- high-speed blender
- airtight storage containers (3 large)

i. Undercover Roasted Veggie Tomato Pasta

- Complete steps 1 through 4. While the veggies are roasting, move on to the next recipe.

- Once the veggies are roasted, proceed with step 6, and refrigerate the sauce in a large airtight container.

- When you are ready to reheat the sauce and serve with pasta, follow steps 5 and 7.

ii. Instant Pot Potato and Cauliflower Red Thai Curry (with Stovetop Option!)

- Prepare and cook the curry in full. Chop the greens and place in a medium bowl. Set aside to have on hand when the curry is finished cooking. While the curry cooks, move on to the next recipe. After cooking, allow the curry to cool on the counter, and refrigerate in a large airtight container.

iii. Mediterranean Smashed Chickpea Salad with Tzatziki Aioli

- Prepare the recipe up to step 3. Refrigerate in a large container.

- When you are ready to serve, proceed with step 4.

TIPS:

- Instant Pot Potato and Cauliflower Red Thai Curry (with Stovetop Option!): If you are cooking the stovetop version, be sure to check on it and give it a stir every 5 minutes or so during the cooking process. If using an Instant Pot, remember to listen for the beep that signals the curry is finished cooking, and do a quick release so it doesn't overcook.

- Be sure to check the Storage tip on the recipe pages for storage and reheating instructions.

- Looking for a couple more dinner options for the week? Try my Italian One-Pot Buttery Tomato, White Beans, and Farro (page 96) and Pumpkin Spice and Everything Nice Salad (page 191) as other weeknight options.

Glow Getter Meal Plan 2

Sloppy Glows (page 90)
School Night Tofu Scramble (page 78)
with Roasted Red Pepper and Walnut Dip (page 298)
Green Goddess Gazpacho (page 219)

Total time: 1 hour, plus cleanup

MAIN EQUIPMENT:

○ chef's knife/paring knife/cutting board

○ large skillet or pot

○ large sieve

○ citrus juicer/reamer

○ high-speed blender

○ airtight storage containers
   (2 large, 2 medium)

i. Sloppy Glows

○ Follow steps 3 (see Tip below) through 5 and step 7. Refrigerate the cooled lentil mixture in a medium airtight container. Clean the skillet or pot.

○ For the Cashew Sour Cream (if using): Soak the cashews overnight or for 1 hour in boiling water. When soaking is complete, drain and rinse. Refrigerate the soaked and drained nuts in a medium airtight container.

○ When you are ready to reheat and serve the Sloppy Glows, proceed with steps 1 and 2, and steps 6 and 8 (reheating the lentil mixture on the stovetop while the buns toast) through to completion.

ii. School Night Tofu Scramble with Roasted Red Pepper and Walnut Dip

○ Follow steps 2 through 5, and remove from heat. Refrigerate the cooled tofu scramble in a large airtight container.

○ When you are ready to reheat and serve the tofu scramble, prepare the Roasted Red Pepper and Walnut Dip. Follow the reheating instructions found in the Storage tip, and proceed with step 6.

iii. Green Goddess Gazpacho

○ Make the gazpacho in full. Refrigerate in a large airtight container or jar.

TIPS:

• Sloppy Glows: Step 2 says to slice half of the onion into rounds for serving. We find this is best done fresh, right before serving, so the onion slices don't dry out. The soaked and drained cashews can be refrigerated for up to 4 days before making the Cashew Sour Cream.

• Green Goddess Gazpacho: If the weather is cold where you are, feel free to swap the gazpacho for a cooked soup, stew, or curry.

• Be sure to check the Storage tip on the recipe pages for storage and reheating instructions.

• To round out your week, try making my Mega Crunch Sun-Dried Tomato–Pepita Taco Salad (page 204) and Bruschetta Veggie Burgers (page 49) as other weeknight options.

Glow Getter Meal Plan 3

Fast Family Fajitas (page 53)

Crispy Potato Stacks (page 87) with Pretty Parsley-Cilantro Pepita Pesto (page 275)

Rebellious Battered Broc-Cauli Burgers (page 113) with Sriracha Aioli (page 289)

Total time: 60 minutes, plus cleanup

MAIN EQUIPMENT:

o high-speed blender or food processor

o chef's knife/paring knife/cutting board

o citrus juicer/reamer

o food processor

o silicone ice cube tray (optional)

o ruler and pencil (optional)

o Microplane (optional)

o airtight storage containers
(2 large, 2 medium, 1 or 2 small)

i. Fast Family Fajitas

o For the Cashew Sour Cream: Soak the cashews overnight or for 1 hour in boiling water. Prepare the Cashew Sour Cream in full, as directed. Alternatively, prepare the 24/7 Avocado-Cilantro Sauce, and rinse out the food processor. Refrigerate the cream or sauce in a medium airtight container.

o Slice the 4 cups (510 g) of fajita veggies and refrigerate the raw sliced veggies in a large airtight container. *Do not* mince the cilantro, as it's best prepared right before serving.

o Prepare the Tex-Mex Flavor Bombs, and refrigerate the mixture in a small airtight container, or freeze in a silicone ice cube tray. Clean the food processor.

o When you are ready to cook and serve the fajitas, proceed with step 2 of the fajita recipe, following it through to completion. (Don't forget to mince the cilantro at this point, too!)

ii. Crispy Potato Stacks with Pretty Parsley-Cilantro Pepita Pesto

○ Prepare the Pretty Parsley-Cilantro Pepita Pesto and refrigerate it in a small airtight container.

○ When you are ready to cook and serve this recipe, let the pesto sit on the counter to come to room temperature while you prep and roast the potatoes. Proceed with step 1 and follow the recipe through to completion.

iii. Rebellious Battered Broc-Cauli Burgers with Sriracha Aioli

○ As detailed in step 3: Chop the broccoli and cauliflower into florets. Refrigerate in a large zip-top bag or airtight container.

○ Make the Sriracha Aioli (directly in a small airtight container), secure the lid, and refrigerate.

○ When you are ready to cook and serve the burgers, let the florets come to room temperature, then proceed with steps 1, 2, and 4 through to completion.

TIPS:

• Fast Family Fajitas: The raw sliced fajita veggies can be stored up to 4 days before you cook and serve the fajitas.

• Crispy Potato Stacks with Pretty Parsley-Cilantro Pepita Pesto: You can change up the pesto by swapping in my Lemony Dill Protein Pesto (page 297), Perfect Basil Pesto (page 294), or Boom! Broccoli Pesto (page 276). After storing, I like to refresh the flavors of the pesto with a squeeze of lemon, if needed.

• Rebellious Battered Broc-Cauli Burgers with Sriracha Aioli: The raw broccoli and cauliflower florets and Sriracha Aioli can be refrigerated up to 3 days before you cook and serve the recipes.

• Be sure to check the Storage tip on the recipe pages for storage and reheating instructions.

• Do you have leftover broccoli and cauliflower to use up? Consider making my Cauliflower "Potato" Salad (page 203) or Charred Broccoli Quinoa Salad with Apple Honey–Dijon Dressing (page 187).

• Looking for a couple more dinner options for the week? Why not make my Glow-rious Greek Pasta with Oregano, Basil, and Lemon Zest Parmesan (page 193) and Weeknight Tex-Mex Quinoa with Cashew Sour Cream (page 75) to round out the week?

Glow Getter Meal Plan 4

Glow Green 30-Minute Pesto Pasta (page 55)
Smoky Black Bean and Brown Rice Veggie Burgers (page 131)
Creamy Buffalo Cauli Tacos (page 67)

Total time: 1 hour 30 minutes (includes cleanup)

MAIN EQUIPMENT:
- medium pot
- chef's knife/cutting board
- citrus juicer/reamer
- food processor
- extra-large rimmed baking sheet
- large skillet
- large sieve
- large mixing bowl
- airtight storage containers
  (3 large, 4 medium, 1 small)

i. Glow Green 30-Minute Pesto Pasta

- Before starting the pesto pasta, cook the rice that's called for in the burger recipe below. While the rice is cooking, proceed with the pasta recipe.

- Slice or chop the mushrooms, zucchini, and broccoli. Refrigerate in 1 large and 1 medium airtight container.

- Prepare the double batch of Pretty Parsley-Cilantro Pepita Pesto. Refrigerate in 1 medium airtight container. Clean the food processor.

- When you are ready to cook and serve the pasta, place the pesto on the counter. Follow step 1 through to completion.

ii. Smoky Black Bean and Brown Rice Veggie Burgers

- Prepare the veggie burgers through step 10. While the burgers are cooking, move on to the next recipe. Refrigerate the cooled patties in 1 large airtight container and the OSG House Sauce in 1 small airtight container.

- When you are ready to reheat and serve the burgers, follow the directions for reheating found in the recipe's Storage tip.

iii. Creamy Buffalo Cauli Tacos

O In step 4, chop the cauliflower as directed but do not mix in the oil. Refrigerate the raw florets in 1 large airtight container.

O Soak the cashews for the Creamy Buffalo Sauce. Also, soak the cashews for the Cashew Sour Cream (or soak the sunflower seeds for the Creamy Cashew or Sunflower Aioli). For both recipes, you can do the 1-hour quick soak in boiling water, or you can soak overnight—your call! After soaking, drain, rinse, and refrigerate separately in 2 medium airtight containers.

O When you are ready to cook and serve the tacos, place the refrigerated cauliflower florets on the counter and proceed with step 2, following the recipe through to completion. Don't forget to mix the cauliflower florets with the 2 tablespoons oil before adding the Buffalo sauce.

TIPS:

• Glow Green 30-Minute Pesto Pasta: The raw sliced or chopped veggies and pesto can be refrigerated for up to 2 days before cooking and serving the recipes. The pesto flavors tend to dilute a bit while storing, so you may need a bit more lemon juice than called for in step 5 of the Glow Green 30-Minute Pesto Pasta recipe.

• Creamy Buffalo Cauli Tacos: The raw cauliflower florets and soaked and drained cashews/seeds can be refrigerated for up to 3 days before cooking and serving the recipes.

• Be sure to check the Storage tip on the recipe pages for storage and reheating instructions.

• This plan's timing includes cleanup while the other meal plans do not. This is because at the end of this meal plan there is downtime while you are waiting for the burgers to finish cooking. You can clean up during this downtime, and wrap up the whole shebang (including cleanup completion) around the 1 hour 30 minute mark.

• To round out your week, try making my Cozy Butternut Squash, Sweet Potato, and Red Lentil Stew (page 215) and Dreamy Peanut Butter Crunch Veggie Noodle Bowls (page 127).

MENUS
TO GET YOUR
GLOW ON

D oes planning a menu and finding dishes that complement one another leave you scratching your head? I know it was that way for me! I've given myself the lofty task of creating a handful of delectable menus for you, my dear readers. *wipes sweat bead from forehead* Don't worry, we've got this!

Putting together menus is challenging because you want to enjoy the fruits of your labor without spending hours upon hours in the kitchen, and, more important, you want *others* to love the thoughtful meal you put together. And by *love*, I mean you want your guests to rave about the meal to you and others . . . "I could not stop eating the delicious food! You're going to have to roll me out the door!" . . . Or is that just me?

With these goals in mind, I've created a variety of menus that will hopefully help you relax a bit in the menu-planning department, lend a helping hand with some tips and tricks, and inspire you to get your glow on all year round. Each menu features *at least* one make ahead–friendly recipe (or is entirely make ahead–friendly). I'm all about saving you (okay, okay, and myself, too!) time and sanity. Oh, and it probably goes without saying, you certainly don't need to make everything from a single menu. Often, I will suggest more ideas than necessary just to make sure you have enough inspiration. Don't forget to snap pictures if you make any of the menus or dishes below and tag them #OhSheGlowsforDinner on social media so I can see them!

Girls' Night

Cozying up with a group of my gals on a frigid winter night is a great way to boost our spirits! We all love Mexican-inspired dishes, so I centered this menu around all of those wonderful flavors. It's always fun to build our own fajitas, catch up, and stuff our faces!

- Fast Family Fajitas (page 53)
- Cilantro-Speckled Green Rice and Avocado Stack (page 207) or Weeknight Tex-Mex Quinoa with Cashew Sour Cream (page 75)
- Zesty Lime and Cayenne Roasted Chickpea and Sweet Potato Salad (page 199)
- Soothing Mint and Ginger Green Tea (page 267)

On the Glow Meal

Any recipe marked as *on the glow* makes a lovely portable meal, but this combo is one of my faves . . . a roasted, protein-packed salad; a zippy, warming soup; a refreshing thermos-ready coconut latte; and a lightly sweet, chewy energy square that's the perfect ending. Take a few quiet minutes away from your workspace and restore your glow with this perfect, portable lunch.

- Charred Broccoli Quinoa Salad with Apple Honey–Dijon Dressing (page 187)
- Glowing Spiced Lentil Soup (page 226)
- Always Hangry PB&J Protein Snacking Bites (page 258)
- Solid Gold Pumpkin Pie Spice Coconut Latte (page 264)

I love to see what you're making!
Share pictures on social media using the hashtags
#OhSheGlowsforDinner and #OhSheGlowsCookbookClub

Oh She Glows Cookbook Club Night

Hosting an Oh She Glows cookbook night? *Wheee*, can I come? It's the perfect opportunity for friends to get together, swap stories and tips, share the recipes, and find new faves! Try to have each member bring a dish, potluck style, for fuss-free hosting.

- Cheesy Lentil Bolognese Casserole (page 59) with Italian Herb Parmesan (page 301)
- Apple Honey–Sriracha Roasted Rainbow Carrots with Cashew Cream (page 141)
- Balsamic Roasted Root Vegetable Medley with Thyme and Cayenne (page 139)
- Charred Broccoli Quinoa Salad with Apple Honey–Dijon Dressing (page 187) or Apple Honey–Dijon Mixed Greens (see Tip, page 285)
- Glow-rious Greek Pasta with Oregano, Basil, and Lemon Zest Parmesan (page 193) with Authentic-Tasting Vegan Feta Cheese (page 327)
- O Canada! Spiced Maple Cream Torte with Warm and Gooey Apple Pie Compote (page 233)

OSG Cookbook Club Tips: I'd suggest assigning the host or hostess the Cheesy Lentil Bolognese Casserole and the Apple Honey–Sriracha Roasted Rainbow Carrots with Cashew Cream because they are easiest to make at home and the casserole can be made a couple of days ahead of time, so there is little work the day of. Other guests can each bring one of the remaining dishes listed (feel free to change up my suggestions!). Since oven space will be tight with the casserole and carrots roasting, it helps if a guest roasts the root vegetables at their own home, cools them on the pan, and then transports them in a Dutch oven. This makes it easy to reheat the root veggies, uncovered, on the stovetop (over medium-low heat for about 15 minutes, stirring occasionally) before serving. Since the vegan feta cheese can soften on warm food, it helps to keep it separate and refrigerated until just before serving. Don't forget to store the O Canada! Spiced Maple Cream Torte in the fridge upon arrival. If someone is making the Charred Broccoli Quinoa Salad, pomegranate arils lend a beautiful pop of color on the dish and look lovely when presenting. Of course, feel free to change up this menu as you wish and do what works for you, swapping in your favorite dishes from the book. Have fun!

Holiday Get-Togethers

I used to stress a lot when hosting a big family meal—for weeks beforehand, I'd be anxious about which dishes complemented one another and how to plan it so everything was finished cooking at the same time. Finally, one year before hosting a big Easter lunch, I decided to come up with a holiday menu that I could use as a "template" for future holidays. I worked for a couple of weeks to plan and test which recipes could be made in advance and which dishes would please the most amount of people. Well, the work was worth it because I barely had to lift a finger come Easter lunch (okay, maybe just a little bit!) and I got to enjoy the meal for fourteen just as much as everyone else. Since I did prep in the days leading up to the meal, all I had to do on the big day was pop some things in the oven and do some light assembly. It felt so good. Below are my tried-and-true holiday meal recipes that can be partially or fully made in the days leading up to your special occasion. Feel free to make as many or as few dishes as you need to customize the menu to your personal gathering.

- Festive Bread-Free Stuffing Balls (page 105)
- Rosemary and Thyme Mushroom Gravy (page 304)
- Ultimate Creamy Salt-and-Vinegar Scalloped Potatoes (page 147) or Creamy Mushroom, Green Bean, and Wild Rice Casserole (page 153)
- Crispy Brussels Sprouts in Garlic Oil (page 151)
- Balsamic Roasted Root Vegetable Medley with Thyme and Cayenne (page 139)
- Crispy Smashed Potatoes (page 173) with Creamy Cashew or Sunflower Aioli (page 293)

To transform this into a spring-friendly holiday menu: Swap the Crispy Brussels Sprouts in Garlic Oil for Apple Honey–Sriracha Roasted Rainbow Carrots with Cashew Cream (page 141); the Balsamic Roasted Root Vegetable Medley with Thyme and Cayenne for Summery Chimichurri Chickpea Pasta Salad (page 185). You can also change up the Festive Bread-Free Stuffing Balls with my Portobello Boats with Rosemary-Lentil Crumble and Balsamic-Apple Glaze (page 47).

Halloween Dinner

Halloween is a busy evening for families, handing out candy to kids and rushing through supper to get your own goblins and superheroes out the door. A light menu of nutritious, kid-favorite dishes will power them through. The recipes below are quick to prepare or can even be made the day before. Sounds like a trick, but it's definitely a treat!

- Flavor Bomb Chimichurri Guacamole (page 163) with tortilla chips
- Sloppy Glows (page 90) or Weeknight Tex-Mex Quinoa with Cashew Sour Cream (page 75)
- 6-Ingredient Chocolate Peanut Butter Oat Crumble Squares (page 252)

Get Your Glow Back

These recipes are my go-to recipes for getting back my glow! They're packed with nutrients and can be whipped up in a flash so you can get under that cozy blanket with a good book (and perhaps a mug of warm, gingery veggie soup!) in no time.

- Cold-Be-Gone Flavor Bomb Noodle Soup (page 213)
- Immunity Glo Shot (page 263)
- 20-Minute Sweet Potato Noodle Bowl with Sesame, Cilantro, Lime, and Avocado (page 102)

Game Night

Crowd-pleasing, filling-but-not-*stuffing*, and make-ahead are key factors for game-night gatherings (I don't want to miss out on the action)! I love serving up plant-based recipes with a traditional game-night spin, so the only thing we complain about is the score . . . and boy, do we like to complain about the score.

- Spicy Potato Nacho Plate (page 71) or Game Night Crispy Potato Bruschetta (page 176)
- Creamy Buffalo Cauli Tacos (page 67)
- Flavor Bomb Chimichurri Guacamole (page 163) with tortilla chips

Date Night In

Eating meals with little ones is pretty chaotic, isn't it? Eric and I are lucky if we can hear ourselves speak over the noise! About once a week, we love to enjoy a nice meal together after the kids go to bed. This menu only requires 30 minutes active prep time (including dessert), so you can sit down to a nice meal in under an hour. Just don't be surprised if someone starts crying the minute your butt hits the chair . . . Eric can get pretty emotional about good food.

- Glow Green 30-Minute Pesto Pasta (page 55) or Velvety Alfredo Mushroom-and-Chickpea Pot (page 84) with crusty fresh bread
- Apple Honey–Dijon Mixed Greens (see Tip, page 285)
- Your favorite wine or beverage of choice
- 6-Ingredient Chocolate Peanut Butter Oat Crumble Squares (page 252)

Summer Dinner Alfresco

A lazy, hazy summer evening and a breezy, light outdoor meal shared with friends . . . what could be better? How about dishes that can be made ahead the day before? Now we're talking!

- Green Goddess Gazpacho (page 219) with all the toppings
- Mega Crunch Sun-Dried Tomato–Pepita Taco Salad (page 204)
- Summery Chimichurri Chickpea Pasta Salad (page 185)
- Kombucha Strawberry-Lime Granita (page 245) or Brainchild Cherry-Lemon Coconut Cream Pops (page 241)
- Mint, Ginger, and Lemon Sparkling Sipper (page 268)

Mother's Day Breakfast for Dinner

If my kids could have their way, they'd probably choose a Mother's Day menu made up of all desserts (they get their sweet tooth from their mama)! This menu works great for brunch or breakfast for dinner, depending on what time of day you'd like to celebrate. The School Night Tofu Scramble with Roasted Red Pepper and Walnut Dip and Fastest No-Bake Jammy Oat Crumble Squares can be made ahead, saving you fuss on the big day.

• School Night Tofu Scramble with Roasted Red Pepper and Walnut Dip (page 78)

• Mama's favorite bread (toasted)

• Optional accompaniments: sliced avocado, fruit salad, Cashew Sour Cream (page 321)

• Fastest No-Bake Jammy Oat Crumble Squares (page 239)

Father's Day Feast

Kids will be proud to serve up a "burger and fries" meal for Dad that they helped to make; enlist them to help season the potato wedges or stir together the OSG House Sauce. Kids also enjoy pouring the cookie chunks into the ice cream maker, too (not to mention "cleaning" the bowl).

• Bruschetta Veggie Burgers (page 49) or Smoky Black Bean and Brown Rice Veggie Burgers (page 131) with OSG House Sauce (page 331)

• Seasoned Crispy Baked Potato Wedges (page 159)

• Peppermint Crunch Ice Cream (page 246) with Chewy Double-Chocolate Sunflower Cookies (page 249)

TIPS FOR
COOKING IN THE
OH SHE GLOWS
KITCHEN

During the recipe-testing process for this cookbook, my recipe testers asked me to include a section on how to follow my recipes for the best possible outcome. I love this idea because I thrive on giving you the most knowledge, tips, tricks, and help to ensure you have success! For the recipe pros out there, you'll likely know many of these things I talk about below. I encourage you to read over this section anyway because many of the things that I do are unique to my own kitchen and habits (such as how I measure flour), so this chapter will help you obtain the best possible results. Knowledge is power, and once you know these things by heart, you'll be able to whiz through the recipes at a faster, more confident pace! Who doesn't want that?

Have fun!

Do whatever you need to do to make cooking an enjoyable experience. Play your favorite music, grab a drink, clear your space before you begin, etc.

Read over the recipe in full

You can roll your eyes over this one (I am, and I'm the one writing it), but it helps so much to read the entire recipe (from headnote to the tips) before you begin—the earlier you can read it over, the better, because occasionally recipes require advance prep, like soaking or chilling overnight. (I also provide a handy "advance prep required" label at the top for those recipes.) Reading over the recipe also helps you visualize (from an enticing head-note description and the various steps) how it should look at various stages of cooking. In the headnote and/or tips section, I love to provide substitution tips or any other info when I think it'll help you achieve a better end result. I want each recipe to be a wealth of information for you and would hate for you to miss all these details.

Allergy and preparation labels

You'll find various allergy and preparation labels near the top of each recipe. Is the family coming over for a special occasion and your aunt has a nut allergy, cousin is gluten-free, sister can't eat soy, and you need a kid-friendly dish, too? Don't despair! The allergy labels help you to quickly identify which recipes will fit your needs. **Please note that *optional ingredients and optional sub recipes are *not* included in the allergy and prepara-tion labels.** I've even created a handy reference tool for you called "Helpful Recipe Lists" (page 340), where you can find them all in one spot. Always be proactive, however, and check the labels of your ingredients to ensure the food is safe for you to consume. Below are the labels described in a bit more detail.

Vegan: This recipe contains no animal products. All of the recipes in this book are vegan. Woohoo!

Gluten-Free: This recipe is free of gluten. Be sure to use certified gluten-free ingredients for these recipes to ensure they are gluten-free, if this is a concern for you.

Nut-Free: There are no nuts or nut products in this recipe. Please be aware that Health Canada does not classify coconut as a nut, whereas the United States does. Since I live in Canada, I follow Health Canada's guidelines, and therefore my recipes that contain coconut are labeled nut-free. Please ensure that you read each recipe's ingredient list closely if you or someone you are cooking for has a coconut allergy.

Soy-Free: This recipe does not contain soy products like tofu, edamame, tempeh, tamari, soy-based miso, etc. I will often use soy-free products like coconut aminos (soy-free seasoning sauce) and chickpea miso to make the recipes soy-free.

Grain-Free: This recipe does not contain grains. A grain is classified as a cultivated cereal crop or the fruit/seed of a cereal. Rice, oats, wheat, and millet are examples of grains. Quinoa is a seed, but since many grain-free diets prohibit quinoa (counting it as a pseudo-cereal grain), I have included it in the grain category.

Oil-Free: This recipe doesn't contain added oils (this includes mayonnaise). However, it may still be rich in healthy fats, like those that include avocado, hemp hearts, chia seeds, and naturally occurring oils such as those found in nut or seed butters.

Kid-Friendly: The recipes in this book marked "kid-friendly" received approval ratings from 60 percent or more of the children who tasted the recipe during the testing stage. Keep in mind that kids might love a recipe one day and hate it the next (or they may hate a recipe the first time, hate it the second, and love it when they're a teenager . . . anything is possible)! If a recipe is not marked "kid-friendly" but has a tip at the bottom to make it so, it will be noted as "kid-friendly option."

Raw/No Bake: This recipe does not require cooking, though a few of these recipes may involve a tiny amount of heating an ingredient, such as melting coconut oil.

Advance Prep Required: One or more components in this recipe must be prepared in advance. Examples can include soaking nuts, chilling a can of coconut milk, or preparing a sauce.

Freezer-Friendly: This recipe has been tested successfully in the freezer. In my Storage tip at the bottom of the recipe directions, I will tell you how long it keeps in the freezer without losing texture or flavor, how to store it, and I'll often include reheating directions. I got your back!

On the Glow: This recipe is particularly suited to being stored and transported, so it makes a wonderful lunch or other "takeout" meal. Be prepared though: Everyone at your work or school is going to want to eat your food. Quick, run and hide!

One Pot or One Bowl: This recipe requires just ONE pot or bowl and minimal fuss. Do you hear the angels singing?! I sure do.

You'll notice in this Allergy and Preparation Label section that "option" often follows some labels. Whenever you see something like "nut-free option," it means that I've provided a tip for turning the recipe into a nut-free recipe (such as by swapping cashews for pepitas in a pesto).

Active prep time and total time

Active prep time: Your active time in the kitchen (chopping, processing, blending, assembling, etc.) ends when you can "walk away" from the kitchen and let it cook (or chill). The active prep time and total time estimates are based on averages from our testing group along with my own experience.

Total time: This is the total amount of time it takes for the recipe from start to finish, including all sub recipes (unless those sub recipes are marked as "optional"; then they are not counted in the timing). For example, my Cheesy Lentil Bolognese Casserole (page 59) calls for Vegan Parmesan (page 317) or Italian Herb Parmesan (page 301) (neither of which is marked as optional), so the total time reflects how long it takes to prep *all* components of this recipe, from the start until it's finished cooking. Keep in mind that these times are also based on averages, and they assume the cook is going at a steady pace without any breaks. Total time does not include soaking time, nor does it include cooling time.

Ingredient list

I'm sure this is common knowledge for most of you, but I've been asked this question so many times over the years. We all know that using the wrong amount of an ingredient can throw off a recipe's taste or texture. You'll want to pay close attention to the order of the wording in the ingredient list, particularly the action word (minced, chopped, diced, etc.). For example, *1 cup minced parsley* is very different from *1 cup parsley, minced*. *1 cup minced parsley* means you mince the parsley <u>before</u> measuring 1 cup, and *1 cup parsley, minced,* means you first measure 1 cup of whole parsley leaves, then mince it after measuring. An easy way to remember it: If the action comes after a comma, you do the action *after* measuring.

Adding "to taste": I know it can feel scary to read that you are to add an ingredient "to taste" when you've never made the recipe before. I've found that this comfort comes with practice . . . getting a feel for your taste buds and how certain ingredients help balance the flavors. When creating recipes, I will often suggest a range, but I always encourage you to add to taste. Start slowly and add a bit at a time, tasting as you cook. You may prefer 1 tablespoon or 3 tablespoons of lemon juice, compared to my suggested 2 tablespoons. I love when you customize recipes to suit your tastes! For those new to plant-based cooking, or even just cooking from scratch in general, you might find that you enjoy the flavor of new-to-you ingredients more if you use the lower end of the range, until you become accustomed to their flavor (nutritional yeast, miso, lemon juice, raw garlic, etc.). I love a lot of flavor, so I always use the upper end of the suggested range for any given ingredient.

A note on measuring flour: Traditionally in recipes, flours are measured using the *spoon and level* method, where flour is spooned into the measuring cup and leveled off with a knife (scraping the excess off the top). I like to keep things as speedy as possible, by using my *scoop and shake until level* method. Simply scoop the flour into your measuring cup (using the measuring cup itself to scoop up the flour), and shake it gently until the flour is level to the top of the cup. My recipes that include flour are always measured this way. However, I recommend you weigh your flour whenever possible for the best result, so I also provide the exact flour weights. If you don't have a kitchen scale, please use the *scoop and shake until level* method.

A note on pepitas: I call for roasted pepitas (hulled pumpkin seeds) often in my recipes. For convenience, I like to keep store-bought roasted pepitas on hand (I tend to buy the bulk-sized bags from Costco). If you use store-bought roasted pepitas that are salted, you may need to reduce the added salt in the recipe. To roast raw pepitas at home, spread them out onto a small baking sheet and toss with 1 teaspoon of olive oil. Roast at 325°F (160°C) for 10 to 13 minutes, until lightly golden.

Storage

On the recipe page you'll find storage information for each recipe. I'll tell you how to store leftovers in the fridge and how long they'll last. If it's a freezer-friendly recipe, I'll let you know how to store it in the freezer and how long it'll keep. Very often, I'll provide tips on reheating, too! No one wants leftovers to go to waste . . . am I right? And now I've taken all the guesswork out of it for you.

7

Tips section

Asterisks: The asterisks correspond with the asterisks in the ingredient list. If an ingredient has one asterisk, match it to the tip with one asterisk, and so on. I do this so that when you read through the ingredient list, you'll easily be able to identify the ingredients that have more information for you below, and you'll be less likely to miss important notes!

Up the glow: This tip is a fun way to amp up the flavors, textures, and nutrients in a recipe. For example, I might say, "Add 3 cups chopped fresh spinach during the last 5 minutes of cooking for an extra boost of green power!" If you ever find a recipe needs a bit more flavor, I encourage you to seek out any flavor-boosting tips found in these Up the Glow tips. Adding these optional ideas as tips allows me to keep the ingredient list streamlined and perfect for those cooking in a hurry!

Make it kid-friendly: If the recipe isn't naturally kid-friendly (maybe it's on the spicy side), I will try to provide a tip on how to make it more kid-friendly. For example, "Omit the red pepper flakes and sriracha to make this kid-friendly. You can top your individual bowl with a drizzle of sriracha or sprinkle of red pepper flakes, to taste."

Make it gluten-, nut-, soy-, or grain-free: To create recipes that many people can enjoy, I try to include a tip to make them free of the more common allergens and sensitivities (assuming my testing has worked successfully). By omitting certain optional ingredients or simply preparing or serving them in a different way, many of the recipes have options for tailoring them to your needs. I only provide swaps and suggestions if I have tested them successfully in my own kitchen!

GO-TO MAINS

Portobello Boats with Rosemary-Lentil Crumble and Balsamic-Apple Glaze

Serves 6 (1 large boat per serving) • **Active prep time** 20 minutes • **Total time** 35 minutes

2 tablespoons extra-virgin olive oil

6 large or 8 medium portobello mushrooms (650 g), stemmed and cleaned*

Fine sea salt

1 cup (70 g) finely chopped onion (1 medium)

3 large garlic cloves (18 g), minced (1½ tablespoons)

1 cup (100 g) walnuts

2 to 4 teaspoons minced fresh rosemary, to taste**

½ cup (10 g) fresh parsley leaves, finely chopped

1 (14-ounce/398 mL) can lentils, drained and rinsed***

2 teaspoons sherry vinegar, or to taste

Freshly ground black pepper

For the Balsamic-Apple Glaze

½ cup ketchup

¼ cup balsamic vinegar

¼ cup applesauce or apple butter

2 tablespoons pure maple syrup

What if I told you that this filling, protein-packed main dish can be ready and on the table in about 30 minutes? Yes, it's true! Not only is this dish a fast vegan protein option, it's also bursting with all kinds of crunchy, chewy textures and savory flavors from the rosemary, parsley, and garlic. Don't forget the Balsamic-Apple Glaze, which takes just a couple of minutes to stir together; its tangy sweetness makes everything pop, so be sure to have it on hand—I bet you'll be reaching for more! Try to select the largest portobello mushrooms you can find, as they'll hold a lot more crumble than smaller ones will. If you are using smaller caps, just ensure you have around 1½ pounds (675 g) of caps total, and add a bit less crumble to each. Feelin' festive? Add some chopped dried cranberries to the crumble! To round out this hearty dish, serve the portobello boats with my Crispy Brussels Sprouts in Garlic Oil (page 151) or Roasted Garlic Cauliflower Rice (page 170).

1. Preheat the oven to 400°F (200°C). Line a large baking sheet with parchment paper.

2. Using 1 tablespoon of the olive oil, brush the tops and bottoms of the portobellos until each is completely coated. Place them stemmed-side down on the prepared baking sheet and sprinkle each with a pinch of salt. Bake for 20 minutes, or until the caps look like they are shriveling up and are fork-tender (very large mushrooms may need 5 minutes more).

recipe continues

recipe continued from previous page

STORAGE

I like to store any leftovers (fully assembled, including the glaze!) in a baking dish covered with aluminum foil in the fridge for up to 4 days. When I want to serve them, all I have to do is pop the covered dish into the oven. Reheat at 400°F (200°C) for 17 to 23 minutes, until warmed through.

TIPS

* If your portobellos are on the small side, simply double the number called for. To clean the portobellos, rub the outside with damp paper towels to remove any debris. With a small spoon, scrape out the black gills inside the cap and discard them.

** You can substitute 1½ teaspoons dried rosemary for the fresh rosemary, adding it to the skillet in step 4 with the walnuts and lentils.

*** One 14-ounce (398 mL) can of lentils is equivalent to 1½ cups cooked lentils, if you prefer to cook them from scratch.

MAKE IT NUT-FREE

Use ¾ cup (120 g) roasted pepitas (see page 338) in place of the walnuts.

3. Meanwhile, in a medium skillet, heat the remaining 1 tablespoon olive oil over medium heat. Add the onion and garlic and stir to coat with the oil. Sauté for 5 to 6 minutes, until the onion is softened.

4. Chop the walnuts into pieces just smaller than pea-sized. Add the walnuts, 2 teaspoons of the rosemary, the parsley, drained lentils, vinegar, and salt (I use about ½ teaspoon) and pepper to taste to the onion mixture in the skillet and stir well to combine. Taste and adjust the seasonings, if desired. Cook for a few minutes, until heated through. Taste and stir in more of the rosemary, if you'd like a stronger rosemary flavor.

5. Make the Balsamic-Apple Glaze: In a small pot, whisk together the ketchup, vinegar, applesauce, and maple syrup and heat over medium-low heat, stirring every now and then, until warmed through.

6. Plate the roasted portobellos stemmed-side up, like a bowl, and divide the crumble evenly among them (I use about ½ cup of the crumble on large portobellos and ¼ cup on smaller ones). Season with a sprinkle of salt and pepper and serve immediately, drizzled generously with the warm glaze.

Bruschetta Veggie Burgers

Makes 7 large burgers • **Active prep time** 20 minutes • **Total time** 55 minutes

I tablespoon extra-virgin olive oil

I cup (140 g) finely chopped red onion

3 large garlic cloves (18 g), minced (1½ tablespoons)

¾ cup (115 g) raw cashews

½ cup (50 g) gluten-free rolled oats

¾ cup lightly packed (22 g) fresh basil leaves

¼ cup (50 g) oil-packed unsalted sun-dried tomatoes, drained and coarsely chopped*

I (14-ounce/398 mL) can lentils, drained and rinsed**

I tablespoon fresh lemon juice

I tablespoon tomato paste

½ to I teaspoon red pepper flakes, to taste

¾ teaspoon fine sea salt, or to taste

Freshly ground black pepper

2½ tablespoons gluten-free oat flour

Buns, for serving (optional)

Topping options

Mashed avocado

Authentic-Tasting Vegan Feta Cheese (page 327)***

Perfect Basil Pesto (page 294) or Roasted Red Pepper and Walnut Dip (page 298)

Sliced tomato

These veggie burgers are bursting with sunny Italian flavors like fresh basil, sun-dried tomatoes, lemon, and garlic, and are a true flavor explosion! When I first served these to my family, I knew they were a hit because everyone gobbled up their servings (not an easy task with two toddlers at the dinner table!). Yep, these burgers just took a DNA test—turns out, they're 100% that dish (thanks, Lizzo). We love topping them with sliced tomatoes, my Perfect Basil Pesto, sliced avocado, and herbed salt and pepper, and they are also absolutely irresistible with my Authentic-Tasting Vegan Feta Cheese! Try serving them with my Seasoned Crispy Baked Potato Wedges (page 159) for a healthier twist on traditional fries. If you're avoiding gluten, use a lettuce wrap or gluten-free bun, or simply serve the patties "naked," piled high with all the fun toppings (my favorite). I like to whip up the toppings while the patties are in the oven. It's important to follow this recipe exactly as written, as veggie burger recipes are tricky to perfect, and if you make changes, they may not hold together. And for best results, be sure to bake them—they are a little too delicate for grilling.

1. Preheat the oven to 350°F (180°C). Line a large baking sheet with parchment paper.

2. In a medium skillet, heat the oil over medium heat. Add the onion and garlic, stir to coat, and sauté for 5 to 6 minutes, until the onion is soft.

3. Meanwhile, in a food processor, process the cashews, oats, and basil for 7 to 10 seconds, until coarsely chopped (be careful not to process the mixture into a fine flour—you want a coarse

recipe continues

recipe continued from previous page

STORAGE

These are best served fresh out of the oven, but you can store the baked patties in an airtight container in the fridge for a couple of days. Reheat them in an oiled skillet over medium heat for 3 minutes per side. I don't recommend freezing them, as they tend to dry out.

TIPS

* If your sun-dried tomatoes are salted, you may need to use less salt to season the patty mixture before baking.

** It's important to use a brand of canned lentils that contains "intact" lentils, which are not compacted together or mushy. One 14-ounce (398 mL) can of lentils is equivalent to 1½ cups cooked lentils, if you prefer to cook them from scratch.

*** If you use the feta as a topping, the recipe will no longer be soy-free.

meal). Add the cooked onion mixture, sun-dried tomatoes, drained lentils, lemon juice, tomato paste, red pepper flakes, and salt and black pepper to taste to the oat mixture in the food processor. Pulse the mixture about 15 times, until chopped (again, avoid overprocessing the mixture, as you want it to have a coarse texture). Taste and adjust the seasonings with more salt, black pepper, and red pepper flakes, if desired.

4. Spoon the mixture into a large bowl. Add the oat flour and stir well to combine. Taste and adjust the seasonings, if desired. Let the dough sit for a few minutes to allow the flour to work its thickening magic.

5. Using a measuring cup, scoop up ½ cup of the mixture (without packing it into the cup too firmly). Flip the cup over into your hand so the mixture pops out onto your palm. Using both palms, shape the mixture into a patty, rotating it between your palms and packing it together tightly so it holds its shape well. (The dough will be a bit wet and sticky, but this is normal. If it's too sticky to shape, stir in another tablespoon of oat flour and let the dough rest for a couple of minutes before trying again.) Transfer the patty to the prepared pan and repeat with the remaining dough, placing the patties a couple of inches (5 cm) apart on the pan. You should have about 7 large patties.

6. Bake for 23 to 25 minutes, until the bottoms are lightly golden. Let the patties sit on the pan for 10 minutes to firm up before handling them. (If you skip the 10-minute sitting period, the burgers may easily break apart.) Serve on a bun, if desired, with your choice of toppings.

Fast Family Fajitas

Makes 6 medium or 8 small fajitas • **Active prep time** 30 minutes • **Total time** 35 minutes

3 Tex-Mex Flavor Bombs (page 314)*

Cashew Sour Cream (page 321) or
24/7 Avocado-Cilantro Sauce
(page 286)**

2 tablespoons extra-virgin olive oil

2 cups (150 g) thinly sliced cremini
mushrooms

1 cup (90 g) thinly sliced onion

1 cup (270 g) thinly sliced red bell
pepper

¼ cup water

1 (14-ounce/398 mL) can black beans,
drained and rinsed***

For serving

1 or 2 ripe large (240 g each) avocados,
pitted

6 medium (8-inch/20 cm) or 8 small
(6-inch/15 cm) soft tortillas

Chopped fresh cilantro and/or diced
fresh tomatoes

Fine sea salt or Tex-Mex Spice Blend
(page 313)

Freshly ground black pepper

Fresh lime juice

This recipe simplifies family fajita night, making it fast enough for a weeknight dinner! It includes my handy Tex-Mex Flavor Bombs, homemade flavor concentrates that bring instant pizzazz to dishes. I keep them stocked in my freezer (along with some Cashew Sour Cream) to use in these quick fajitas, which helps me get the whole recipe on the table in under 20 minutes! No more measuring and fussing with a bunch of spices—all you need for an authentically smoky, lightly spicy fajita are a few flavor bombs.

1. Prepare the Tex-Mex Flavor Bombs and the Cashew Sour Cream (or 24/7 Avocado-Cilantro Sauce).

2. In a large skillet, heat the oil over medium heat. Add the mushrooms, onion, and bell pepper and stir to coat with the oil. Raise the heat to medium-high and sauté, uncovered, stirring occasionally, for about 6 minutes, until the veggies start to soften.

3. Add the flavor bombs to the vegetables and cook, stirring frequently, until the flavor bombs melt, 2 to 3 minutes.

4. Add the water to the skillet and stir until the veggies are coated in sauce. Simmer, uncovered, until the veggies have absorbed the sauce and are cooked to your liking, 2 to 4 minutes more.

5. Stir in the black beans, cook for another minute, until heated through, then remove from the heat.

recipe continues

recipe continued from previous page

STORAGE

Store leftover fajita filling (separately from any toppings) in an airtight container in the fridge for up to 4 days. Reheat in an oiled skillet over medium heat until warmed through.

TIPS

* If you don't have flavor bombs in your freezer already, not to worry: Simply make the mixture before you begin this recipe and use 6 tablespoons in place of the 3 frozen flavor bombs called for—then freeze the rest so you'll have some stocked for future fajita nights! Add the unfrozen flavor bomb mixture in step 2, then immediately proceed to step 3.

** If you don't have time to make the Cashew Sour Cream or 24/7 Avocado-Cilantro Sauce, vegan mayo works in a pinch!

*** One 14-ounce (398 mL) can of black beans is equivalent to 1½ cups cooked black beans, if you prefer to cook them from scratch.

MAKE IT GLUTEN- AND GRAIN-FREE

Use gluten-free (and grain-free, if needed) tortillas or lettuce leaves.

MAKE IT NUT-FREE

Omit the Cashew Sour Cream and use 24/7 Avocado-Cilantro Sauce, Creamy Sunflower Aioli (see page 293), or vegan mayo instead.

6. Meanwhile, slice an avocado or two. Portion the avocado among 6 tortillas, then top with cilantro and Cashew Sour Cream.

7. When the sautéed vegetables are ready, taste and season with salt, pepper, and a squeeze of lime juice. Divide the veggies evenly among the tortillas, roll up, and enjoy!

Glow Green 30-Minute Pesto Pasta

Serves 6 • **Active prep time** 25 to 30 minutes • **Total time** 25 to 30 minutes

2 tablespoons extra-virgin olive oil

8 ounces (225 g) cremini mushrooms, thinly sliced

I medium green zucchini, diced into ½-inch (I cm) pieces (2½ cups)

3 cups (265 g) diced (½-inch/I cm pieces) broccoli florets (from I small bunch)

Fine sea salt and freshly ground black pepper

14 ounces (5 cups/I.25 L) dry rotini pasta

Double batch Pretty Parsley-Cilantro Pepita Pesto (see page 275)

6 to 7 teaspoons fresh lemon juice, or to taste

This is what I like to call one of my *Top Chef* recipes because you'll be amazed by the delicious, fresh meal pulled together in record time. When I have my game face on, I can have this family-favorite dish ready and on the table in 25 minutes! Say what? That's what I'm talking about. It's bursting with green summer vegetables but isn't boring in any way because it's all coated in the dreamiest, most flavorful pesto made with fresh parsley, cilantro, garlic, and lemon (and those ingredients make it naturally detoxifying, too). When I discovered how much my son, Arlo, loves pesto of all kinds (he literally eats it off a spoon—#proudmama), this dish quickly became one of our summer staples and I hope it will be for you, too. If you prefer a veggie-heavy pasta, you can increase the amount of chopped veggies and reduce the pasta as desired, until you find your perfect ratio.

1. Bring a large pot of water to a boil.

2. Meanwhile, in an extra-large skillet, heat the oil over medium-low heat. Add the mushrooms, zucchini, broccoli, a generous pinch of salt, and a bit of pepper and stir well to combine. Raise the heat to medium-high and sauté, uncovered, stirring occasionally, for 10 minutes, then check the tenderness of the veggies. Cover and cook, reducing the heat if necessary and stirring in a splash of water if the veggies begin to stick to the pan, for 4 to 6 minutes more, until the veggies are fork-tender. After cooking, drain any water that is left in the skillet.

recipe continues

recipe continued from previous page

STORAGE

Store in an airtight container in the fridge for up to 3 days. Serve leftovers chilled or at room temperature, adding a squeeze of lemon juice and a sprinkle of salt to revive the flavors, if desired. I don't recommend reheating this, as the flavors diminish quite a bit.

TIP

This pasta is wonderful garnished with lemon zest!

MAKE IT GLUTEN- AND GRAIN-FREE

Use gluten-free (and grain-free, if needed) pasta.

UP THE GLOW

Sprinkle on hemp hearts for a protein boost, or try my Italian Herb Parmesan (page 30!) or Herbamare for mega flavor.

3. When the water comes to a boil, cook the pasta according to the package directions until al dente. Drain and rinse with cold water to stop the cooking process and return the drained pasta to the pot.

4. While the veggies and pasta are cooking away, prepare a double batch of the Pretty Parsley-Cilantro Pepita Pesto. (See the double-batch Tip at the bottom of the pesto recipe.)

5. Add the cooked veggies and all of the pesto to the pot with the pasta. Stir well to combine. Taste and add the lemon juice, little by little until the flavors pop, to taste, and season with additional salt and pepper as desired. Serve and enjoy!

Cheesy Lentil Bolognese Casserole

Serves 8 • **Soak time** I hour or up to overnight
Active prep time 45 minutes • **Total time** I hour I5 minutes

I batch Vegan Cheese Sauce 2.0 (page 290)

4 teaspoons Italian seasoning, homemade (page 312) or store-bought

14 ounces (5 cups/400 g) dry fusilli or rotini pasta

2 tablespoons extra-virgin olive oil

I large sweet onion, diced (about 2 cups/280 g)

4 large garlic cloves (24 g), minced (2 tablespoons)

¼ to ¾ teaspoon fine sea salt, to taste, plus more as needed

8 ounces (225 g) cremini mushrooms, thinly sliced

3 cups (750 mL) chunky marinara sauce*

I (14-ounce/398 mL) can lentils, drained and rinsed**

2 tablespoons tahini***

½ teaspoon freshly ground black pepper, or to taste

I teaspoon red pepper flakes, or to taste

Paprika, for garnish

Italian Herb Parmesan (page 301) or Vegan Parmesan (page 317), for serving

Our entire family is in love with this cheesy, creamy, comforting, and hearty casserole! The lentil-mushroom Bolognese and my perfected velvety vegan cheese sauce are incredibly delicious together. Imagine coming home at the end of a long day and having this casserole all ready to bake . . . nothing is better! (This is also my favorite recipe to make for new moms . . . they're always delighted when I drop off a casserole and all they have to do is bake it!) It's the kind of recipe to make on a slow weekend, when you have a full hour to cook (and hopefully a grateful cater to clean the pile of dishes afterward!). I also provide handy make-ahead tips to simplify things further. This casserole is lovely served with a simple side salad (see the Tip on page 285) and some crusty fresh bread.

Don't have time to make the cheese sauce and bake the casserole? For an easy weeknight meal, just serve the lentil Bolognese straight from the pot after you add the cooked pasta and season to taste! For a delightful tangy/salty pop, I love adding some chopped oil-packed sun-dried tomatoes in step 6.

I. Prepare the Vegan Cheese Sauce 2.0 and Italian seasoning (if not using store-bought), and set both aside.

2. Preheat the oven to 400°F (200°C). Lightly oil a 9 by 13-inch (3 L) or 8 by 12-inch (3 L) casserole dish.

3. Bring a large pot of water to a boil. Add the pasta and cook according to the package directions until al dente (be sure not to overcook it). Drain and set aside.

recipe continues

recipe continued from previous page

TIPS

* If the unbaked casserole is going to sit in the fridge for a couple of days *before* you bake it, feel free to stir in an extra ½ cup marinara sauce to help counteract any moisture loss.

** One 14-ounce (398 mL) can of lentils is equivalent to 1½ cups cooked lentils, if you prefer to cook them from scratch.

*** The tahini lends a lovely creaminess and depth of flavor to the Bolognese sauce, but if you're allergic to sesame or don't have any tahini on hand, the sauce will still turn out great without it.

If your child is not a mushroom fan, process the mushrooms in a food processor until minced. They'll be virtually undetectable, but your meal will still retain its immune-boosting benefits!

MAKE IT AHEAD

You can assemble the entire casserole in advance to bake later—just prepare the recipe through step 9 (don't bake it!), wrap it up, and refrigerate for 1 to 3 days. When you're ready to bake it, uncover the dish and bake at 400°F (200°C) for 30 to 35 minutes, until heated through.

MAKE IT GLUTEN-FREE

Use gluten-free pasta.

MAKE IT NUT-FREE

Use the nut-free options when preparing the Vegan Cheese Sauce 2.0 and the Italian Herb Parmesan.

4. Meanwhile, in a large Dutch oven or pot (about 5 quarts/5 L), stir together the oil, onion, and garlic. Add a pinch of salt, stir, and sauté over medium heat for 4 to 6 minutes, until the onion is softened and translucent.

5. Stir in the mushrooms and Italian seasoning, raise the heat to medium-high, and cook, uncovered, for another 7 to 9 minutes, until the liquid released by the mushrooms has evaporated.

6. Add the marinara sauce, lentils, and tahini and stir to combine. Add the cooked pasta and stir until it's coated in the lentil-veggie mixture.

7. Taste and season with the salt, black pepper, and red pepper flakes. Turn off the heat.

8. Spoon the pasta mixture into the prepared casserole dish and spread it out evenly.

9. Pour all the cheese sauce over the top of the pasta mixture, spreading it out with the back of a spoon until it covers the entire surface. Garnish with paprika (it adds a beautiful pop of red) and pepper, if desired.

10. Bake the casserole, uncovered, for 20 to 24 minutes, until heated through.

11. While the casserole bakes, prepare the Italian Herb Parmesan or Vegan Parmesan.

12. Serve the casserole with a generous sprinkle of parmesan on top of each portion, with more in a bowl on the side.

STORAGE

Store leftovers in an airtight container in the fridge for up to 7 days. They're delicious served chilled, straight from the fridge!

Green Powerhouse Roasted Protein Bowl

Makes 4 large bowls • **Active prep time** 30 minutes • **Total time** 50 minutes

I small bunch broccoli, cut into I-inch (2.5 cm) florets (3 heaping cups/210 g)

3 large Yukon Gold potatoes, cut into ½-inch (1 cm) cubes (3 cups/420 g)*

1½ tablespoons extra-virgin olive oil

Fine sea salt and freshly ground black pepper

I cup (185 g) uncooked quinoa

1¾ cups water

I batch Boom! Broccoli Pesto (page 276)

2 tablespoons fresh lemon juice, more if needed

4 tablespoons (40 g) roasted salted pepitas (see page 338)

2 tablespoons plus 2 teaspoons hemp hearts

5 large green onions (105 g), thinly sliced (1 cup)

I large (240 g) or 2 medium (400 g total) ripe avocados, pitted and chopped

If I ever have a plant-based restaurant or café, this nutritious bowl will definitely be on the menu! But until then, I'll make this recipe for my family again and again. I love that it can be changed up simply by swapping in whatever veggies we have on hand. It just checks all the boxes for us, and whenever I make it for family and friends, everyone raves about it. This cozy bowl features Yukon Gold potatoes and broccoli, which are roasted until crisp and charred. It's all tossed with warm, lemony quinoa and my beloved Boom! Broccoli Pesto. Crunchy pepitas, protein-packed hemp hearts, and creamy avocado round out the healthy toppings. On chilly days, I love sipping a hot Soothing Mint and Ginger Green Tea (page 267) with this bowl; the two together feel like a big warm hug. This powerhouse bowl is lovely with all different kinds of pesto as well, so feel free to experiment with using my Perfect Basil Pesto (page 294) or Pretty Parsley-Cilantro Pepita Pesto (page 275) to change up the flavors.

1. Preheat the oven to 400°F (200°C). Line an extra-large (15 by 21-inch/38 by 53 cm) baking sheet (or two large baking sheets) with parchment paper.

2. Place the broccoli and potatoes on the prepared baking sheet. Toss with the oil until thoroughly coated (I like to massage the oil into the broccoli florets so they get coated nicely). Spread into an even layer and season with a generous amount of salt and pepper.

recipe continues

recipe continued from previous page

STORAGE

Store in an airtight container in the fridge for up to 4 days. Reheat in an oiled skillet over medium heat until warmed through. It's great enjoyed chilled, too!

TIP

* Fingerling, yellow, or red potatoes work great, too! There's no need to peel them.

UP THE GLOW

Boost the protein by adding chickpeas, adzuki beans, great northern beans, kidney beans, or lentils (try French green lentils to keep the green theme going!).

MAKE IT AHEAD

The pesto and quinoa can both be made 2 days ahead and stored in separate airtight containers in the fridge.

3. Roast the potatoes and broccoli for 15 minutes, then remove from the oven and flip. Roast for 10 to 20 minutes more, until the potatoes and broccoli are fork-tender and golden brown with some charred spots.

4. Meanwhile, in a large (4- to 5-quart/4 to 5 L) pot, combine the quinoa and water. Bring to a low boil over high heat, then quickly reduce the heat to medium. Cover with a tight-fitting lid and gently simmer for 12 to 14 minutes, until the water has been absorbed and the quinoa is fluffy. Remove from the heat, fluff with a fork, and replace the lid to keep the quinoa warm.

5. While the vegetables and quinoa are cooking, prepare the Boom! Broccoli Pesto.

6. Add the lemon juice and 1/2 teaspoon salt to the quinoa and stir until combined. Stir in all the roasted veggies.

7. Grab four large shallow bowls. Spoon 1 1/2 cups of the quinoa-veggie mixture into each bowl. Spoon a generous 1/4 cup of the pesto on the side of the quinoa mixture, then scatter 1 tablespoon of the pepitas, 2 teaspoons of the hemp hearts, 1/4 cup of the green onion, and one-quarter of the avocado over each bowl. Season with salt, pepper, and a squeeze of lemon juice, to taste, if desired. Serve warm.

Instant Pot Potato and Cauliflower Red Thai Curry
(with Stovetop Option!)

Serves 4 (1⅓ cups per serving) • **Active prep time** 10 minutes • **Total time** 35 minutes

1 tablespoon extra-virgin olive oil

1 (14-ounce/398 mL) can light coconut milk

1 (14-ounce/398 mL) can diced tomatoes, with their juices

½ small head cauliflower, cut into ½-inch (1 cm) florets (2 cups/230 g)

2 large yellow potatoes, peeled and cut into ½-inch (1 cm) cubes (2 cups/340 g)

2 tablespoons red curry paste*

1 teaspoon dried onion flakes**

½ teaspoon garlic powder

¾ teaspoon fine sea salt, or to taste

⅛ to ¼ teaspoon cayenne pepper, to taste (optional)

Lots of freshly ground black pepper

½ cup (100 g) dried red lentils

3 cups (85 g) baby spinach, chopped

Serving suggestions

Cooked jasmine rice

Minced fresh cilantro

Fresh lime juice

Cashew Sour Cream (page 321)

I love the thick, stewlike texture of this hearty, flavorful potato curry, and serving it over a cup of fluffy rice lends just the right amount of chewiness! This dish is one of those crave-worthy comfort foods that I reach for again and again—and why wouldn't I? It only takes 10 minutes to prep, and the flavor is out of this world! The secret is the red Thai curry paste, an addictive and aromatic, sweet-and-savory blend of crushed shallots, lemongrass, garlic, ginger, chiles, and smoky spices. I created this recipe out of a need for more "hands-off" pantry dinner options that I can prepare quickly when I have a lot going on. Normally, I don't think of curry as a summer option, but I actually find myself making this for dinner in my Instant Pot when it's hot outside and I don't want to turn on the oven and heat up the kitchen—it works like a charm! Just be sure to pair it with a glass of ice water (wink wink). Not to worry if you don't have an Instant Pot. I've also included directions for making this curry on the stovetop. For a delicious grain-free option, try serving it over Roasted Garlic Cauliflower Rice (page 170)—it's a great way to use up any extra cauliflower that didn't make it into the curry!

1. In an Instant Pot or comparable multicooker, stir together the oil, coconut milk, diced tomatoes with their juices, cauliflower, potato, red curry paste, onion flakes, garlic powder, salt, cayenne pepper, and black pepper until well combined.

recipe continues

recipe continued from previous page

STORAGE

Store leftover curry in an airtight container in the fridge for up to 5 days, or freeze leftovers in an airtight container for up to 1 month. Reheat in a saucepan over medium heat for 3 to 5 minutes, until heated through.

TIPS

* Curry paste varies greatly in its heat intensity. I use Thai Kitchen brand and find that 2 to 2½ tablespoons of curry paste is perfect in this recipe. Some brands are more intense and spicy, so you may want to start with 1½ tablespoons, adding more if desired after cooking.

** Using ½ teaspoon onion powder in place of the dried onion flakes works great, too.

2. Add the red lentils on top of the mixture and gently press the lentils into the liquid (do not stir the lentils into the mixture, as this can result in a burn message). There will *just* be enough liquid to cover most of the veggies, but this is normal.

3. Secure lid in the lock position and check that the steam release handle is pointing to the "Sealing" position.

4. Press the "Pressure Cook" button (or "Manual," on some machines) and set the cook time to 5 minutes on high pressure. After 5 to 7 seconds, you'll hear a couple of beeps and the screen will say "On." The cooking process has begun!

5. You'll hear a few beeps when the cooking time is up. Immediately do a quick pressure release to avoid overcooking the curry. (I use a wooden spoon handle to shift the steam release handle to the "Venting" position to release the pressure.) Once all the pressure has been released, the float valve will sink and you won't hear steam anymore.

6. Carefully open the lid and stir in the spinach. Allow it to wilt, uncovered, for a couple of minutes. Press "Cancel" to turn the heat off.

7. Serve over rice, if you'd like, with your desired garnishes. Rest assured that the curry is delicious all on its own, too!

Stovetop Option

Combine all the ingredients except the chopped spinach in a large pot, stir, and bring to a low boil over medium-high heat. Reduce the heat to medium, cover, and simmer, stirring every 5 minutes, for 20 to 30 minutes, then add the spinach and cook for 5 minutes more, until the veggies and lentils are tender. If you notice that the curry is cooking too quickly or seems like it's sticking to the pot at any point, reduce the heat as necessary. Garnish and serve as directed.

Creamy Buffalo Cauli Tacos

Makes 8 medium tacos • **Soak time** I hour or up to overnight
Active prep time I5 minutes • **Total time** 40 minutes

For the Creamy Buffalo Sauce

I cup (I50 g) raw cashews

2 to 3 tablespoons sriracha*

½ cup water

¾ teaspoon fine sea salt, to taste

For the cauliflower

I large head cauliflower
(2½ pounds/1.125 kg)

2 tablespoons extra-virgin olive oil

Fine sea salt and freshly ground
black pepper

To assemble

8 medium (8-inch/20 cm) soft tortillas
or butter lettuce leaves

I ripe large avocado, pitted and sliced

I cup (65 g) shredded cabbage or
lettuce

Cashew Sour Cream (page 32I) or
Creamy Cashew or Sunflower Aioli
(page 293)

Have you ever tasted spicy, rich, and creamy roasted cauliflower florets so good you couldn't stop eating them straight from the pan? Well, say howdy to these cashew-sriracha delights. The Buffalo sauce couldn't be simpler, and the cashews add light sweetness and major creaminess without the need for butter. We love these tacos topped with a generous amount of Cashew Sour Cream or Creamy Cashew or Sunflower Aioli and sliced avocado to help cool the spicy cauliflower, and I love how vibrant shredded purple cabbage adds crunch and makes them look simply gorgeous. The roasted Buffalo cauliflower is also great on its own or thrown on top of a salad. Pair these creamy cauliflower tacos with a cooling side, like my Flavor Bomb Chimichurri Guacamole (page 163) and tortilla chips for a fun family meal!

I. Make the Creamy Buffalo Sauce: Place the cashews in a small bowl and add boiling water to cover. Soak for I hour, then drain. (Alternatively, soak the cashews in room-temperature water to cover for at least 8 hours or up to overnight, then drain.)

2. Preheat the oven to 425°F (220°C). Line an extra-large (I5 by 21-inch/38 by 53 cm) baking sheet (or two medium baking sheets) with parchment paper.

3. Transfer the drained cashews to a high-speed blender and add the sriracha, water, and salt. Blend on high until super smooth. If you are using a standard blender, you may need to add a little more water, a couple tablespoons at a time, to get the sauce going.

recipe continues

recipe continued from previous page

STORAGE

Store the cauliflower in an airtight container in the fridge for up to 3 days. (Store any toppings separately.) Reheat the cauliflower on a parchment-lined baking sheet in a preheated 400°F (200°C) oven for 9 to 10 minutes. Assemble the tacos while the cauliflower is reheating, then top with the cauliflower.

TIP

* I love Simply Natural sriracha. Using 2 tablespoons provides a medium heat level, while 3 tablespoons provides a hot heat level. The heat level will vary by brand, so be sure to add it to taste. If you like your tacos even spicier, feel free to drizzle some more sriracha on top before diving in!

MAKE IT GLUTEN-FREE
OR GRAIN-FREE

Use butter lettuce leaves or grain-free or gluten-free wraps, or turn this dish into a salad.

UP THE GLOW

Add some chickpeas to your taco toppings for more protein.

4. Prepare the cauliflower: Stem the cauliflower and chop it into 1½-inch (4 cm) florets (you should have about 6 heaping cups). Place the florets in a large zip-top bag (or a very large bowl) and add the oil. Toss until fully coated.

5. Add the Creamy Buffalo Sauce to the cauliflower, seal the bag, and toss and "massage" until fully coated. Keep mixing until all the cauliflower is covered in sauce; you don't want to see any white patches. Spread the cauliflower over the prepared baking sheet in a single layer, leaving ½ inch (1 cm) between the florets. Sprinkle with salt and pepper.

6. Roast the cauliflower for 15 to 25 minutes, until just fork-tender and lightly golden on the bottom. The cook time will depend on the size of your florets—I cook mine for about 22 minutes. Be sure to not overcook them, as you want a tiny bit of resistance when you bite into a floret, and you don't want them to be mushy.

7. Meanwhile, divide the tortillas among individual plates and top with your desired toppings, so all you have to do is add the cauliflower (and any crispy bits stuck to the parchment paper!) after it's finished cooking (prep win!).

8. Remove the cauliflower from the oven, let it sit for a couple of minutes, then divide it among the prepared tacos. Serve immediately.

Spicy Potato Nacho Plate

Serves 4 • **Soak time** I hour or up to overnight (for the Cashew Sour Cream)
Active prep time 25 minutes • **Total time** 45 minutes

Seasoned Crispy Baked Potato Wedges (page 159)*

I cup Cashew Sour Cream (page 321)

I cup cooked black beans or Saucy Little Black Bean Skillet (page 167)

½ to ¾ cup shredded lettuce

I ripe large (240 g) avocado, pitted and diced, or I cup guacamole

½ to ¾ cup salsa

Sriracha or other hot sauce

STORAGE

Store leftover components in separate airtight containers in the fridge for up to 3 days.

TIP

* Don't have time to make the potato wedges? Swap them out for tortilla chips for a more traditional (and super-fast!) nacho plate.

MAKE IT NUT-FREE

Omit the Cashew Sour Cream and serve with Sriracha Aioli (page 289) instead.

Move over, "loaded baked potato" . . . there's a new spud dish in town! You won't miss the sour cream and bacon bits from conventional baked potatoes when you lay your eyes on this spectacular seasoned-potato-nacho dish. These nachos are the perfect game-night food. Eric and I often make them after the kids are in bed (shhhh!) when we're craving a stick-to-your-ribs meal to eat in front of the TV. The prep time is minimal; we even like to split it up so one of us preps the potato wedges while the other preps the toppings. Easy peasy, I tell you, and that way, we never miss the kickoff or puck drop (go Leafs!). If you have some on hand, my Flavor Bomb Chimichurri Guacamole (page 163) is a dream on these nachos!

I. Prepare the Seasoned Crispy Baked Potato Wedges.

2. While the potato wedges cook, get your toppings ready: Prepare the Cashew Sour Cream, black beans, shredded lettuce, and diced avocado, and gather the salsa and sriracha.

3. To keep the potato wedges as warm as possible, I'll often serve the potato nachos directly from the baking sheet. If you prefer, you can spoon the potato wedges onto a medium platter, but they'll cool quickly. Layer on the toppings (I try to go as fast as possible so the potatoes stay warm!). If you have some Cashew Sour Cream left over, serve it on the side in a small bowl with a spoon so you can add more as you go (trust me, you'll want more). Serve immediately, and expect the entire plate to vanish before your eyes.

Italian Herb Parmesan–Crusted Portobellos with Sneaky Protein-Packed Mashed Potatoes

Makes 6 large portobello caps • **Active prep time** 40 minutes • **Total time** 40 minutes

1 batch Italian Herb Parmesan (page 301)*

1 tablespoon extra-virgin olive oil

1 tablespoon balsamic vinegar

6 large portobello mushrooms (600 to 700 g), stemmed and cleaned**

Fine sea salt

Sneaky Protein-Packed Mashed Potatoes (page 164), for serving

Freshly ground black pepper

This easy recipe could turn a mushroom hater into a raving fan, and it's one of my very favorite ways to enjoy portobello mushrooms! The key is the Italian Herb Parmesan (made with lively fresh thyme, woody rosemary, and toasty pepitas)—it gives the dish such a lovely, crunchy texture, which is the perfect complement to the hearty chewiness of the roasted mushrooms. The Sneaky Protein-Packed Mashed Potatoes make this dish rich and hearty, but the crusted portobellos are great on their own, too (and the prep time decreases to just 20 minutes if you are only making the portobellos with parmesan). If you have leftover roasted portobellos, I love storing them individually in small airtight containers, complete with the potatoes and parm topping. They make delicious *on the glow* lunches if you have a microwave handy!

1. Preheat the oven to 400°F (200°C). Line a large rimmed baking sheet with parchment paper.

2. Prepare the Italian Herb Parmesan. Transfer it to a small bowl and cover it so it doesn't dry out. Quickly wash the processor bowl and blade so they're ready to use to make the Sneaky Protein-Packed Mashed Potatoes later on.

3. In a small bowl, whisk together the oil and vinegar. With a pastry brush, brush both sides of the portobellos with the oil-vinegar mixture until fully coated, stirring the oil-vinegar

recipe continues

recipe continued from previous page

STORAGE

Wrap the fully assembled portobellos individually in aluminum foil or place them in an airtight container and store in the fridge for up to 4 days. To reheat, unwrap the assembled portobellos and place in a baking dish lined with parchment paper (you can also add leftover mashed potatoes to the baking dish, if you have some). Bake, uncovered, in a preheated 400°F (200°C) oven for 15 to 17 minutes, until heated through and golden. Refresh the parmesan flavors with a tiny sprinkling of sherry vinegar and salt just before serving.

TIPS

* For this recipe, use 2 teaspoons sherry vinegar in the parm instead of 1 teaspoon, as it needs a stronger flavor when paired with the mushrooms.

** To clean the portobellos, rub the outside with a damp paper towel to remove any debris. With a small spoon, scrape out the black gills inside the cap and discard them.

mixture as needed to recombine as you go. Place the caps stemmed-side up on the prepared baking sheet and sprinkle each one with a small pinch of salt.

4. Bake the mushrooms for 18 to 22 minutes, until the caps look like they are shriveling up and are fork-tender.

5. Meanwhile, prepare the Sneaky Protein-Packed Mashed Potatoes.

6. Remove the portobellos from the oven and pour off any liquid that has collected in the caps while they were cooking. Top each cap with 3 tablespoons of the parmesan and spread it evenly to cover the surface of the mushroom. Serve one or two portobello(s) on a bed of warm mashed potatoes, seasoned with a sprinkle of salt and pepper and topped with any leftover parm.

Weeknight Tex-Mex Quinoa with Cashew Sour Cream

Serves 4 • **Active prep time** 20 minutes • **Total time** 40 minutes

¼ to ½ cup Cashew Sour Cream (page 321)

For the quinoa

1 tablespoon extra-virgin olive oil

1 large jalapeño (70 g), seeded and diced

3 large garlic cloves (18 g), minced (1½ tablespoons)

1½ cups (200 g) diced (¼-inch/5 mm pieces) peeled sweet potato (1 small)

1 (14-ounce/398 mL) can black beans, drained and rinsed*

1 (14-ounce/398 mL) can fire-roasted diced tomatoes, with their juices

1 cup (185 g) uncooked quinoa

1 cup low-sodium vegetable broth

2 to 3 teaspoons Tex-Mex Spice Blend (page 313), to taste

Fine sea salt and freshly ground black pepper

Topping suggestions

½ cup packed (12 g) fresh cilantro, minced

1 to 2 ripe large (240 g each) avocados, pitted and diced

1 large lime, sliced into wedges

This is one of our family's go-to weeknight meals. We love it served either bowl-style, loaded with toppings, or as a burrito filling. The charred fire-roasted tomatoes and my sweet-and-smoky Tex-Mex Spice Blend are the perfect pair in this simple yet addictive dish. Oh, and did I mention it's also killer served with my Vegan Cheese Sauce 2.0 (page 290) and corn chips for scooping? Oh my word. This one-pot wonder is incredibly easy, and everyone loves adding their own toppings. When we have leftovers, I love to pack them up for a ready-made *on the glow* lunch, topped with all the fixin's—I squeeze lots of lime juice over the avocado to keep it fresh. You'll also love this quinoa dish topped with my Pretty Parsley-Cilantro Pepita Pesto (page 275), Easy Chimichurri Sauce (page 272), or Flavor Bomb Chimichurri Guacamole (page 163) for a delicious twist. Really, there are at least a dozen ways to enjoy it, so get creative and change it up when you feel so inclined! In the summer, I grill halved bell peppers and use them as "bowls" for the quinoa mixture.

1. Prepare the Cashew Sour Cream. Set aside.

2. Make the quinoa: In a medium pot (at least 3 quarts/3 L), heat the oil over medium heat. Add the jalapeño and garlic and stir to coat with the oil. Sauté until softened, 4 to 6 minutes.

recipe continues

recipe continued from previous page

STORAGE

Store in an airtight container in the fridge for up to 3 days, or freeze in a freezer bag with the air pressed out or in an airtight container for up to 1 month. To reheat, thaw (if necessary) and transfer to a saucepan. Stir in a bit of vegetable broth to moisten and heat over medium heat until warmed throughout. Add a pinch or two of Tex-Mex Spice Blend and a squeeze of lime juice to revive the flavors, if desired.

TIPS

* One 14-ounce (398 mL) can of black beans is equivalent to 1½ cups cooked black beans, if you prefer to cook them from scratch.

This recipe is a one-pot recipe if the Cashew Sour Cream is made in advance or omitted from the recipe.

MAKE IT NUT-FREE

Top the fajitas with Flavor Bomb Chimichurri Guacamole or avocado instead of Cashew Sour Cream.

UP THE GLOW

Add fresh or frozen corn kernels during step 3. Chopped roasted red peppers, stirred in after cooking, are also nice!

3. Stir in the sweet potato, black beans, diced tomatoes with their juices, quinoa, broth, and 2 teaspoons of the Tex-Mex Spice Blend.

4. Increase the heat to medium-high and bring to a low boil, then reduce the heat to medium-low, and cover with a tight-fitting lid. Gently simmer, stirring a few times throughout to check if the mixture is sticking, for 23 to 30 minutes, until the sweet potato is tender and the broth has been absorbed. Reduce the heat during the last several minutes of the cooking time. If at any point the quinoa mixture begins to dry up or stick to the pot, reduce the heat or add a splash of broth and stir to rehydrate.

5. Taste the mixture and add more Tex-Mex Spice Blend, if desired (I tend to stir in 1 teaspoon more). Season with salt and pepper.

6. Spoon into bowls and add your desired toppings. I love adding a generous dollop of Cashew Sour Cream, minced cilantro, lots of avocado, and a squeeze of lime juice.

School Night Tofu Scramble with Roasted Red Pepper and Walnut Dip

Serves 6 (¾ cup scramble per serving) • **Active prep time** 20 minutes • **Total time** 25 minutes

1 batch Roasted Red Pepper and Walnut Dip (page 298)

1 tablespoon extra-virgin olive oil

1 cup (140 g) diced yellow or sweet onion (1 medium)

3 large garlic cloves (18 g), minced (1½ tablespoons)

1 small red bell pepper (180 g), diced (1 cup)

1 cup (180 g) diced tomato (2 medium)

½ cup (95 g) oil-packed unsalted sun-dried tomatoes, drained and chopped*

½ teaspoon ground turmeric, or to taste

1 teaspoon ground cumin

1 (16-ounce/450 g) package firm or extra-firm tofu, drained and patted dry**

½ cup (10 g) fresh parsley, minced

2 teaspoons fresh lemon juice, or to taste, plus more for serving

½ to 1 teaspoon fine sea salt, to taste

Freshly ground black pepper

⅛ teaspoon cayenne pepper, or to taste

Freshly sliced bread (optional)

Cashew Sour Cream (page 321; optional)

In our house, we love "breakfast for dinner" nights. They're fast and satisfying, and the whole family tends to enjoy them (miracles do happen!). One of my favorite ways to serve tofu is in a veggie-packed scramble. Its neutral flavor soaks up all the flavorful ingredients around it, and its texture is light, fluffy, and filling all at once. I've packed this scramble with sunny Mediterranean flavors like garlic, red bell pepper, both fresh and sun-dried tomatoes, and gorgeous bright green parsley. It's all topped with my creamy Roasted Red Pepper and Walnut Dip for even more flavor and staying power. For a speedy weeknight option, we love to serve the tofu scramble on whole-grain toast spread with Cashew Sour Cream (or store-bought vegan mayo, mashed avocado, or hummus in a pinch!), and top it with a generous spoonful of red pepper dip. Or serve it with my Seasoned Crispy Baked Potato Wedges (page 159) for the ultimate "breakfast for dinner" combo. Have fun changing up the veggies and herbs for what you have on hand, and experiment with different toppings, like my Perfect Basil Pesto (page 294).

1. Make the Roasted Red Pepper and Walnut Dip and set aside.

2. In a large skillet or pot, heat the oil over medium heat. Add the onion and garlic and stir to coat with the oil. Sauté for 4 to 5 minutes, until the onion is softened.

3. Add the diced bell pepper and tomatoes and stir to combine. Raise the heat to medium-high and sauté for another 5 minutes,

recipe continues

recipe continued from previous page

STORAGE

Store in an airtight container in the fridge for up to 4 to 5 days. Reheat in an oiled skillet over medium heat, stirring occasionally, for 4 to 5 minutes.

TIPS

* If your sun-dried tomatoes contain sodium, be sure to add the salt gradually and taste as you go to make sure you don't overseason the scramble.

** Firm or extra-firm tofu blocks work best in this recipe. If your tofu feels soft and waterlogged, be sure to press it in a tofu press for at least 30 minutes to extract the excess liquid before you begin. If you don't have a tofu press, lay two thick dish towels on top of each other on the counter and place a few sheets of paper towels on top. Slice the tofu into 9 or 10 rectangles and set them on the paper towels in a single layer. Place two more thick dish towels on top of the slabs and place a cutting board on top. Set several heavy books on top of the cutting board and press for 30 minutes.

MAKE IT NUT-FREE

Use the nut-free option when preparing the Roasted Red Pepper and Walnut Dip, and omit the optional Cashew Sour Cream.

UP THE GLOW

Add a sprinkle of nutritional yeast for a light cheesy flavor.

until the bell pepper starts to soften. During the last couple of minutes, stir in the sun-dried tomatoes, turmeric, and cumin to combine.

4. Break the tofu block into 4 or 5 large chunks. Using your hands, hold each chunk over the skillet and crumble it into ½-inch (1 cm) pieces. Stir the tofu into the veggie mixture until thoroughly combined. The tofu will turn a gorgeous yellow color thanks to the turmeric. Stir in the parsley. Reduce the heat to medium and cook for 3 to 5 minutes, until heated through.

5. Add the lemon juice, salt, black pepper, and cayenne pepper, to taste, stirring as you go.

6. Toast the bread, if using, and spread Cashew Sour Cream over one side of each slice. Top with a generous spoonful of the warm tofu scramble, followed by a dollop of the Roasted Red Pepper Walnut Dip. Garnish with a squeeze of lemon juice and a sprinkle of salt and black pepper, if desired, then serve.

Mmm! Maple Baked Beans and Greens

Serves 4 (1 cup per serving) • **Active prep time** 20 minutes • **Total time** 50 minutes

1½ tablespoons extra virgin olive oil

1 medium onion, diced (1½ cups/210 g)

⅓ cup (60 g) chopped pitted Medjool dates*

7 to 8 tablespoons pure maple syrup, to taste

4 to 5 tablespoons apple cider vinegar, to taste

¼ cup tomato paste

1½ tablespoons blackstrap molasses

1 to 1½ tablespoons whole-grain mustard, to taste

2 teaspoons smoked paprika

1½ teaspoons liquid smoke

2 (14-ounce/398 mL) cans navy beans, drained and rinsed**

¾ teaspoon fine sea salt, or to taste

Freshly ground black pepper

4 very large chard leaves, stemmed and finely chopped (4 cups/160 g)

As a kid, I used to love canned baked beans, but somehow I don't think they would impress me much as an adult, with my (slightly) more sophisticated palate. My weeknight-friendly version uses just the right amount of sauce for moisture, while keeping the focus on the complex sweet, smoky, and tangy flavors of the apple cider vinegar, liquid smoke, tomato paste, pure maple syrup, and smoked paprika. I also packed some green power into this typically low-on-veggies dish by adding several servings of finely chopped chard (which cooks down a lot so it doesn't overwhelm the other ingredients!). Chard haters will rejoice because the amazing flavors of the sauce completely disguise the chard. Eric, a skeptical bitter-greens eater, says, "I'd never know this was chard!" What's even better? While this dish is baking, a delicious maple aroma fills the entire house—it's seriously enticing enough to wake someone from a deep winter slumber! For a simple dinner, we love to serve these baked beans over toast and pair them with a tangy green salad such as my Apple Honey–Dijon Mixed Greens (see page 285). If you're feeding a crowd or simply want to have extra meals on hand for a couple of days, this recipe doubles beautifully. For heat lovers, try stirring a bit of cayenne pepper into your portion. It adds a great kick!

1. Preheat the oven to 350°F (180°C).

2. In a large oven-safe pot (I use a large 5-quart/5 L enameled Dutch oven), heat the oil over medium heat. Add the onion,

recipe continues

recipe continued from previous page

STORAGE

Store in an airtight container in the fridge for up to 4 days, or freeze in a freezer bag with the air pressed out or in an airtight container for up to 2 months.

TIPS

* I love to store pitted dates in the freezer for several hours to make them easier to chop—they don't stick together nearly as much.

** Two 14-ounce (398 mL) cans of navy beans are equivalent to 3 heaping cups total cooked navy beans, if you prefer to cook them from scratch.

stir to coat with the oil, and sauté for 5 to 7 minutes, until softened.

3. Add the dates, maple syrup, vinegar, tomato paste, molasses, mustard, smoked paprika, and liquid smoke to the pot and stir well until combined.

4. Increase the heat to medium-high and bring the mixture to a simmer. Simmer for a couple of minutes. Stir in the drained beans and season the mixture with salt and pepper.

5. Cover the pot with an oven-safe lid (or aluminum foil, if necessary) and, using oven mitts, carefully transfer the pot to the oven. Bake the beans for 20 minutes. Carefully remove the pot from the oven, uncover, and stir in the chard. Cover and bake for another 10 minutes, or until the mixture is bubbling and the greens have darkened slightly.

6. Stir, then carefully taste and add more vinegar, maple syrup, mustard, salt, or pepper, to taste, if desired.

Velvety Alfredo Mushroom-and-Chickpea Pot

Serves 4 (I cup per serving) • **Active prep time** 20 minutes • **Total time** 30 minutes

2 tablespoons extra-virgin olive oil

2 cups (280 g) diced yellow onion (I large)

6 large garlic cloves (36 g), minced (3 tablespoons)

16 ounces (450 g) cremini mushrooms, thinly sliced (7 heaping cups)

½ to ¾ teaspoon fine sea salt, to taste

I cup plus 2 tablespoons low-sodium veggie broth

4½ tablespoons smooth raw cashew butter

6 tablespoons (30 g) nutritional yeast

I (14-ounce/398 mL) can chickpeas, drained and rinsed*

½ to I teaspoon red pepper flakes, to taste

3 to 4 teaspoons white wine vinegar, to taste

Freshly ground black pepper

Cayenne pepper (optional)

For serving (optional)

Roasted Garlic Cauliflower Rice (page 170), cooked rice, or crusty bread

Minced fresh parsley, for garnish

This savory, warming dinner comes together in 30 minutes with ingredients I usually have on hand. I could throw on some thick socks, tuck in under a warm blanket, and eat a hearty bowl of this meal on a cold day, and I'd be perfectly happy! Creamy, rich cashew butter, umami-rich nutritional yeast, immune-boosting garlic, and flavorful veggie broth come together to create the sauce for this creamy, dreamy mushroom-and-chickpea "Alfredo." It's downright decadent, especially when paired with crusty bread for scooping. I also love it served over freshly cooked rice, which amps up the staying power of this comfort-food bowl. To save a bit of prep work, I'll often buy presliced mushrooms. (Okay, okay, I often buy prepeeled garlic cloves, too! Whatever saves time and sanity, I say.)

I. In a large pot, heat the oil over medium heat. Add the onion and garlic and stir to coat with the oil. Sauté for 5 to 6 minutes, until the onion is softened.

2. Add the mushrooms and a pinch of salt and stir to combine. Increase the heat to medium-high and sauté, uncovered, stirring occasionally, for 8 to 10 minutes more, until most of the liquid released by the mushrooms has evaporated (there should be I to 2 tablespoons of liquid left in the pot). If any bits stick to the pan, add a touch of the broth and stir to scrape them up.

recipe continues

recipe continued from previous page

STORAGE

Store leftovers in an airtight container in the fridge for up to 4 days, or freeze in a freezer bag with the air pressed out or in an airtight container for up to 1 month. To reheat, thaw completely (if frozen) and transfer to a saucepan. Cover and heat over medium heat, stirring frequently, for 5 to 8 minutes. Reduce the heat, if necessary, to prevent it from sticking to the pot, and add a splash of broth for moisture, if needed.

TIP

* One 14-ounce (398 mL) can of chickpeas is equivalent to 1½ cups cooked chickpeas, if you prefer to cook them from scratch.

3. In a small bowl, whisk together the broth and cashew butter until smooth. (If your cashew butter is quite firm, throw the broth and cashew butter into a blender and blend until smooth.)

4. Add the broth–cashew butter mixture, nutritional yeast, chickpeas, and red pepper flakes to the pot. Reduce the heat to medium and simmer, uncovered, stirring every few minutes, for 5 to 8 minutes more.

5. Taste and season with the vinegar, black pepper, and additional salt and red pepper flakes, to taste. If you like a kick of heat, stir in a bit of cayenne, too. Serve with desired accompaniments, garnished with parsley, if you like.

Crispy Potato Stacks with Boom! Broccoli Pesto

Serves 5 (3 stacks per serving) • **Active prep time** 20 minutes • **Total time** 45 minutes

3 large russet potatoes (950 g total)

1½ to 2 tablespoons extra-virgin olive oil

Fine sea salt and freshly ground black pepper

I batch Boom! Broccoli Pesto (page 276)*

I heaping cup (165 g) thinly sliced English cucumber

I large or 2 medium tomatoes, sliced

I to 2 cups sprouts or microgreens (optional)

Fresh lemon juice (optional)**

These pesto-covered potatoes are simply irresistible, in that stick-to-your-ribs, (healthy!) comfort food kinda way. Thick russet potato slices are lightly brushed with oil and seasoned with sea salt, then baked until buttery and crispy. I love slathering on my favorite pesto and stacking them with fresh tomato, sprouts/microgreens, and cucumber. The crunchy and creamy textures are just crave-worthy, not to mention that the vibrant flavors will have your taste buds dancing with each and every bite! If you have some on hand, these stacks are over-the-top when sprinkled with a finishing salt, such as a large-flake sea salt like Maldon, or my Vegan Parmesan (page 317), just before serving. These stacks are lovely served alongside my Mega Crunch Sun-Dried Tomato–Pepita Taco Salad (page 204) for a nutritious, veggie-packed meal.

I. Preheat the oven to 425°F (220°C). Line an extra-large (15 by 21-inch/38 by 53 cm) baking sheet (or two large baking sheets) with parchment paper.

2. Using a sharp knife, slice the potatoes lengthwise into ½- to ¾-inch-thick (I to 2 cm) slabs. (I get about 5 slabs per large russet potato and end up with about 15 total when using 3 large russets. Don't fuss about the number too much, though!)

3. Place the potato slabs on the prepared baking sheet. Using a pastry brush (or simply your hands), fully coat both sides of each potato slab with the oil. Arrange the slabs ½ inch (I cm)

recipe continues

recipe continued from previous page

STORAGE

Store the potato slabs and toppings (except the tomato and cucumber) in separate airtight containers in the fridge for up to 4 days. Reheat the potato slabs in an oiled skillet over medium heat for a few minutes on each side (I like to sprinkle on a little sea salt first to revive their flavors). Remove from the heat and add the toppings. I like to slice tomato and cucumber fresh just before serving, as opposed to storing sliced tomatoes in the fridge.

TIPS

* To change up the pesto, try swapping it for Pretty Parsley-Cilantro Pepita Pesto (page 275) or Lemony Dill Protein Pesto (page 297).

** You can reserve any leftover lemon juice from the pesto recipe to drizzle over the stacks, if you like.

apart on the pan and sprinkle each slab generously with salt and a small amount of pepper.

4. Roast the potatoes for 25 to 35 minutes, until tender and golden brown in some spots, flipping them once halfway through baking. I prefer these slightly overcooked so they'll crisp up a bit around the edges . . . yum!

5. While the potatoes roast, prepare the Boom! Broccoli Pesto, cucumber, and tomato.

6. When the potatoes are ready, immediately assemble the potato stacks: Season the potatoes with another generous sprinkle of salt. Generously coat the surface of each slab with about 1½ tablespoons of the pesto and top each with cucumber, tomato, and a small handful of sprouts, if desired. You can cut the tomato slices to fit the slabs, if you're feeling fancy! Squeeze a little lemon juice over the stacks, if desired, and season with additional salt and pepper before serving, if you like. Serve warm.

Sloppy Glows

Serves 4 (¾ cup per serving) • **Soak time** I hour or up to overnight (for the Cashew Sour Cream)
Active prep time I5 minutes • **Total time** 30 minutes

4 hamburger buns

I extra-large red onion

2 tablespoons extra-virgin olive oil

4 medium garlic cloves (16 g), minced

2 teaspoons chili powder

I½ teaspoons ground cumin

I¼ cups tomato sauce, plus more
if needed

⅔ cup (II5 g) jarred roasted red
peppers, drained and diced

⅓ cup (65 g) oil-packed unsalted sun-
dried tomatoes, drained and chopped

I (14-ounce/398 mL) can lentils, drained
and rinsed*

I½ to 2 tablespoons vegan
Worcestershire sauce, to taste

I½ to 2 tablespoons unpacked brown
sugar, to taste

½ to ¾ teaspoon fine sea salt, to taste

Freshly ground black pepper

½ to I teaspoon apple cider vinegar,
to taste

Cashew Sour Cream (page 32I;
optional)

Sloppy Glow? What did you just call me? I guess the nickname
could be worse. And really, "Sloppy Glow" isn't that far from
the truth . . . most days I'm a hot mess in the kitchen, and in
life, really. I say, embrace your inner Sloppy Glow and ditch
the perfectionism! It's perfectly acceptable to be falling apart
at the seams, wearing joggers for days straight (this was so me
during the development of this cookbook), or in the case of *these*
Sloppy Glows, bursting out of a bun! Whether you are a Sloppy
Glow, a hot mess, or even a proud perfectionist, I think you're
going to fall in love with these saucy, flavor-packed lentils, made
special with roasted red peppers, tangy vegan Worcestershire
sauce, and just a hint of brown sugar and served up in a toasty
bun. Our whole family loves Sloppy Glows; I love mine paired
with Cashew Sour Cream, sliced pickles, and mashed avocado
with a sprinkle of sea salt—the creaminess and crunch are
the perfect contrast to the tangy lentil mixture! If you'd like
an accompaniment, pair your Sloppy Glows with my Charred
Broccoli Quinoa Salad with Apple Honey–Dijon Dressing
(page 187). If you'd like to make the lentil mixture a little (or a
lot) spicy, stir in a bit of sriracha, red pepper flakes, or cayenne
pepper.

I. Preheat the oven to 400°F (200°C). Open each bun and place
them split-side up on a large baking sheet. Set aside.

2. Slice the red onion in half. Slice one half into very thin
rounds, rinse, drain, and set aside to garnish the burgers later.
Finely chop the other half (you should have I cup).

recipe continues

recipe continued from previous page

STORAGE

Store in an airtight container in the fridge for up to 4 days, or freeze in a freezer bag with the air pressed out or in an airtight container for up to 2 months. To reheat, thaw completely (if frozen) and transfer to a preheated oiled skillet over medium heat. Cover and cook for 2 to 4 minutes. I like to revive the flavor a bit with the tiniest sprinkle of chili powder and salt, and a drizzle of tomato sauce, if the lentil mixture gets dry in the skillet.

TIP

* One 14-ounce (398 mL) can of lentils is equivalent to 1½ cups cooked lentils, if you prefer to cook them from scratch.

MAKE IT GLUTEN- OR GRAIN-FREE

Use gluten-free buns or serve the lentils over a cooked gluten-free grain, such as brown rice or quinoa. To make it grain-free, use grain-free buns.

3. In a large skillet or pot, heat the oil over medium heat. Add the 1 cup finely chopped onion and the garlic and stir to coat with the oil. Sauté for 5 to 6 minutes, until the onion has softened. (It's important that the onions are tender.)

4. Stir in the chili powder and cumin and cook for a minute more, until fragrant.

5. Add the tomato sauce, roasted red peppers, sun-dried tomatoes, drained lentils, Worcestershire sauce, brown sugar (starting with 1½ tablespoons), salt, and black pepper to taste. Stir to combine. Raise the heat to medium-high and bring to a rapid simmer. Reduce the heat to medium and gently simmer, uncovered, stirring occasionally, for 5 to 8 minutes, until slightly thickened.

6. While the lentil mixture simmers, toast the buns in the oven for 6 to 10 minutes, until lightly toasted (this adds a lovely texture contrast to the soft lentil mixture).

7. Stir the vinegar into the lentil mixture. Taste and add more salt, pepper, Worcestershire sauce, and sugar, if desired. Reduce the heat to low and cover until ready to serve.

8. Add a big scoop of the warm lentil mixture to the bottom of each toasted bun and top with the sliced onions (if you're not a fan of onion, you can skip this). Add a generous dollop of Cashew Sour Cream to each, if desired, and close the buns. Serve immediately.

Undercover Roasted Veggie Tomato Pasta

Serves 4, with leftover sauce (makes 5½ cups sauce)
Active prep time 15 minutes • **Total time** 55 minutes

1 medium green or yellow zucchini (275 g)

1 medium sweet onion (280 g)

2 large red bell peppers (510 g total), seeded

2 medium carrots (210 g total), peeled

5 large garlic cloves (30 g)

3 tablespoons plus 1 teaspoon extra-virgin olive oil

¼ teaspoon fine sea salt, or to taste

¼ teaspoon freshly ground black pepper, or to taste

16 ounces (5¾ cups/450 g) dry pasta

1 (28-ounce/796 mL) can fire-roasted diced tomatoes, with their juices

¼ to ½ teaspoon white wine vinegar, to taste

⅓ cup lightly packed (9 g) fresh basil leaves, finely chopped (optional)

Ah, age two. Precisely the age when both of my kids started using the word "no" with a vengeance, refusing all kinds of foods they'd previously loved. It's also precisely the age when both of my kids started picking things out of dishes . . . like chopped veggies, lentils, and, well, *anything*. You better not show a speck of texture, or it's going to be refused! I went from thinking I had nailed this kid-friendly-healthy-eating thing to feeling discouraged and defeated most days. A few years ago, I came up with this sneaky pasta sauce out of sheer desperation—I needed to find a way to get more vegetables (hell, *any* vegetables!) into my kids' bellies. During certain toddler phases, they were even turning away smoothies, but the one thing they rarely rejected was our dear old friend pasta. So I roasted a bunch of veggies and blended them into a homemade tomato sauce. Not only is it easy for busy people (just 15 minutes of prep!), but it's incredibly nutritious, unique-tasting, thick, rich, and luxuriously smooth, perfect for even the most discerning of family members. Not in the mood for pasta? This sauce works beautifully as a tomato soup! Simply heat it up after blending and season to taste. Serve with fresh bread for dipping or crumbled crackers on top.

1. Preheat the oven to 425°F (220°C). Line an extra-large (15 by 21-inch/38 by 53 cm) baking sheet with parchment paper.

recipe continues

recipe continued from previous page

STORAGE

Store leftover sauce in an airtight container in the fridge for up to 5 days or in the freezer for up to 1 month. Thaw (if frozen) and reheat in a pot over medium heat until heated through.

MAKE IT GRAIN-FREE

Use grain-free pasta.

MAKE IT GLUTEN-FREE

Use gluten-free pasta.

UP THE GLOW

Add my Italian Seasoning (page 312) to taste in step 6. For an extra-decadent sauce, stir in a bit of vegan butter during the last step—it's lovely!

2. Chop the zucchini, onion, and bell peppers into ½-inch (1 cm) pieces and slice the carrots crosswise into ¼-inch-thick (5 mm) coins (it's important to cut the vegetables to the specified sizes so they cook within the appropriate time frame), adding them to the prepared baking sheet as you go. You should have 2 cups zucchini, 1½ cups onion, 3 cups bell peppers, and 1¼ cups carrots. Put the garlic cloves on a square of aluminum foil, drizzle with 1 teaspoon of the oil, and fold the foil to completely enclose the garlic.

3. Toss the veggies with 2 tablespoons of the oil until thoroughly coated. Sprinkle with the salt and pepper. Place the foil packet with the garlic on the baking sheet.

4. Roast the veggies and garlic uncovered, for 40 to 45 minutes, until the veggies are lightly charred (this adds mega flavor!) and fork-tender. You can remove the garlic a bit earlier to avoid burning it, if necessary. After cooking, carefully unwrap the garlic and discard the foil.

5. Meanwhile, bring a large pot of water to a boil. When the veggies have about 10 minutes left in the oven, add the pasta to the boiling water and cook until al dente according to the package directions. Drain the pasta and return it to the pot.

6. In a high-speed blender, add the fire-roasted tomatoes with their juices, the roasted veggies and garlic, and the remaining 1 tablespoon oil. Blend on medium speed until smooth. (Depending on the size of your blender, you may have to do this in a couple of batches.) The sauce will be luxuriously thick.

7. Add your desired amount of sauce to the pot with the drained pasta and stir to combine. Depending on how much pasta you prepared, you may have sauce left over, so be sure to see the storage information. Stir in the vinegar to taste (start with ¼ teaspoon and add more little by little from there) and season with additional salt and pepper, if needed. Stir in the basil (if using—if you have a picky eater who might spot that speck of green and gasp, you can sprinkle it over individual plates instead). Cover and simmer over medium heat for about 5 minutes to allow the flavors to develop even more. Serve and enjoy!

Italian One-Pot Buttery Tomato, White Beans, and Farro

Serves 5 (1 cup per serving) • **Active prep time** 20 minutes • **Total time** 40 to 45 minutes

⅓ cup 5-Ingredient Vegan Butter (page 318) or extra-virgin olive oil

2 cups (280 g) diced onion (1 large)

¼ cup (33 g) minced garlic (6 large cloves)

1 tablespoon Italian seasoning, homemade (page 312) or store-bought

1 teaspoon dried red pepper flakes, or to taste

1 cup (145 g) dry quick-cooking 10-minute farro, rinsed and drained*

2¼ cups water

1¼ cups marinara sauce

1 (14-ounce/398 mL) can white beans, drained and rinsed**

⅓ cup (65 g) oil-packed unsalted sun-dried tomatoes, drained and minced

2½ tablespoons nutritional yeast

½ to ¾ teaspoon fine sea salt, to taste

Freshly ground black pepper

½ to 1½ teaspoons white wine vinegar or fresh lemon juice, to taste

¾ cup packed (23 g) fresh basil leaves, minced (optional)

Every plant-based eater needs a go-to grains-and-beans dish in their back pocket, and this one is ours! And it just so happens to be one of the most omnivore-friendly dishes in the book (as rated by my dear family, friends, and recipe testers). This is a fantastic dinner option when you want something that can be made in one pot and without much fuss. I love making it when I have last-minute company coming over, because I usually have most of the ingredients on hand, and it's just so nourishing and flavorful. The bright acidity of the marinara combined with the Italian seasoning and fresh basil make this one-pot meal irresistible. I call for more butter or oil in this recipe than I normally do, but it's necessary to balance out the acidity from the tomatoes. White beans boost the protein and fiber content, and 10-minute quick-cooking farro gives it a nutty chewiness. Take your meal over the top with a sprinkle of Italian Herb Parmesan (page 301) or Vegan Parmesan (page 317) just before serving. It's also dreamy served with a swirl of Cashew Sour Cream (page 321) or Creamy Cashew or Sunflower Aioli (page 293), toasted bread, and a tangy green salad such as my Apple Honey–Dijon Mixed Greens (see page 285). Leftovers reheat like a dream, and we even love to use them in wraps for instant *on the glow* Italian burritos!

1. In a large pot, melt the butter over medium heat. Add the onion and garlic and stir to coat with the butter. Increase the heat to medium-high and sauté, reducing the heat as necessary

recipe continues

recipe continued from previous page

STORAGE

Store in an airtight container in the fridge for up to 4 days, or freeze in a freezer bag with the air pressed out or in an airtight container for up to 2 months. To reheat, thaw completely (if frozen), transfer to a lightly oiled skillet, cover, and heat over medium heat, stirring occasionally, for 4 to 5 minutes.

TIPS

* It's crucial that you use a quick-cooking farro (often labeled "precooked," "10-minute," or "Italian" farro)—be sure the package says it cooks in only 10 to 12 minutes. Regular farro, which has a cooking time of 30 minutes or longer, and semi-pearled farro do not work in this recipe. Even though the package of quick-cooking farro indicates it cooks in 10 to 12 minutes, I find it takes longer to cook in a thick tomato sauce, so stick with the cook time indicated in the recipe.

** I like using large white beans like butter beans or great northern beans in this recipe. However, if all you have on hand are navy beans or cannellini beans, feel free to use them! One 14-ounce (398 mL) can of white beans is equivalent to 1½ cups cooked white beans, if you prefer to cook them from scratch.

MAKE IT KID-FRIENDLY

Reduce or omit the red pepper flakes as needed.

to prevent burning, for 7 to 9 minutes, until the onion is very soft (it's important to sauté the onion until soft so it's not the least bit crunchy in the finished dish).

2. Stir in the Italian seasoning and red pepper flakes and cook for 1 minute, or until fragrant.

3. Add the farro to the pot, stir, and cook for another minute.

4. Add the water, marinara sauce, drained beans, sun-dried tomatoes, nutritional yeast, salt (start with ½ teaspoon, or even less, if your marinara sauce has a lot of sodium), and black pepper, to taste. Stir well to combine.

5. Increase the heat to high and bring the mixture to a low boil. Immediately reduce the heat to medium and simmer rapidly, uncovered, stirring frequently, for 18 to 23 minutes. After 18 minutes of cooking, carefully taste the farro. If it isn't tender and cooked through, keep cooking for a few minutes longer, then check. The farro should be tender, but it will still have a *slight* chewiness when ready, and the sauce should be thickened.

6. Remove from the heat and stir in the vinegar to taste, along with the basil. (You can also sprinkle the basil on top of the dish just before serving for a pop of color!) Taste and add more red pepper flakes, salt, and black pepper, to taste, if desired. Serve on its own or with some crusty bread for dipping.

Speedy 8-Ingredient Pantry Dal

Serves 4 (1¼ cups per serving) • **Active prep time** 8 minutes
Total time 22 to 37 minutes (depending on the veggies used)

1 tablespoon virgin coconut oil or extra-virgin olive oil

4 cups diced (peeled, if necessary) veggies (see headnote)

½ cup (100 g) dried red lentils

½ cup water, plus more if needed

1 (14-ounce/398 mL) can diced tomatoes, with their juices

1 (14-ounce/398 mL) can light coconut milk

1½ teaspoons garlic powder

1½ teaspoons dried onion flakes*

1 tablespoon good-quality curry powder, or to taste**

¾ to 1 teaspoon fine sea salt, to taste

Freshly ground black pepper

Chopped fresh cilantro, for garnish

Cooked basmati rice or grain of choice (optional), for serving

Fresh lime juice, for serving

With only eight ingredients and 8 minutes of prep time, this dish can be whipped up lightning fast using pantry staples and whatever veggies you have on hand. No being stuck in the kitchen or last-minute trips to the store for this one! I started with the traditional legumes and spices that make up an authentic dal and added veggies to make it a speedy, nutritionally rounded dinner option. You can choose the quick curry powder option or take a couple of extra minutes and use my custom spice combo. I love it both ways! If you have some on hand, baby spinach is a great addition—simply stir it in at the end of cooking. We love this dish with 2 cups (220 g) of chopped zucchini and 2 cups (110 g) of broccoli, but feel free to use any veggies you have on hand to make this truly a "pantry" recipe! A few ideas: carrot and zucchini, potatoes and peas, peeled sweet potato and red bell pepper, or cauliflower and broccoli.

1. In a large pot, warm the oil over medium-low heat. Add the veggies to the pot and stir to coat with the oil.

2. Add the lentils, water, diced tomatoes with their juices, coconut milk, garlic powder, onion flakes, curry powder, salt, and pepper to taste. Stir to combine.

3. Increase the heat to high and bring to a low boil. Reduce the heat to medium and gently simmer, uncovered, stirring

recipe continues

recipe continued from previous page

STORAGE

Store in an airtight container in the fridge for up to 5 days, or freeze leftovers in an airtight container for up to 1 month.

TIPS

* Onion powder will work instead, but I would suggest adding it to taste in ¼-teaspoon increments to prevent its flavor overpowering the dish.

** If you don't have your favorite curry powder on hand, you can substitute the following: 1½ teaspoons ground turmeric, 1½ teaspoons ground coriander, 1 teaspoon ground cumin, ½ teaspoon ground ginger (or more to taste), and ¼ teaspoon cayenne pepper (optional). Don't forget to use the 1½ teaspoons of both garlic powder and onion flakes, as well.

MAKE IT KID-FRIENDLY

Use the spice blend in the Tips, and omit the optional cayenne. Use veggies that are already hits with your child.

occasionally, for 15 to 30 minutes, until the veggies and lentils are tender; the cook time will depend on the type and size of veggies you use (check on them frequently). If any lentils stick to the bottom of the pot, scrape them up and reduce the heat, if necessary. (If you're using potatoes, I suggest covering the pot while cooking because they don't contain as much liquid as other veggies; you may need to add more water to thin the mixture.)

4. Garnish with cilantro and serve over rice, if desired, with some fresh lime juice squeezed over the top.

20-Minute Sweet Potato Noodle Bowl with Sesame, Cilantro, Lime, and Avocado

Serves 2 · **Active prep time** 20 minutes · **Total time** 20 minutes

1 large or 2 medium sweet potatoes (465 g)

2 tablespoons extra-virgin olive oil

½ cup lightly packed (11 g) fresh cilantro leaves, minced

2 large green onions (40 g), thinly sliced

1 ripe medium (200 g) avocado, pitted and diced

¾ cup canned black beans (half a 14-ounce/398 mL can), drained and rinsed*

¼ teaspoon plus ⅛ teaspoon fine sea salt, or to taste

Freshly ground black pepper

1 tablespoon fresh lime juice, or to taste

4 teaspoons tahini, for serving (optional)

This is a fun and healthy weeknight dinner when you don't have much energy to cook but still crave something satisfying. The creamy black beans, cozy sweet potato "noodles," and velvety tahini are accented by fresh, crunchy green onion and bright cilantro for the perfect flavor and texture contrast. When spiralizing sweet potato, I use my small countertop spiralizer. I love that it takes just one minute to spiralize a large sweet potato into 6 cups of beautiful tendrils! If you don't have a spiralizer, you can use a julienne peeler, but your prep time will be significantly longer. Julienne peelers tend to produce thinner strands as well, so your cook time may be a bit shorter.

1. Peel the sweet potato and trim both ends so they are flat. Using a spiralizer with the spaghetti blade attached, spiralize the sweet potato into long strands (you should have 6 packed cups sweet potato noodles). Place the strands in a heap on the cutting board and coarsely chop them in about 6 spots to shorten them just a bit.

2. In a large nonstick wok or skillet, add the oil, then place the noodles on top. With your hands, toss and massage the noodles until they're fully coated in the oil. Cover the wok with a tight-fitting lid and set it over medium heat. Gently cook the noodles, stirring occasionally and reducing the heat if necessary, for 7 to 15 minutes, until tender. (The cooking time will vary based on

recipe continues

recipe continued from previous page

STORAGE

Store leftover sweet potato noodles in an airtight container in the fridge for up to 4 days. To reheat, transfer the noodles to a preheated oiled pan over medium heat, cover, and cook for 1 to 3 minutes, until heated through.

TIP

* One 14-ounce (398 mL) can of black beans contains 1½ cups of beans, twice what you need for this recipe, so I like to freeze the unused portion in a small airtight container for the next time I make this dish. If you have cooked black beans on hand, you can use ¾ cup of those instead.

UP THE GLOW

Add a generous sprinkle of my Tex-Mex Spice Blend (page 313) and/or red pepper flakes for a flavor boost!

the thickness of the noodles and the type of pan you use. If you are using a thin-bottomed skillet, your cooking time may be shorter than if you are using a heavy-bottomed skillet.) The finished noodles shouldn't be *crunchy*, but they shouldn't be mushy, either. They should be tender, like pasta. Check on them every minute or two while cooking, especially the first time you make them, to ensure your cook time is appropriate. If the noodles stick to the wok while cooking, add a splash of water and stir with a wooden spoon to scrape up any stuck bits.

3. Meanwhile, prepare the cilantro, green onions, and avocado. When the sweet potato noodles are almost ready, stir in the black beans, cover, and cook for a minute or two, until heated through.

4. Remove the wok from the heat and stir in the cilantro and green onions. Season with salt, pepper, and lime juice, to taste.

5. Portion into bowls and top with the avocado. Drizzle each bowl with a couple teaspoons of the tahini (if using). Season with more salt, pepper, and lime juice, if desired. Serve immediately.

Festive Bread-Free Stuffing Balls

Makes 18 to 20 balls • **Active prep time** 30 minutes • **Total time** 1 hour

I tablespoon extra-virgin olive oil

8 ounces (225 g) cremini mushrooms

3 large garlic cloves (18 g), minced
(1½ tablespoons)

I teaspoon fine sea salt, or to taste

I cup (20 g) fresh parsley leaves

I cup packed (30 g) torn stemmed kale
leaves

⅓ cup packed (40 g) dried cranberries

½ cup plus 2 tablespoons (65 g)
gluten-free rolled oats

I (14-ounce/398 mL) can lentils, drained
and rinsed*

I cup (100 g) walnut halves

4 teaspoons fresh thyme leaves,
or 2 teaspoons dried

2 teaspoons minced fresh oregano,
or 1 teaspoon dried

I teaspoon minced fresh rosemary,
or ½ teaspoon dried

I tablespoon ground flaxseed

2½ teaspoons sherry vinegar**

Freshly ground black pepper

These festive lentil balls have all the joyous, savory flavors of traditional stuffing, but they're protein-packed, bite-sized, and even gluten-free! I love them paired with my Rosemary and Thyme Mushroom Gravy (page 304), which is also a great way to use some of the fresh herbs called for in this recipe. They make the perfect addition to your dinner plate; for a nourishing meal, I love pairing them with simple roasted veggies or serving them alongside my Creamy Mushroom, Green Bean, and Wild Rice Casserole (page 153), Romesco Roasted Potatoes and Green Beans (page 157), or Crispy Brussels Sprouts in Garlic Oil (page 151) for a celebratory weekend or holiday meal. This recipe moves quickly, so read through the entire recipe and have your ingredients and tools at the ready before you begin.

1. Preheat the oven to 350°F (180°C). Line a large baking sheet with parchment paper.

2. In a large pot, heat the oil over medium heat. Finely chop the mushrooms until they're about the size of peas (no larger, or the balls may not hold together). Add the mushrooms, garlic, and a pinch of salt and stir to combine. Sauté for about 6 to 8 minutes, until the mushroom water cooks off and the mushrooms are tender. Reduce heat to medium-low if necessary to prevent burning.

3. Meanwhile, in a food processor, place the parsley and kale and pulse 20 to 25 times, until the greens are chopped to about the size of almonds or a bit smaller. Transfer the greens to a small bowl.

recipe continues

recipe continued from previous page

STORAGE

Store leftovers in an airtight container in the fridge for 2 to 3 days. To reheat, heat about 1 tablespoon oil in a skillet over medium heat, add the balls, and gently fry, tossing occasionally, until heated through and golden, 5 to 6 minutes.

TIPS

* It's important to use a brand of canned lentils that contains "intact" lentils, which are not compacted together or mushy (to avoid the dough being too wet). One 14-ounce (398 mL) can of lentils is equivalent to 1½ cups cooked lentils, if you prefer to cook them from scratch.

** Don't have any sherry vinegar on hand? You can swap it out for white wine vinegar in a pinch.

MAKE-AHEAD

Refrigerate the uncooked balls on a plate or baking sheet wrapped tightly in plastic wrap or aluminum foil for up to 24 hours before baking so there's less fuss the day of the big meal. Allow them to come to room temperature before baking as directed in step 9, to ensure accurate cook times. The uncooked balls can also be frozen in a freezer bag with the air pressed out for up to 2 weeks. Simply pop the frozen balls on a parchment-lined baking sheet and bake for 30 to 32 minutes, until heated through and golden.

4. Finely chop the dried cranberries and add them to the bowl with the greens. Set aside.

5. Place the oats in the food processor (no need to clean it out first!) and process until they're finely chopped and resemble coarse flour, about 30 seconds. Add the drained lentils and walnuts to the processor bowl with the oat flour and process the mixture ten to thirteen times, until the walnuts are broken down into pea-sized pieces. Set aside.

6. To the pot with the mushrooms and garlic, add the cranberry-greens mixture and the thyme, oregano, and rosemary. Sauté over medium heat for 1 minute, then turn off the heat.

7. In a small cup, stir together the flaxseed and vinegar, then pour it into the skillet. Stir to combine. Add the lentil-oat mixture and stir until thoroughly combined. At first, the mixture will seem dry, but keep mixing until the dough easily sticks together when pressed between your fingers. If it is too dry to hold together, add water, a teaspoon at a time, and mix again (I typically need to add 3 teaspoons). Stir in salt and pepper to taste.

8. With lightly dampened hands, shape the dough into 18 to 20 balls, using about 2½ lightly packed tablespoons of the dough for each and packing them well so they hold together. Place them on the prepared baking sheet about 2 inches (5 cm) apart as you go.

9. Bake for 20 to 23 minutes, until lightly golden on the bottom and firm to the touch. Let cool for 5 to 10 minutes before serving.

The Mama Bear Bowl: Cauli-Power Savory Steel-Cut Oatmeal

Makes 4 cups • **Active prep time** 5 minutes • **Cook time** 30 minutes • **Total time** 40 minutes

3¼ cups water

I cup (172 g) gluten-free uncooked steel-cut oats*

2 teaspoons minced or grated fresh garlic**

½ teaspoon fine sea salt, or to taste

I (10-ounce/300 g) package frozen cauliflower rice***

Freshly ground black pepper

Garlic powder

Topping suggestions

Herbamare

Perfect Basil Pesto (page 294)

Hummus

Sliced avocado

Sliced green onion

Chopped tomatoes or marinara sauce

Minced fresh parsley or cilantro

Crackers

Hemp hearts

Roasted pepitas (see page 338) or nuts

Cooked beans or lentils

Roasted or grilled veggies

Spices and seasonings (smoked paprika, garlic powder, etc.)

This is one of those handy "base" recipes that's perfect for fast dinners, lunches, and breakfasts. Shortly after my second little one, Arlo, was born, I started to call it my "Mama Bear Bowl" since I relied on it during those *hangry* breastfeeding months. Not only is it packed with nutrition (hello, cauliflower, steel-cut oats, and protein-rich toppings!), it takes just a few minutes to throw together in a pot and leaves you with several meals' worth to reheat all week long (or all day long, like I often did). It really doesn't get much easier. I've given you instructions for cooking it on the stovetop, but I love to make it in my Instant Pot so I don't have to watch it or stir it. My favorite toppings are sliced avocado, sea salt, garlic powder, pepper, Perfect Basil Pesto, chopped tomatoes or salsa, crackers, and roasted salted pepitas (for a little crunch)! If I have time, I also love to load it with roasted veggies like broccoli, red bell pepper, mushrooms, and tomatoes. One of my friends tops hers with the cooked veggies from my Fast Family Fajitas (page 53) and can't get enough of it. One thing is for sure: This bowl is going to leave you energized and satisfied!

I. In a medium pot, bring the water to a low boil over high heat. Add the oats, garlic, and salt. Reduce the heat to medium and cook, uncovered, stirring occasionally and reducing the heat as necessary to avoid burning, for 22 to 30 minutes, depending

recipe continues

recipe continued from previous page

STORAGE

Store leftovers in an airtight container in the fridge for 5 to 7 days, or freeze them for 1 to 2 months. To reheat, thaw completely (if frozen), then transfer to a small pot, add a splash of water, and heat over medium heat until warmed through.

TIPS

* Be sure to use regular steel-cut oats, as quick-cooking steel-cut oats do not work in this recipe as written.

** I use a Microplane for grating.

*** I often use one (300 g) package frozen cauliflower crumbles (also called "riced cauliflower" or "cauliflower rice"). To make cauliflower rice at home, place 11 ounces (310 g) cauliflower florets in a large food processor and pulse until the cauliflower is broken down into pieces resembling rice. You should have 2½ cups cauliflower rice.

how chewy you like your oats. The oats are ready when most of the water has been absorbed and they are softened but still a bit chewy. (I tend to cook them for between 26 and 29 minutes.)

2. Meanwhile, in another medium pot, bring a few inches of water to a simmer over medium-high heat and place a steamer basket on top (or simply use a countertop steamer appliance). Place the cauliflower rice in the steamer, cover, and steam for 7 to 14 minutes (the timing will depend on the size of the cauliflower rice and whether it is cooked from fresh or frozen), until soft and tender. Turn the heat off and remove the lid. (I don't recommend cooking the cauliflower and the oats in the same pot. In my trials, the cauliflower rice and oats ended up crunchy, so it's best to cook them separately.)

3. When the oats are ready, add the steamed cauliflower rice and stir well. Season with the salt, pepper, and garlic powder to taste. Portion into bowls and serve with your favorite toppings.

The Mama Bear Bowl Instant Pot Method

1. In an Instant Pot or other multicooker, stir together 3 cups water, the oats, frozen cauliflower rice, garlic, and salt. (Not to worry if your cauliflower rice is a big frozen block . . . simply leave it on top, as there's no need to break it down before cooking.)

2. Secure the lid in the lock position and check that the steam release handle is pointing to the "Sealing" position.

3. Press the "Pressure Cook" (or "Manual") button and set the cook time to 7 minutes on high pressure. After 5 seconds, you'll hear a couple of beeps and the screen will say "On." The cooking process has begun! *happy dance*

4. Once finished, you'll hear a few beeps letting you know that the cooking is over. Let the Instant Pot do a natural pressure release (simply wait 10 minutes for most of the pressure to dissipate on its own).

5. Carefully release any remaining steam before removing the lid. The oatmeal will look watery, but not to worry—this is normal! Stir the oatmeal until well combined, and let it sit, uncovered, for 5 to 10 minutes to thicken before serving as directed in step 3 of the stovetop directions.

Rebellious Battered Broc-Cauli Burgers with Sriracha Aioli

Makes 5 burgers • **Active prep time** 25 minutes • **Total time** 30 minutes

For the Battered Broc-Cauli

½ cup (70 g) chickpea flour*

½ cup (65 g) almond flour*

¼ cup (30 g) arrowroot starch

1¼ teaspoons fine sea salt, or to taste, plus more for garnish

½ teaspoon baking soda

¾ cup unsweetened plain almond milk

2 tablespoons grapeseed oil

4 large garlic cloves (24 g), grated on a Microplane (2 tablespoons)

½ small to medium head cauliflower (400 g)

½ small to medium bunch broccoli (250 g)

For serving

I batch Sriracha Aioli (page 289)

5 burger buns (gluten- or grain-free, if desired)

Sliced dill pickles

Pretty Quick-Pickled Red Onions (page 302; optional)

Ah, these burgers remind me fondly of my teenage years . . . rebellious and eyebrow-raising! A broccoli floret burger, a concept I discovered at Parka Food Co. in Toronto, is a revelation. Who knew that vegetables don't have to mimic a round patty to make a hearty, "hits the spot" burger? My twist pairs broccoli and cauliflower florets, which are dipped in a simple gluten-free chickpea- and almond-flour batter and roasted (instead of fried) until soft and tender. Tangy dill pickles keep the burger tradition going (and add a very necessary crunch!), while my fiery Sriracha Aioli lends a decadent creaminess and a spicy punch. If you aren't a fan of sriracha's heat, you can reduce the amount called for in the aioli or simply top the burgers with my Creamy Cashew or Sunflower Aioli (page 293) instead. It's important to use the amount of broccoli and cauliflower florets called for here (weigh them to be sure, if you can), as there's *just* enough batter for the quantity I've listed in the recipe. Use any leftover raw broccoli and cauliflower in my Boom! Broccoli Pesto (page 276), Green Powerhouse Roasted Protein Bowl (page 61—switch it up by using half broccoli and half cauliflower), or Instant Pot Potato and Cauliflower Red Thai Curry (page 65). These burgers are delicious served with my Cauliflower "Potato" Salad (page 203) alongside, too.

recipe continues

recipe continued from previous page

STORAGE

These burgers are best served fresh, but you can store leftover broccoli and cauliflower in an airtight container in the fridge for up to 2 days. Reheat on a lightly oiled baking sheet in a preheated 425°F (220°C) oven for about 7 minutes, until heated through.

TIP

* Chickpea flour (also called gram flour or besan) can be found at large supermarket chains in the international aisle, at ethnic grocers, and online. I recommend weighing both flours for best results (at least the first time you make it, if you can).

MAKE IT KID-FRIENDLY

Reduce the amount of sriracha in the aioli, or swap out the aioli for their preferred condiments.

MAKE IT AHEAD

Prepare the Sriracha Aioli and cut the vegetables the night before and store them in separate airtight containers in the fridge. When you are ready to prepare the recipe, place the chopped broccoli and cauliflower florets on the counter for at least 10 minutes, preheat the oven, and proceed with the recipe directions.

1. Make the Battered Broc-Cauli: Preheat the oven to 450°F (230°C). Line an extra-large (15 by 21-inch/38 by 53 cm) baking sheet with parchment paper.

2. In a very large bowl (you'll be adding the cauliflower and broccoli to it, so make sure it's big—I use a huge bamboo salad bowl), whisk together the chickpea flour, almond flour, arrowroot starch, salt, and baking soda until combined. While whisking, slowly stream in the milk, then the grapeseed oil, and whisk until smooth. Whisk in the garlic. Set the batter aside.

3. This recipe works best when the florets are similar in size, so draw a 2 by 1½-inch (5 by 4 cm) rectangle on parchment paper to use as a floret sizing guide. Chop the cauliflower into medium 2-inch-long, 1½-inch-wide (5 by 4 cm) florets, placing each floret on the rectangle to check for correct sizing, until you have 2 slightly heaping cups (200 g), about 10 florets. Slice the stems a bit thinner if need be, so they are ¼ to ½ inch (5 mm to 1 cm) thick at the most (overly thick stems won't cook through in time). Repeat this process for the broccoli—you should have 2 slightly heaping cups (125 g) of broccoli florets, about 10 florets.

4. Add the cauliflower and broccoli florets to the bowl of batter. Using your hands (this works way better than a spoon), coat the florets very well with the batter, getting it into all the nooks and crannies of the veggies.

5. Remove the battered cauliflower florets first, one at a time, scooping a bit of batter with each floret as you go, and place them 1 inch (2.5 cm) apart on the prepared baking sheet. The batter will pool a bit under the florets.

6. Swirl the spongy broccoli tops into the batter left in the bowl to coat each one a bit better, placing each one on the baking sheet, 1 inch (2.5 cm) apart, as you go. If there is any leftover batter in the bowl, scoop it up and spread it onto any bare patches on the florets.

7. Bake the cauliflower and broccoli for 12 to 14 minutes, until the stems are *just* fork-tender. Be careful not to overbake them, or they'll get mushy. At the 11-minute mark, do a quick fork check for doneness, piercing the stems. We're looking for an al dente texture here: tender but with some resistance when you slide a fork into the stems. If they're not ready, cook them for a little longer, checking the stems again every minute. If you have any overly thick florets, you may need to leave those in by themselves to cook a bit longer. The broccoli tends to cook a bit faster than the cauliflower, but this slight texture contrast is no biggie once they're on the burgers.

8. Meanwhile, prepare the Sriracha Aioli.

9. Put your buns in the oven (the bread buns, not your actual buns, as that could tickle!) on a separate baking sheet during the last 4 to 5 minutes of the broc-cauli cook time to lightly toast them.

10. To assemble the burgers, spread a tablespoon of the aioli over the bottom of each bun. Top it with plenty of sliced pickles, covering the bottom of the bun (you don't want to skip this crunch!), followed by about 4 florets (2 broccoli and 2 cauliflower). Dollop another tablespoon of the aioli on top of the florets, top with a few pickled red onions (if using), close the buns, and prepare for the burgers to be going, going, GONE in a flash.

Savory Herb and Veggie Chickpea Pancakes

Serves 2 (3 or 4 small pancakes per serving) • **Active prep time** 20 minutes • **Total time** 25 minutes

Sriracha Aioli (page 289), for serving

1 tablespoon coconut oil or extra-virgin olive oil

¼ cup (15 g) diced green onions, plus more for serving

⅓ cup (50 g) diced tomato

1 large garlic clove (6 g), minced

⅓ cup (45 g) finely chopped red bell pepper

½ cup (70 g) chickpea flour*

2 tablespoons nutritional yeast

¼ teaspoon fine sea salt, or to taste

Freshly ground black pepper, to taste

½ cup water

¼ cup packed (5 g) fresh parsley or basil, minced

If you've ever wondered what meal I make when I'm dining solo and don't want much fuss, this is it. Depending on how hungry I am, I can polish off a batch all by myself. It's family-friendly, too—my kids love picking up the pancakes with their hands and dipping them into their favorite sauce. It's easy to change up the veggies depending on what you have in the crisper, making it super versatile, too. This version is packed with crispy red bell pepper and green onion, sweet ripe tomato, and fresh parsley. Using chickpea flour as the base is a fun way to sneak in plant-based protein and fiber. Because the pancakes are so mild in flavor, it's essential (to me, anyway) to top these with a punchy, vibrant sauce like my Sriracha Aioli. I just slather that stuff on . . . livin' my best life over here! Other tasty topping ideas include sliced avocado, hummus, sea salt, and lemon juice; Perfect Basil Pesto (page 294); vegan mayo and smoked paprika; 24/7 Avocado-Cilantro Sauce (page 286); and Creamy Cashew or Sunflower Aioli (page 293). My Saucy Little Black Bean Skillet (page 167) is lovely spooned over the top, and it'll boost the protein even more. It's important to use a nonstick skillet (or nonstick pancake griddle) for this recipe, as the pancakes tend to stick horribly to uncoated skillets (yes, even when the pan's been liberally oiled . . . sigh). This recipe also doubles beautifully, if you need more servings.

1. Prepare the Sriracha Aioli. Set aside.

2. In a large nonstick skillet, melt the coconut oil over medium heat. Add the green onions, tomato, garlic, and bell pepper and

recipe continues

recipe continued from previous page

STORAGE

Store in an airtight container in the fridge for up to 2 days. To reheat, transfer the pancakes to a preheated lightly oiled griddle or skillet over medium heat and cook for 1 to 2 minutes on each side, until heated through. Freezing is not recommended.

TIP

* Use the "scoop and shake until level" method (see page 41) when measuring the chickpea flour.

stir to coat with the oil. Sauté, stirring occasionally, for 4 to 5 minutes, until softened.

3. Heat a large pancake griddle or skillet over medium-high heat for a few minutes (or wash and dry the skillet you used for the veggie mixture and use it again).

4. While the griddle heats, in a large bowl, whisk together the chickpea flour, nutritional yeast, salt, pepper, and water until very smooth. Add the parsley and the sautéed veggies. Whisk again until combined. The batter will be runny like crepe batter, not as thick as traditional pancake batter.

5. When a drop of water sizzles on the griddle, it's ready. Reduce the heat to medium or a touch above medium. Grease the griddle with oil.

6. For each pancake, spoon 2 tablespoons of the batter onto the griddle (I use a 1/8-cup measuring spoon for this), quickly spreading it out with the back of the spoon until it's about 3 inches (8 cm) wide. Space the pancakes a couple of inches (5 cm) apart on the griddle. Cook for 2 to 4 minutes, until a golden crust forms. Reduce the heat if necessary to avoid burning (you're looking for a golden brown crust, not a blackened bottom). Flip and cook for 2 to 3 minutes, until golden on the second side. (It may take a trial run to determine the right cook time and appropriate heat for your stove and the pan you're using. Lightweight skillets tend to cook faster and require lower heat to avoid burning the pancakes, whereas griddles or heavy skillets can withstand a higher heat. Some stovetops/burners can run hot, too.)

7. Transfer the first batch of pancakes to a wire rack. Spray the griddle with oil and cook the remaining batter as directed above.

8. Serve the pancakes with the aioli dolloped on top, along with a handful of sliced green onion for added crunch.

Mediterranean Smashed Chickpea Salad with Tzatziki Aioli

Serves 5 (about ⅔ cup per serving) • **Active prep time** 20 minutes • **Total time** 20 minutes

For the Tzatziki Aioli

6 tablespoons vegan mayo

2 large garlic cloves (12 g), minced

1 teaspoon lemon zest (optional)

5 to 6 teaspoons fresh lemon juice, to taste

¼ cup packed (8 g) fresh dill, minced

½ medium English cucumber (130 g), unpeeled

For the Chickpea Salad

1 (19-ounce/540 mL) can chickpeas, drained and rinsed*

¾ cup (105 g) finely chopped red onion, rinsed and drained

½ cup packed (100 g) jarred roasted red peppers, drained and chopped

⅓ cup (65 g) oil-packed unsalted sun-dried tomatoes, drained and finely chopped

½ cup (75 g) finely chopped seeded Roma (plum) tomato (1 large)

1½ teaspoons dried basil, or to taste

¼ teaspoon fine sea salt, or to taste

Freshly ground black pepper

Minced fresh dill

Fresh lemon juice

This creamy, crunchy, and tangy salad is a fantastic, easy dinner when you don't feel like cooking but still want a nourishing meal. The base is made with my special Tzatziki Aioli, which adds such a lovely Greek flavor to this dish, and sunny Mediterranean veggies like crunchy red onion, sweet roasted red peppers, tangy sun-dried and fresh tomatoes, savory dried basil, and protein-packed chickpeas. I love that you can serve this salad so many different ways, so it feels fresh every time: Stuff it into wraps or pitas, serve it on top of whole-grain toast or salads, or scoop it up with your favorite crackers! This salad is also wonderful on top of Crispy Roasted Potato Rounds (see page 176). We like to slice the potatoes into substantial ¼-inch-thick (5 mm) slabs instead of rounds for this dish. This salad is fantastic served with Green Goddess Gazpacho (page 219) for the most refreshing hot-weather meal, and you can use up any leftover fresh dill by making my Rustic Roasted Carrot and Dill Hummus (page 179).

1. Make the Tzatziki Aioli: In a small bowl, stir together the mayo, garlic, lemon zest (if using), lemon juice, and dill. Shred the cucumber on the standard-sized holes (not the very tiny holes) of a box grater. Fold a clean, thick kitchen towel in half (or use layered paper towels) and place ½ cup of the grated cucumber on the towel. Press out as much water as you can (this step is important to keep the cucumber from making the aioli watery). Stir the cucumber into the aioli and set aside.

recipe continues

recipe continued from previous page

STORAGE

Store leftovers in an airtight container in the fridge for 2 to 3 days. Stir well before serving. If necessary, spruce up the flavors by stirring in a touch more salt, pepper, mayo, or lemon juice, to taste.

TIP

* One 19-ounce (540 mL) can of chickpeas is equivalent to 2 cups cooked chickpeas, if you prefer to cook them from scratch.

MAKE IT SOY-FREE

Use soy-free mayonnaise.

UP THE GLOW

To take this dish to the next level, crumble my Authentic-Tasting Vegan Feta Cheese (page 327) on top. It's an absolute dream!

2. Make the chickpea salad: To a large bowl, add the chickpeas and mash with a potato masher until flaky, leaving about a quarter of the chickpeas whole for texture. Stir in the red onion, roasted red peppers, sun-dried tomatoes, Roma tomato, and basil.

3. Pour all the aioli over the chickpea mixture and stir well to coat and combine. Taste and season with salt, pepper, dill, and lemon juice until the flavors pop to your liking.

4. Serve as desired (see the headnote for suggestions!).

Humble Creamy Mushrooms and Toast

Serves 2 • **Soak time** 1 hour or up to overnight • **Active prep time** 15 minutes • **Total time** 20 minutes

Creamy Cashew or Sunflower Aioli (page 293) or Cashew Sour Cream (page 321)

1 tablespoon extra-virgin olive oil

1 cup (125 g) finely chopped yellow onion

2 tablespoons (24 g) minced garlic (4 large cloves)

1 teaspoon Italian seasoning, homemade (page 312) or store-bought

8 ounces (225 g) cremini mushrooms, sliced (3½ cups)

Fine sea salt and black pepper

2 to 4 slices of your favorite bread

½ to 1 teaspoon white wine vinegar, to taste

STORAGE

Refrigerate leftovers in an airtight container for up to 4 days. To reheat, transfer the mushroom mixture to a preheated oiled skillet over medium heat, cover, and cook for 3 to 4 minutes, until heated through.

MAKE IT GLUTEN-FREE

Use gluten-free bread.

MAKE IT NUT-FREE

Use the sunflower option for the Creamy Cashew or Sunflower Aioli.

Sliced cremini mushrooms are sautéed in savory garlic, onion, and Italian seasonings until tender, and a splash of white wine vinegar lends a touch of sophistication and brightness. This recipe is a fun way to use up leftover Cashew Sour Cream—it's divine spread on toast. Be sure to prepare the Creamy Cashew or Sunflower Aioli or Cashew Sour Cream in advance so it has a chance to thicken up a bit so it's the right texture for spreading. If you need more than a couple of servings, it'll easily scale up, so don't be afraid to double the recipe.

1. Prepare the Creamy Cashew or Sunflower Aioli or Cashew Sour Cream.

2. In a medium skillet, heat the oil over medium heat. Add the onion and garlic and sauté for 5 to 6 minutes, until the onion is softened.

3. Stir in the Italian seasoning, mushrooms, and a pinch each of salt and pepper. Increase the heat to medium-high and cook, uncovered, stirring occasionally, for 10 minutes, or until the liquid released by the mushrooms has evaporated and the mushrooms soften to your liking.

4. Near the end of cooking the mushrooms, toast the bread. Spread each piece of toasted bread generously with the aioli or sour cream (I like using 1½ to 2 tablespoons per slice).

5. Taste the mushroom mixture and season with the vinegar and additional salt and pepper. Spoon the hot mushrooms over the warm toast, season with an additional sprinkle of salt and a grind of pepper, and serve.

Kitchen Sink Sheet Pan Buddha Bowl

Serves 4 • **Active prep time** 35 minutes • **Total time** 1 hour

1 batch Roasted Garlic Cauliflower Rice (page 170)*

1 large sweet potato or yellow potato (500 g)

1 (14-ounce/398 mL) can chickpeas, drained and rinsed**

3 cups chopped fresh veggies of choice***

2 tablespoons extra-virgin olive oil

Fine sea salt

Double batch 24/7 Avocado-Cilantro Sauce (see page 286)

Garlic powder

Tex-Mex Spice Blend (page 313; optional)

Topping suggestions

Hemp hearts

Sliced avocado

Sliced green onion

Shredded cabbage or lettuce

Ah, Buddha bowls . . . don't they make the best kind of dinner? Full of different flavors and textures, they really hit all the right spots. I love this Buddha bowl recipe because it allows me to use up any veggies I have lingering in my crisper. It's a handy "everything but the kitchen sink" dinner recipe. Roasting is incredibly forgiving for veggies on their last legs, so if you have any soft and spongy carrots, peppers, mushrooms, squash, or taters, just chop them up and throw them in the oven. Once they're roasted and seasoned, you'll never know they were past their prime. Each time you make this bowl, you can change up the veggies, as well as swap out the cauliflower rice for whatever grain you have on hand, so you'll never get bored. I also enjoy incorporating seasonal produce whenever I can. This Buddha bowl is delicious topped with a generous amount of my rich and creamy 24/7 Avocado-Cilantro Sauce. To create a totally new variation, you can change things up and try serving it with my Rustic Roasted Carrot and Dill Hummus (page 179), Easy Chimichurri Sauce (page 272), pesto (pages 275, 276, 294, 297), Apple Honey–Dijon Dressing (page 285), or Creamy Cashew or Sunflower Aioli (page 293).

1. Position two oven racks near the center of the oven. Preheat the oven to 425°F (220°C). Line two extra-large (15 by 21-inch/ 38 by 53 cm) rimmed baking sheets with parchment paper.

2. Prep the Roasted Garlic Cauliflower Rice and spread it over one of the prepared baking sheets, but don't put it in the oven yet.

recipe continues

recipe continued from previous page

STORAGE

Store the cauliflower rice, roasted veggies and chickpeas, and sauce in separate airtight containers in the fridge for up to 4 days. To reheat, spread the veggies in an even layer on a lightly oiled baking sheet. Bake in a preheated 400°F (200°C) oven for 4 to 5 minutes, then spread the cauliflower rice in an even layer beside the veggies and bake for 5 to 6 minutes more. Top with the sauce and enjoy.

TIPS

* To change up this recipe, try swapping out the cauliflower rice for a cooked grain like quinoa, millet, farro, or rice.

** One 14-ounce (398 mL) can of chickpeas is equivalent to 1½ cups cooked chickpeas, if you prefer to cook them from scratch.

*** Carrots, yellow potatoes, cremini mushrooms, butternut squash, bell peppers, and brussels sprouts are all lovely options. If you're using broccoli florets, remove them after 20 minutes of roasting to avoid burning.

MAKE IT SOY-FREE

Use soy-free vegan mayo in the 24/7 Avocado-Cilantro Sauce.

3. Peel the sweet potato, if desired, and chop it into 1-inch (2.5 cm) chunks (you should have about 3 cups). Place the sweet potato on the second baking sheet.

4. With a clean kitchen towel, pat the chickpeas mostly dry, then add them to the baking sheet with the sweet potato.

5. Add the chopped or sliced veggies to the baking sheet with the sweet potato and chickpeas, and drizzle the oil all over the top. Massage the oil thoroughly into the veggies and chickpeas, then spread everything out into a single layer. Sprinkle salt generously over the top.

6. Roast the veggies and chickpeas for 10 minutes, then add the cauliflower rice to the oven to join the chickpeas and veggies and roast both baking sheets for 20 to 25 minutes more, removing the cauliflower rice earlier if it starts to brown.

7. Meanwhile, prepare a double batch of 24/7 Avocado-Cilantro Sauce. Prep any toppings so they are ready to go.

8. To serve, spoon a couple of scoops of the cauliflower rice into each of four shallow serving bowls and top with the roasted veggies and chickpeas and the toppings of your choice. Transfer the avocado-cilantro sauce to a medium zip-top bag, snip off one corner, and generously pipe the sauce all over the bowls (or simply dollop it over the top). Finally, sprinkle on some garlic powder and Tex-Mex Spice Blend, if desired, and serve.

Dreamy Peanut Butter Crunch Veggie Noodle Bowls

Serves 4 • **Active prep time** 30 minutes • **Total time** 35 minutes

I batch Dreamy Peanut Butter Sauce with Ginger and Lime (page 330)

4 ounces (115 g) dry soba noodles or spaghetti noodles of your choice

1 tablespoon extra-virgin olive oil

1 medium red bell pepper (270 g), seeded and thinly sliced (2 cups)

3 heaping cups (225 g) thinly sliced green or red cabbage (½ small)*

1 cup (140 g) frozen shelled edamame

2 tablespoons coconut aminos (soy-free seasoning sauce)**

2 medium carrots (225 g), peeled and julienned (1¾ cups)

4 large green onions (75 g), thinly sliced (1 cup)

½ cup lightly packed (11 g) fresh cilantro, minced

Fine sea salt

Lime wedges, for serving

Chopped salted roasted peanuts, for serving

I came up with this delicious, crunchy, creamy bowl when I needed a speedy, gluten-free dinner option for a girls' get-together, and it now makes regular appearances at our dinner table. First things first, I created a seriously dreamy peanut butter sauce, because all of us are peanut butter fanatics. Addictive peanut butter, tangy fresh lime juice, flavorful garlic, and warming ginger form the base of this can't-live-without-it sauce. Gorgeous red cabbage, crispy julienned carrot, and zesty red bell pepper create a rainbow-hued base full of textures and fresh flavors. Edamame adds plant-based protein, though you can easily swap it for chickpeas if you can't have soy. If you also need this bowl to be grain-free, rest assured that it's delicious even without the noodles. This light and vibrant dish makes a delightful outdoor, summery meal with my refreshing Mint, Ginger, and Lemon Sparkling Sipper (page 268) alongside. Keep the peanut butter theme going by whipping up my melt-in-your-mouth 6-Ingredient Chocolate Peanut Butter Oat Crumble Squares (page 252) for the quickest, simplest no-bake dessert.

1. Prepare the Dreamy Peanut Butter Sauce with Ginger and Lime. Set aside.

2. Cook the noodles according to the package directions. Drain the noodles and rinse with water.

3. Meanwhile, in a large wok, place the oil, bell pepper, and cabbage. Sauté, uncovered, over medium-high heat for

recipe continues

recipe continued from previous page

STORAGE

Store the veggie noodle mixture and the sauce in separate airtight containers in the fridge for up to 3 days. Reheat the veggie noodle mixture in a preheated skillet or wok over medium heat, covered, for a few minutes, until warmed through. The sauce can be warmed in a small pot over low heat, if desired.

TIPS

* Be sure to avoid using the core of the cabbage, as it is too thick. Slice the cabbage thinly, about 1/8 inch (3 mm) thick, for best results.

** You can swap the coconut aminos for 1 1/2 tablespoons low-sodium tamari.

MAKE IT GLUTEN-FREE

Use gluten-free noodles and ensure that all other ingredients are gluten-free.

MAKE IT SOY-FREE

Swap out the edamame for chickpeas and use coconut aminos for both the noodle bowl and the Dreamy Peanut Butter Sauce with Ginger and Lime.

MAKE IT GRAIN-FREE

Use grain-free noodles, such as legume-based ones.

5 minutes, until slightly softened (you're looking for an al dente texture: tender but with a bit of firmness remaining).

4. Add the edamame and coconut aminos. Stir to combine. Sauté for 3 minutes, until the edamame is thawed and heated through.

5. Add the carrots and green onions. Cook for 1 minute or so, just until tender.

6. Turn off the heat and stir in the cilantro and the drained noodles. Taste and season with salt and lime juice (I add a pinch of salt and a couple squeezes of lime juice). Reheat the mixture over low heat, if necessary.

7. Plate the mixture (using tongs makes it easy!) and add a generous drizzle of peanut butter sauce. Garnish with a lime wedge (it's nice to squeeze some extra lime juice over the top) and a handful of chopped peanuts. Dig in and enjoy!

VEGAN • NUT-FREE • SOY-FREE OPTION • FREEZER-FRIENDLY
KID-FRIENDLY OPTION • ON THE GLOW

Smoky Black Bean and Brown Rice Veggie Burgers

Makes 10 patties • **Active prep time** 30 minutes • **Total time** 1 hour 15 minutes

---

⅓ cup (70 g) uncooked short-grain brown rice*

1½ tablespoons extra-virgin olive oil

1½ cups (210 g) diced sweet onion (1 medium)

3 tablespoons (36 g) minced garlic

2 cups (145 g) chopped cremini mushrooms (almond-sized pieces)

1 to 1¼ teaspoons fine sea salt, plus more as needed

¾ cup packed (15 g) fresh cilantro

⅓ cup (50 g) raw pepitas

2 tablespoons tomato paste

1½ teaspoons smoked paprika

⅛ to ¼ teaspoon chipotle chile powder, plus more to taste**

1 (14-ounce/398 mL) can black beans, drained and rinsed***

1 cup (90 g) coarse panko-style bread crumbs****

2 tablespoons gluten-free oat flour

For serving

OSG House Sauce (page 331)

Burger buns (optional)

Sliced tomato

Lettuce

Sliced avocado

Bread-and-butter or dill pickle slices

These veggie burgers are the answer to my nut-free-burger dreams. They feature chewy black beans, hearty mushrooms, and nutty brown rice, with a smoky, gentle heat from the smoked paprika and chipotle powder. My family loves them topped with my sweet, creamy, and tangy OSG House Sauce and sliced pickles. Creamy avocado, chopped cilantro, and sliced tomatoes are fabulous toppers, too, and all add a pretty punch of color. This recipe calls for short-grain brown rice; I've included my speedy method of cooking brown rice to help save you time, but you can use leftover cooked brown rice instead if you have some on hand. Pair these burgers with a light salad in the warmer months such as my Cauliflower "Potato" Salad (page 203) or my Zesty Lime and Cayenne Roasted Chickpea and Sweet Potato Salad (page 199). In chilly months, we serve them with my Heavenly Chili-Spiced Jalapeño and Garlic Veggie Stew (page 223), Cold-Be-Gone Flavor Bomb Noodle Soup (page 213), or Glowing Spiced Lentil Soup (page 226) for a cozy cold-weather meal.

1. To a medium pot, add the rice and enough water to cover by a few inches. Bring the water to a boil over high heat, then reduce the heat to medium to medium-high and simmer, uncovered, for 30 to 35 minutes, until the rice is soft and tender, checking every so often to ensure there is enough water to keep the rice covered. It's important that the rice is not too chewy or the burgers won't hold together as well. Drain. When the rice has 15 minutes left to cook, continue with the recipe.

recipe continues

recipe continued from previous page

STORAGE

Store the cooked patties in an airtight container in the fridge for up to 3 days. To reheat, fry the baked patties in an oiled nonstick skillet over medium-high heat for 3 minutes per side. You can also freeze the baked patties in a freezer bag for up to 3 weeks. Reheat the frozen patties in a preheated 350°F (180°C) oven for 16 to 17 minutes until warmed through. The patties will be delicate.

TIPS

* Do you have leftover cooked rice on hand? Simply use ¾ cup plus 3 tablespoons cooked short-grain brown rice in this recipe.

** Chipotle powder's heat level varies greatly from brand to brand—some are very hot while others are barely spicy. I love Simply Organic chipotle powder (it is *very* spicy, which is why I only call for a small amount) and tend to use a heaping ¼ teaspoon. Whichever brand you use, be sure to add it a little bit at a time, to taste.

*** One 14-ounce (398 mL) can of black beans is equivalent to 1½ cups cooked black beans.

**** ShaSha Co. Organic Spelt Bread Crumbs are my favorite.

If you love a slightly crispy burger texture, after the cooling period, fry the baked patties in an oiled nonstick skillet over medium-high heat for 2 minutes per side before serving.

MAKE IT KID-FRIENDLY

Reduce or omit the chipotle chile powder.

MAKE IT SOY-FREE

Use soy-free vegan mayo.

2. Preheat the oven to 350°F (180°C). Line an extra-large (15 by 21-inch/38 by 53 cm) baking sheet with parchment paper.

3. In a large skillet, heat the oil over medium heat. Add the onion and garlic and stir to coat with the oil. Sauté for 4 to 5 minutes, until the onion is softened.

4. Add the mushrooms and a small pinch of salt and stir to combine. Increase the heat to medium-high and sauté for 6 to 7 minutes, until the liquid released by the mushrooms has evaporated and the mushrooms are softened.

5. While the mushrooms are cooking, in a food processor, place the cilantro and pepitas. Add the cooked mushroom mixture. Pulse 20 to 25 times, until coarsely chopped. Do not overprocess, as you want the mixture to have some texture.

6. Add the tomato paste, salt (starting with ¾ to 1 teaspoon), smoked paprika, chipotle powder (starting with ⅛ teaspoon), drained beans, and all of the cooked rice. Pulse about 10 times, until combined but just coarsely chopped. There will still be large bean pieces and the mixture will be quite wet.

7. Transfer the mixture to a large bowl and stir in the bread crumbs and oat flour until combined. Add more salt and chipotle powder, to taste, if desired. Let the dough sit at room temperature for a few minutes to firm up a bit.

8. Using a ⅓-cup measuring cup, scoop the burger mixture and pack it tightly. Turn the mixture out of the measuring cup into your palm and shape it into a round, tightly packed patty (wet your hands slightly to prevent sticking, if needed). Place the patty on the prepared baking sheet and repeat with the rest of the mixture. You should have about 10 patties.

9. Bake the patties for 23 to 25 minutes, until lightly golden on the bottom and firm to the touch. Let the patties cool on the pan for 5 to 7 minutes to firm up a bit more before serving.

10. Meanwhile, prepare the OSG House Sauce.

11. Assemble your burgers on buns, as desired.

Instant Marinated Chickpeas on Avocado Toast

Serves 3 • **Active prep time** 15 minutes • **Total time** 15 minutes

1 (14-ounce/398 mL) can chickpeas, drained and rinsed*

⅓ cup packed (9 g) fresh basil leaves, minced

3 tablespoons finely chopped oil-packed unsalted sun-dried tomatoes, drained

2 tablespoons minced red onion

2 tablespoons extra-virgin olive oil

2 tablespoons fresh lemon juice

1 teaspoon red wine vinegar, or to taste

⅛ teaspoon Herbamare or fine sea salt

¼ teaspoon freshly ground black pepper

Red pepper flakes (optional)

For serving

1 to 2 ripe medium (200 g each) avocados, pitted

Toasted sliced bread, matzo crackers, or rice cake thins

Fine sea salt and freshly ground black pepper

Fresh lemon juice

I love to whip up this light meal when I don't want to turn on my oven or put in much effort but still want a delicious, protein-packed dish. The Instant Marinated Chickpeas require zero wait time, so this meal comes together quickly! The tangy chickpeas and fresh herbs are a lovely contrast to the crunchy toast and creamy, buttery avocado. You could also serve this as a salad topper or in lettuce cups, and it's fabulous topped with my Pretty Quick-Pickled Red Onions (page 302). The chickpeas will keep well in the fridge, so you can make this ahead and pack it for work and school lunches or simply prep it to serve right away—we love it both ways.

1. In a medium bowl, stir together the chickpeas, basil, sun-dried tomatoes, red onion, oil, lemon juice, vinegar, Herbamare, pepper, and red pepper flakes to taste (if using). Taste and adjust the seasonings if desired.

2. To serve, mash the avocado onto slices of toast (or crackers/ rice thins) and sprinkle with a touch of salt. Stir the chickpea mixture to redistribute the juices and spoon it over the bread (or crackers), scooping up as much of the liquid in the bowl as you can (you can even mash some of the chickpeas, if you like, to help stop them from rolling off the toast, but this isn't necessary!). Season with additional salt, pepper, and an extra squeeze of lemon juice. Serve immediately.

recipe continues

recipe continued from previous page

STORAGE

Store the chickpeas in an airtight container in the fridge for up to 3 days. The oil tends to solidify in the fridge, so let it sit at room temperature before serving.

TIP

* One 14-ounce (398 mL) can of chickpeas is equivalent to 1½ cups cooked chickpeas, if you prefer to cook them from scratch.

MAKE IT GLUTEN-FREE AND GRAIN-FREE

Serve the chickpeas on half an avocado or on gluten-free (grain-free, if needed) toast or crackers, or use as a salad topper.

MAKE IT KID-FRIENDLY

Omit the onion and sun-dried tomatoes, and reduce the lemon juice and vinegar if your child isn't a fan of these strong flavors.

SATISFYING SIDES *and* SMALL BITES

Balsamic Roasted Root Vegetable Medley with Thyme and Cayenne

Serves 10 as a side dish • **Active prep time** 40 minutes • **Total time** 1 hour 20 minutes

1 small (2-pound/900 g) butternut squash

3 medium carrots (350 g)

3 medium parsnips (350 g)*

2 medium/large sweet potatoes (650 g)

3 large yellow or red potatoes (650 g)

⅓ cup plus 1 teaspoon vegan butter, melted, or extra-virgin olive oil**

1 tablespoon plus 1 teaspoon pure maple syrup, plus more if needed

3 tablespoons balsamic vinegar, plus more if needed

1½ teaspoons fine sea salt

¼ teaspoon freshly ground black pepper

Dried or fresh thyme leaves

Cayenne pepper (optional)

I created this irresistible roasted root veggie medley to get us through the long Canadian winters. The combo of sweet and earthy root vegetables and tangy balsamic dressing is cold-weather perfection. This recipe is a handy meal-prep option, since it makes two huge pans of roasted veggies that you can enjoy all week long. Chop once, enjoy for several days! And of course, because those delicious roots are in season during the cold winter months, it's a lovely dish to serve as part of a holiday spread (see page 32 for my beloved holiday menu!).

1. Preheat the oven to 375°F (190°C) and position the oven racks near the middle of the oven. Line two extra-large (15 by 21-inch/ 38 by 53 cm) rimmed baking sheets with parchment paper.

2. Peel and seed the squash. Peel the carrots, parsnips, sweet potatoes, and potatoes. Chop the squash and all the veggies into small ¼- to ½-inch-thick (5 mm to 1 cm) pieces—be sure they're no bigger, or they'll take an extra-long time to cook. You should have 5½ cups butternut squash, 2 cups carrots, 2 cups parsnips, 4 cups sweet potatoes, and 4 cups yellow potatoes. Place them on the prepared pans as you chop them.

3. In a small bowl, whisk together ⅓ cup of the melted butter, 1 tablespoon of the maple syrup, and 1 tablespoon of the vinegar until combined. Drizzle half the liquid (about 3½ tablespoons)

recipe continues

recipe continued from previous page

STORAGE

Store in an airtight container in the fridge for up to 5 days. Reheat in an oiled skillet, over medium heat, covered, stirring occasionally, for 5 to 6 minutes, until warmed through.

TIPS

* Slice out and compost/discard the thick core of the parsnip before chopping. The core is fibrous and difficult to chew, and may be too firm even after cooking.

** 5-Ingredient Vegan Butter (page 318) is fantastic in this dish, but feel free to use your favorite store-bought vegan butter instead! If you don't have either of those, extra-virgin olive oil works really well instead.

MAKE IT SOY-FREE

Use soy-free vegan butter, 5-Ingredient Vegan Butter, or olive oil.

MAKE IT AHEAD

I love that you can peel and chop the veggies and prepare the dressing the day before to save time the day of your meal. If you're storing the prepped veggies in the fridge ahead of time, just be sure to let them sit at room temperature for about 45 minutes before you start cooking; this ensures that the vegan butter won't harden upon contact and that my suggested bake time will be accurate.

over each pan of veggies and toss well until thoroughly coated. Really take your time rubbing the sauce into the veggies to make sure they're fully coated. Spread the veggies into a single layer, then season each pan with $1/2$ teaspoon of the salt and $1/8$ teaspoon of the pepper.

4. Roast, uncovered, for 30 minutes, then rotate the pans (no need to flip the veggies) and roast for another 15 to 20 minutes, until the veggies are fork-tender. I suggest checking on them after 40 minutes, and then every 5 or so minutes after that, until you get a sense of the timing in your oven. When ready, the carrots tend to have a small amount of bite to them (an al dente texture), while the other veggies are usually more tender. I really enjoy this slight texture difference while eating the medley!

5. Meanwhile, prepare the balsamic dressing: In a small bowl, whisk together the remaining 2 tablespoons vinegar, 1 teaspoon maple syrup, 1 teaspoon melted butter, and $1/2$ teaspoon salt.

6. Transfer the roasted veggies to a large shallow serving dish (I like to lift the ends of the parchment paper and slide the veggies right into the dish). Drizzle all of the dressing on top, and gently toss to coat the veggies. Sprinkle with thyme to taste, and season with a small sprinkling of cayenne pepper (a little bit goes a long way, and adds a lovely kick of heat and flavor depth), if desired. Taste and season with the remaining salt and black pepper (or even an extra drizzle of balsamic vinegar or maple syrup!), if desired. Serve warm.

Apple Honey–Sriracha Roasted Rainbow Carrots with Cashew Cream

Serves 6 • **Soak time** I hour or up to overnight
Active prep time I5 minutes • **Total time** 35 to 40 minutes

For the Sriracha-Garlic Cashew Cream *(makes 1¼ cups)*

¾ cup (115 g) raw cashews

½ cup plus I tablespoon water

I large garlic clove (6 g)

2 tablespoons sriracha, or to taste

I tablespoon extra-virgin olive oil

¼ to ½ teaspoon fine sea salt, to taste

For the Rainbow Carrots

2 bunches rainbow carrots*
(2 pounds 6 ounces/1.1 kg total)

½ to I tablespoon sriracha

I tablespoon apple honey or honey of
your choice, plus more for serving**

I tablespoon extra-virgin olive oil

¼ to ½ teaspoon fine sea salt

Freshly ground black pepper

Have you ever stood over a pan of roasted carrots, unable to stop eating them? I'm pretty excited about this recipe, to say the least. Nourishing and colorful rainbow carrots are roasted in a sweet-and-spicy glaze, then drizzled, hot out of the oven, with a velvety, lightly spicy cashew cream. The glaze is made with light and flowery apple honey for a sweet touch and spicy sriracha for lively heat. You'll go wild for this combo! This recipe is not only delicious and gorgeous, it's deceptively simple, too. A quick glaze for the rainbow carrots and simple blending of ingredients for the cream, and boom, you're done! You may have leftover Sriracha-Garlic Cashew Cream—it's fabulous on avocado toast or dolloped over grains. These roasted carrots are also lovely served with my Lemony Dill Protein Pesto (page 297) instead of the cashew cream, for a flavor-packed nut-free option.

I. Place the cashews in a small bowl and add boiling water to cover. Soak for I hour, then drain. (Alternatively, soak the cashews in room-temperature water to cover for at least 8 hours or up to overnight, then drain.)

2. Make the rainbow carrots: Preheat the oven to 425°F (220°C). Line an extra-large (I5 by 2I-inch/38 by 53 cm) baking sheet with parchment paper.

recipe continues

recipe continued from previous page

STORAGE

Store the carrots and cashew cream in separate airtight containers in the fridge for up to 5 days. Let the cream sit on the counter to come to room temperature before serving. Transfer the carrots to a parchment-lined baking sheet and bake in a preheated 425°F (220°C) oven for 8 to 10 minutes, until heated through. Drizzle on the cashew cream just before serving.

TIPS

* Small, thin rainbow carrots work best for this recipe, as they'll cook much faster than thicker ones. If you do have some large carrots (bigger than a nickel in diameter), slice them in half lengthwise. If they're thicker than an inch (2.5 cm) in diameter, quarter them lengthwise. The carrots should be a similar thickness so they cook in the same amount of time. If you can't find rainbow carrots, you can use regular carrots, but you may need to increase the cooking time a bit.

** I love Bee Free Honee, which is an apple-based honey substitute. Use whatever you like, though!

3. There is no need to peel rainbow carrots since their skin is so delicate—three cheers! Trim the green stems off the carrots, leaving a couple of inches (5 cm) at the top to give them a cute, spiky "hairdo." Gently scrub the carrots and pat dry.

4. In a small bowl, whisk together the sriracha and honey. Set aside.

5. Place the carrots on the prepared baking sheet, drizzle with the oil, and toss until fully coated.

6. Spoon all the sriracha-honey mixture over the oiled carrots and roll the carrots around on the baking sheet until fully coated. (I use my hands to do this.) Space the carrots ½ inch (1 cm) apart on the baking sheet. Sprinkle the salt evenly over the carrots.

7. Roast, uncovered, for 20 to 25 minutes, until just fork-tender. Be sure not to overcook them—a small amount of resistance when inserting a knife is a good thing! Keep an eye on them during the last 5 minutes of cooking to ensure that they don't burn (a little char is delicious, though). The size and freshness of the carrots will impact the cooking time, so don't be surprised if you need to cook them a bit longer, upward of 30 minutes total.

8. Meanwhile, prepare the Sriracha-Garlic Cashew Cream: To a high-speed blender, add the water, drained cashews, garlic, sriracha, oil, and salt. Blend on high until smooth. Taste and add more salt, if necessary.

9. Drizzle a generous amount of the cashew cream and additional honey over the roasted carrots. I add freshly ground pepper, too. (Pro tip: To get the cream to look extra pretty, I transfer it to a small zip-top bag, snip off a corner, and pipe it onto the carrots.) Serve immediately, as they'll cool quickly.

Sizzling Maple-Sriracha Garlic Chickpeas

Serves 3 (½ cup per serving) • **Active prep time** 5 minutes • **Total time** 13 minutes

2 teaspoons grapeseed or avocado oil

1 (14-ounce/398 mL) can chickpeas, drained and rinsed*

1 to 2 teaspoons sriracha, to taste**

2 large garlic cloves (12 g), grated on a Microplane

¼ cup plus 1 tablespoon pure maple syrup

3 tablespoons low-sodium tamari***

¼ cup unseasoned rice vinegar

Plain-Jane chickpeas, step aside! These chickpeas have a gooey, sticky coating that is sweet, tangy, and spicy all at once. If there's anyone in your life who has ever claimed that chickpeas (or plant-based recipes in general . . . *gasp*) are bland and boring, just put this dish in their piehole! I love serving these saucy chickpeas in simple lettuce cups with a sprinkle of sliced green onion and sesame seeds, or scooped onto a salad for a light, protein-packed meal. If you want a more substantial meal, they're quick and filling when served over a bed of your favorite cooked veggies and grains or thrown into a hearty wrap. We especially love this recipe spooned on top of The Mama Bear Bowl: Cauli-Power Savory Steel-Cut Oatmeal (page 108) for a winter-friendly lunch or dinner.

1. In a large nonstick skillet, heat the oil over medium-high heat for about 2 minutes, tilting the skillet to coat with the oil.

2. After preheating, add the drained chickpeas to the pan and spread them out into a single layer. Cook, stirring occasionally, for 5 to 7 minutes, until the chickpeas are golden and browned in some spots.

3. Meanwhile, prepare the sauce: In a small bowl, whisk together the sriracha, garlic, maple syrup, tamari, and vinegar.

4. Carefully pour all the sauce into the skillet (it'll sizzle as it hits the pan). Toss the chickpeas until they're completely coated in the sauce, then spread into a single layer once again.

recipe continues

recipe continued from previous page

STORAGE

These chickpeas are best served freshly cooked, but you can store them in an airtight container in the fridge for up to 3 days. Reheat the chickpeas in an oiled skillet over medium heat, stirring occasionally, for a few minutes, until warmed through.

TIPS

* One 14-ounce (398 mL) can of chickpeas is equivalent to 1½ cups cooked chickpeas, if you prefer to cook them from scratch.

** Using 1 teaspoon sriracha produces a mild to medium spice level, while 2 teaspoons produces a medium to hot spice level.

*** Double-check that your tamari is gluten-free, if necessary.

Reduce the heat to medium and gently simmer the chickpeas in the sauce, uncovered, tossing them occasionally, for 4 to 5 minutes, until the sauce cooks down and thickens, and the chickpeas absorb some of the sauce. There should still be a nice coating left in the pan (about ¼ cup sauce) when they're finished cooking. The chickpeas will continue to absorb sauce after cooking.

5. Serve as desired (see the headnote for tips!).

Ultimate Creamy Salt-and-Vinegar Scalloped Potatoes

Serves 8 • **Soak time** 1 hour or up to overnight (for the cheese sauce)
Active prep time 25 minutes • **Total time** 1 hour 25 minutes

1 batch Garlic Cashew Cheese Sauce (page 282)

1 batch Vegan Parmesan (page 317, cashew version)

2 pounds (900 g) Yukon Gold or yellow potatoes, peeled

Fine sea salt

A few generous pinches of fresh or dried thyme leaves, for garnish (optional)

Creamy, comforting, and stick-to-your-ribs, scalloped potatoes are simply dreamy. I don't know why it took me this long to make a vegan version, but I'm so glad that I did! And boy, did this recipe take a million trials to get just right . . . it was so worth it, though! This dish is garlicky and tangy (think "salt and vinegar" flavor!), with a hint of spice, crunch from the parm, and a bit of chew from the layered potatoes. It's absolutely addictive, and if you are anything like us, you'll find that you can't stop at one helping! For best results, it's important that you use a mandoline to slice the potatoes thinner than ⅛ inch (2 mm is ideal); see Kitchen Tools and Appliances on page 332 for my mandoline recommendation. If you don't own a mandoline and would rather not thinly slice the potatoes by hand, I've included a chopped potato version (see Tips). Often, acids such as vinegar or lemon juice can give cashew sauce a feta-like consistency once baked, so don't worry if this happens to your Garlic Cashew Cheese Sauce after baking . . . the flavor is just as delicious!

1. Prepare the Garlic Cashew Cheese Sauce, followed by the Vegan Parmesan (I like to make the parm quite coarse in texture to give this recipe some crunch). Set aside.

2. Preheat the oven to 425°F (220°C). Liberally oil a 9 by 13-inch (3 L) casserole dish, making sure to coat the sides and bottom completely.

recipe continues

recipe continued from previous page

STORAGE

This casserole can be tightly wrapped and stored in the fridge for up to 5 days. To reheat, cover with aluminum foil and bake in a preheated 425°F (220°C) oven for 20 to 25 minutes, until heated through.

MANDOLINE-FREE VERSION

Prepare the recipe as written, but dice the peeled potatoes into ½-inch (1 cm) cubes instead of slicing them. Add the cubes to the prepared casserole dish and carefully stir in all of the Garlic Cashew Cheese Sauce (alternatively, you can mix them in a large bowl). Spread out the potatoes in the dish and top with the Vegan Parmesan. Cover with foil, prick a few slits in the foil, and bake for 45 minutes. Uncover and bake for 10 minutes more, or until bubbling and golden brown on top and fork-tender.

MAKE IT AHEAD

You can save some time by prepping the sauce and vegan parm 1 to 2 days before you plan to make the casserole and storing them in separate airtight containers in the fridge. Let the sauce sit at room temperature for about an hour before you begin to ensure it's soft and spreadable, since it will thicken in the fridge.

3. Using a mandoline, slice the peeled potatoes into very thin (less than 2 mm) slices (no thicker, or they'll take a long time to cook through).

4. Spread a single layer of sliced potatoes over the bottom of the casserole dish, just barely overlapping them by about ⅛ inch (3 mm) and covering the bottom of the dish. Sprinkle a small pinch of salt over the sliced potatoes. Pour a scant 1 cup of the cashew cheese sauce over the potatoes so it covers the potatoes' surface completely (you can use the measuring cup or your fingers to help spread the sauce over all the potatoes). The sauce will look very thin and watery, but don't worry, because it thickens while baking. Repeat this layering process (remembering to lightly salt each layer of potatoes) until you have used all the sauce and sliced potatoes. (There should be five layers if you use a 9 by 13-inch/3 L casserole and your potato slices are 2 mm thick.) Make sure your final layer is sauce, and use all the remaining cheese sauce on this final layer. It will look like a swimming pool of sauce, but this is normal and it will firm up as it bakes.

5. Sprinkle all the parmesan over the sauce. Cover the casserole dish with aluminum foil. Using a sharp knife, cut about four 1-inch (2.5 cm) slits into the foil to vent steam.

6. Bake the casserole for 1 hour. After 1 hour, remove the foil and check for doneness by sliding a knife into the center of the casserole. You are looking for no resistance when you insert the knife (if your potatoes were sliced thicker than 2 mm, the casserole may take longer to bake). If there is resistance to the knife, replace the foil and bake for 5 to 15 minutes more, then test again.

7. Serve with a sprinkling of thyme leaves, if desired, and prepare to fall into a heavenly trance while enjoying each and every bite!

Crispy Brussels Sprouts in Garlic Oil

Serves 6 as a side dish • **Active prep time** 15 minutes • **Total time** 40 minutes

2 pounds (900 g) brussels sprouts*

3 tablespoons extra-virgin olive oil

5 large garlic cloves (30 g), grated on a Microplane (2½ tablespoons)

½ to ¾ teaspoon fine sea salt, to taste

Freshly ground black pepper (optional)

I will literally stand over a pan of these brussels sprouts and pop them into my mouth before they've had time to cool down (probably burning my mouth . . . agh, not again!), because they are *that* good. When I served these to Eric for the first time, he said, "If you told my twentysomething self that I would be inhaling a plate of brussels sprouts, I never would've believed you!" *Mission accomplished.* If you've ever had less-than-appealing, soggy boiled brussels (something out of a horror movie, I'd say), you really need to give this method a shot—roasting them until they are charred and sweetly caramelized is the only way I make them anymore. Whenever I serve these, friends and family say it's the best way they've ever tried brussels sprouts (I suppose they could be lying, but who would lie about brussels sprouts?). I love them as is, but you can take them to the next level by dipping them in Sriracha Aioli (page 289), Creamy Cashew or Sunflower Aioli (page 293), or good ol' barbecue sauce.

1. Preheat the oven to 400°F (200°C). Lightly oil an extra-large (15 by 21-inch/38 by 53 cm) baking sheet (or two large baking sheets).

2. Trim the stems off the brussels sprouts and slice the sprouts in half (quarter any jumbo sprouts and leave any teeny tiny ones whole).

recipe continues

recipe continued from previous page

STORAGE

Store in an airtight container in the fridge for up to 4 days. To reheat, transfer the sprouts to a preheated lightly oiled skillet over medium-low heat, cover, and cook for 3 to 5 minutes, until warmed through.

TIP

* Two pounds (900 g) of small to medium brussels sprouts is 6½ to 7 cups.

3. In a small bowl, whisk together the oil and garlic until combined. It will look quite thick and you'll wonder if it will really coat all those sprouts, but not to worry, it will! Place the sprouts on the prepared baking sheet and drizzle with all the garlic oil, scooping every last bit out of the bowl. Toss until the brussels sprouts are *completely* coated. Spread them into an even layer on the pan and season with the salt.

4. Roast for 15 minutes. Remove the pan from the oven and flip the sprouts (their bottoms will be brown in spots). Roast for 10 to 20 minutes more, until the sprouts are tender and browned (this adds mega flava!) and any loose leaves are blackened.

5. Serve immediately, seasoned with salt and pepper, if desired, and with a yummy dipping sauce, if you like (see the headnote for ideas!).

Creamy Mushroom, Green Bean, and Wild Rice Casserole

Serves 8 to 10 as a side dish • **Soak time** 1 hour or up to overnight (for the Cashew Sour Cream)
Active prep time 30 to 35 minutes • **Total time** 1 hour 20 minutes

1 cup (190 g) uncooked wild rice blend

1 batch Cashew Sour Cream (page 321)

2 tablespoons extra-virgin olive oil

2 pounds (900 g) cremini mushrooms, sliced

Heaping 1 cup (95 g) chopped (1-inch/ 2.5 cm pieces) green beans*

6 medium garlic cloves (24 g), grated on a Microplane (2½ tablespoons)

¼ cup coconut aminos (soy-free seasoning sauce)**

2 teaspoons pure maple syrup

2 teaspoons smoked paprika

¼ teaspoon cayenne pepper (optional, but recommended)

½ cup low-sodium vegetable broth

1 to 1½ tablespoons apple cider vinegar, to taste

1 teaspoon fine sea salt**

Freshly ground black pepper

½ cup (50 g) sliced almonds or panko-style bread crumbs

Creamy, heavenly, umami delight . . . that's what this casserole brings to the table. The Cashew Sour Cream creates a velvety sauce and the smoked paprika and cayenne add subtle warmth, bringing out its rich flavor. A touch of apple cider vinegar gives it all vibrance. This casserole is delicious when topped with panko-style bread crumbs, but to take it over the top or for special occasions, I highly recommend topping it with the sliced almonds—their lightly sweet, toasty flavor is irresistible in this dish! This is a fantastic casserole to serve as a holiday or special occasion meal, with my Festive Bread-Free Stuffing Balls (page 105) or Balsamic Roasted Root Vegetable Medley with Thyme and Cayenne (page 139) alongside. Turn this delightful dish into a protein-packed entrée by adding a 14-ounce (398 mL) can of chickpeas (drained and rinsed) in step 4 when you add the Cashew Sour Cream. If storing leftover casserole in the fridge, the chickpeas will take on a lovely, soft texture.

1. Cook the rice according to the package directions. While the rice cooks, prepare the Cashew Sour Cream and set aside.

2. Ten minutes before the rice is ready, preheat the oven to 400°F (200°C). Oil an 8 by 12-inch (3 L) or 9 by 13-inch (3 L) casserole dish.

3. In a large (5-quart/5 L) pot, place the oil, mushrooms, green beans, garlic, coconut aminos, maple syrup, smoked paprika,

recipe continues

recipe continued from previous page

STORAGE

Store leftovers in an airtight container in the fridge for up to 4 days, or freeze in a freezer bag with the air pressed out or in an airtight container for up to 2 months. Reheat in a preheated 400°F (200°C) oven, uncovered, for 25 to 30 minutes, until warmed through.

TIPS

* Frozen chopped (not French-cut) green beans work great as a swap for fresh. Simply add the frozen green beans during the last few minutes of cooking the mushroom mixture.

** Low-sodium tamari can be used as a swap for the coconut aminos (however, note that tamari contains soy). Simply add 3 tablespoons low-sodium tamari (do not use full-sodium tamari, as it'll be too salty), and reduce the salt to ½ to ¾ teaspoon, adding more salt, to taste, before transferring the mixture to the casserole dish.

MAKE IT GLUTEN-FREE

Use the sliced almond topping option instead of bread crumbs.

and cayenne pepper. Stir well to combine. Set heat to medium-high and sauté, uncovered, stirring occasionally, for 10 to 12 minutes, until the mushrooms begin to soften. The mixture should be simmering rapidly once the mushrooms start to release their liquid. There will still be a lot of liquid (1 to 1½ cups or so) left in the pot, but we want this, as it will form the base of the sauce.

4. Add the Cashew Sour Cream, broth, and the drained cooked wild rice blend to the pot with the mushrooms and stir to combine. Season with the vinegar, salt, and black pepper to taste and stir to combine. Remove from the heat. The mixture will look very soupy and liquidy, but it will thicken in the oven.

5. Spoon the mixture into the prepared casserole dish using a large spoon or spatula and even out the top. Scatter the sliced almonds evenly over the top. Bake, uncovered, for 20 to 26 minutes, until lightly golden, bubbling, and heated through. Serve and enjoy!

Romesco Roasted Potatoes and Green Beans

Serves 6 as a side dish • **Active prep time** 20 minutes • **Total time** 50 minutes

For the roasted vegetables

2 pounds (900 g) Yukon Gold, yellow, or red potatoes, chopped into ½-inch (1 cm) cubes

1½ tablespoons extra-virgin olive oil

1 pound (450 g) green beans, chopped into 1-inch (2.5 cm) pieces

Fine sea salt and freshly ground black pepper

For the Romesco-Inspired Roasted Red Pepper Sauce
(makes a generous 1⅓ cups)

¾ cup (185 g) raw walnuts

2 medium garlic cloves (8 g)

3 tablespoons extra-virgin olive oil

1 cup lightly packed (230 g) jarred roasted red peppers, drained

1½ tablespoons red wine vinegar

1½ teaspoons smoked paprika

¼ teaspoon cayenne pepper, or more to taste

½ teaspoon fine sea salt

Freshly ground black pepper

2 large green onions, finely chopped, for garnish

I made this for my girlfriends at one of our get-togethers, and everyone wanted the recipe and told me I had to put it in my cookbook. Who am I to deny my gals a big warm-and-cozy bowl of roasted potatoes and green beans, all coated with the most irresistible sweet-and-smoky roasted red pepper and walnut sauce? My family loves this side dish, too. I love serving it with simple bowls of homey Cold-Be-Gone Flavor Bomb Noodle Soup (page 213) for a quick and comforting meal, or you can turn it into a meal by serving it with a tangy green salad such as my Apple Honey–Dijon Mixed Greens (see Tip, page 285) and roasted chickpeas.

1. Make the roasted vegetables: Preheat the oven to 400°F (200°C). Position two oven racks near the middle of the oven. Line two large baking sheets with parchment paper.

2. Place the chopped potatoes in a mound on one baking sheet, drizzle with 1 tablespoon of the oil, and toss to coat. Spread out the potatoes in an even layer over the pan. Place the green beans in a mound on the second baking sheet, drizzle with the remaining ½ tablespoon oil, and toss to coat. Spread out the green beans into an even layer over the pan. Sprinkle both the potatoes and green beans with a generous amount of salt and pepper.

3. Roast the potatoes and green beans for 30 to 35 minutes, until the potatoes are golden brown and fork-tender and the

recipe continues

recipe continued from previous page

STORAGE

Store leftovers in an airtight container in the fridge for up to 3 days. To reheat, add a bit of olive oil to a skillet and cook, covered, over medium-low heat for 3 to 5 minutes, until warmed through. The romesco sauce can be stored in a freezer bag with the air pressed out or in an airtight container in the freezer for up to 1 month.

MAKE IT NUT-FREE

Swap out the walnuts for ½ cup (80 g) roasted pepitas; see page 338.

MAKE IT KID-FRIENDLY

Set aside a small portion of the vegetables and serve a little romesco sauce on the side for dipping. Reduce the cayenne pepper as needed.

UP THE GLOW

Add chickpeas (roasted are nice), sliced toasted almonds, or hemp hearts for a protein boost. Finely chopped arugula is also just the thing for a green-powered crunch!

beans are wilted and lightly charred in some spots, flipping halfway through roasting (pro tip: Sometimes I skip flipping them and it's no big deal!).

4. Meanwhile, prepare the sauce: In a small skillet, toast the walnuts over medium heat for 4 to 8 minutes, until fragrant.

5. In a food processor, process the garlic until minced. Add the toasted walnuts, oil, roasted red peppers, vinegar, smoked paprika, cayenne pepper, and salt and black pepper to taste. Process until smooth.

6. Transfer the *hot-out-of-the-oven* potatoes and green beans to a large bowl. Add all of the romesco sauce and toss until fully coated. Serve warm, with the green onions sprinkled on top. The dish cools down fast, so be sure to serve it as quickly as possible!

Seasoned Crispy Baked Potato Wedges

Serves 4 (10 wedges per serving) • **Active prep time** 10 minutes • **Total time** 40 minutes

1 teaspoon sweet paprika

1 teaspoon dried onion flakes

½ teaspoon garlic powder

¼ teaspoon cayenne pepper*

1 teaspoon fine sea salt, plus more for serving

3 large russet potatoes (800 g)

2 tablespoons grapeseed oil

Sriracha Aioli (page 289) or other sauce, for dipping

These golden wedges are savory and zingy and have a lively heat, making them an irresistible side dish or snack. Eric and I were inhaling a plate of them one evening, and after his first bite, he said, "These aren't your mama's fries!" I replied, "My mom's or yours?!" "*Neither* of ours." Sorry, Mamas (I didn't say it!). Serve these crispy delights dunked in Sriracha Aioli, Creamy Cashew or Sunflower Aioli (page 293), Roasted Red Pepper and Walnut Dip (page 298), or Cashew Sour Cream (page 321) and ketchup. These fries also make the perfectly seasoned, comforting base for my Spicy Potato Nacho Plate (page 71).

1. Preheat the oven to 425°F (220°C). Grease an extra-large (15 by 21-inch/38 by 53 cm) nonstick baking sheet with oil. (I don't use parchment paper because I find the wedges get a bit crispier when baked directly on a greased baking sheet!)

2. In a small bowl, mix together the paprika, onion flakes, garlic powder, cayenne, and salt.

3. Do not peel the potatoes, as roasting them in their skins makes them crispier. Slice the potatoes into ½-inch-thick (1 cm) wedges.

4. Place the wedges in a mound in the center of the prepared baking sheet. Drizzle with the oil and toss until fully coated. Spread the wedges into a single layer over the pan, spacing them 1 inch (2.5 cm) apart. Place the wedges skin-side down wherever possible so the seasoning adheres better.

recipe continues

recipe continued from previous page

STORAGE

Store leftover wedges in an airtight container in the fridge for up to 4 days. Reheat on a lightly greased baking sheet in a preheated 400°F (200°C) oven for 7 to 9 minutes, until heated through.

TIP

* Not a fan of spicy food? Simply omit the cayenne pepper.

5. Sprinkle a generous amount of the seasoning onto the flesh of each potato wedge (I like to sprinkle each wedge one by one rather than shaking it all over them at once, so less seasoning falls onto the baking sheet and goes to waste). If you run out of seasoning, simply sprinkle a bit of each individual spice onto the remaining wedges.

6. Bake for 30 to 35 minutes, until golden brown and tender, flipping the wedges once halfway through.

7. Meanwhile, prepare the Sriracha Aioli.

8. Serve immediately, with the aioli for dipping, or your favorite sauce.

Flavor Bomb Chimichurri Guacamole

Makes 1¾ cups • **Active prep time** 12 minutes • **Total time** 12 minutes

2 tablespoons Easy Chimichurri Sauce (page 272), or to taste, plus more for serving, if desired

3 tablespoons (22 g) finely chopped red onion, rinsed and drained*

½ cup (90 g) diced ripe tomato

⅛ teaspoon fine sea salt, or to taste

Freshly ground black pepper

1 cup (155 g) chopped ripe avocado (from about 2 medium)

Minced fresh parsley, for garnish

STORAGE

Guacamole is best served fresh. However, you can store it in a small airtight container in the fridge for up to 24 hours. Be sure to choose a container that will hold the guacamole without much extra space above it so your guacamole will stay nice and green. You can also pour a thin layer of olive oil over the top before covering the container to prevent oxidization.

TIP

* Rinsing helps reduce the "sharpness" of the onion and makes it more pleasing to enjoy raw. You can skip this, if desired, though.

UP THE GLOW

Sprinkle on some hemp hearts for a protein boost.

When I first tasted my Easy Chimichurri Sauce, I knew I had to find a way to use it in guacamole. The sauce is just so bright and versatile, and when it's added to guacamole, all the flavors sing! The red wine vinegar, parsley, and red chile of the chimichurri sauce stand in for the traditional lime juice, cilantro, and serrano pepper, creating a unique spin on this go-to dip. While it's not the *prettiest* dip, I find that sprinkling a bit of minced parsley on top helps it in the looks department. But really, who cares what it looks like when it tastes this good? Try it on top of my Weeknight Tex-Mex Quinoa with Cashew Sour Cream (page 75) for the perfect effortless supper.

1. Prepare the Easy Chimichurri Sauce. Set aside.

2. In a medium bowl, combine the red onion and tomato. Stir in 1 tablespoon of the chimichurri sauce, along with the salt and pepper.

3. Gently fold in the chopped avocado until just combined. I like my guacamole to have texture with chunks of avocado, so I avoid overmixing it.

4. Fold in the remaining 1 tablespoon chimichurri sauce until just combined.

5. Spoon the guacamole into a small serving bowl. Garnish with a small pinch of salt and a scattering of minced parsley. I like to drizzle even more sauce over the top, too. Serve immediately.

Sneaky Protein-Packed Mashed Potatoes

Serves 6 (¾ cup per serving) • **Active prep time** 25 minutes • **Total time** 25 minutes

3 or 4 large yellow potatoes (750 g)

2 tablespoons extra-virgin olive oil

I cup (125 g) finely chopped sweet or yellow onion (I medium)

5 medium garlic cloves (20 g), minced (2 tablespoons), plus 2 medium garlic cloves, grated on a Microplane

I heaping teaspoon fresh thyme leaves, or ½ teaspoon dried

I (14-ounce/398 mL) can chickpeas, drained and rinsed*

½ cup vegetable broth

Fine sea salt and freshly ground black pepper

3 tablespoons vegan butter, homemade (page 318) or store-bought, plus more if needed

Garlic powder

These mashed potatoes are hiding a protein- and fiber-rich secret! Cooked chickpeas infused with thyme, garlic, and onion are pureed and stirred into an ultra-comforting mashed potato base. And no one will be the wiser—especially bean-fearing kids! This mash contains both cooked and raw garlic for added depth of flavor and vegan butter to give it the creamiest texture and buttery taste. I created this mash to serve as a base for my Italian Herb Parmesan–Crusted Portobellos (page 72)—it's the ultimate stick-to-your-ribs healthy duo. If you're making this as a side dish, I recommend topping it with my Italian Herb Parmesan (page 301) for a flavor explosion, or try my Rosemary and Thyme Mushroom Gravy (page 304) for a rich, cozy, company-worthy side dish. Don't have time for anything extra? Simply sprinkle the mash with a little fresh thyme for a pretty presentation and add a pat of vegan butter on top.

1. Bring a medium pot of water to a boil over high heat.

2. Meanwhile, peel the potatoes and chop them into small ½- to 1-inch (1 to 2.5 cm) pieces (you should have 4 slightly heaping cups).

3. When the water comes to a boil, reduce the heat to medium-high, add the chopped potatoes, and boil for 11 to 14 minutes, until fork-tender.

4. Meanwhile, in a large pot, heat the oil over medium heat. Add the onion and minced garlic and stir to coat with the oil. Sauté, stirring frequently, until the onion softens, about 5 minutes.

recipe continues

recipe continued from previous page

STORAGE

Store in an airtight container in the fridge for up to 4 days. Add a little almond milk or vegan butter when reheating for added creaminess.

TIP

* One 14-ounce (398 mL) can of chickpeas is equivalent to 1½ cups cooked chickpeas, if you prefer to cook them from scratch.

MAKE IT SOY-FREE

Use my homemade butter (page 318) or soy-free store-bought butter.

5. Add the thyme, drained chickpeas, broth, salt, and pepper to taste and stir to combine. Increase the heat to medium-high and simmer, uncovered, for 3 minutes more to infuse with the flavor of the herbs.

6. Carefully transfer the chickpea mixture to a food processor and process for about 1 minute, until it has a smooth texture similar to a thin hummus.

7. When the potatoes are finished cooking, drain them and return them to the pot. Add the butter and grated raw garlic. Using a potato masher, mash the potatoes until smooth.

8. Spoon the chickpea puree into the mashed potatoes and stir well to combine. Season to taste with salt, pepper, and garlic powder. Serve immediately or gently reheat over low heat for a few minutes, if needed, before serving.

Saucy Little Black Bean Skillet

Makes 2 generous cups • **Active prep time** 10 minutes • **Total time** 20 minutes

2 tablespoons extra-virgin olive oil

I cup (140 g) diced onion (I medium)

4 medium garlic cloves (16 g), minced (1½ tablespoons)

I large jalapeño (70 g), seeded and diced (optional)

Fine sea salt

I cup (180 g) diced fresh tomato (I large)

2½ to 3 teaspoons Tex-Mex Spice Blend (page 313), to taste*

2½ tablespoons tomato paste

I (14-ounce/398 mL) can black beans, drained and rinsed**

½ cup (11 g) fresh cilantro leaves, chopped

I like to call these saucy black beans the LBD (little black dress) of vegan protein recipes, as you can use them in wraps or scatter them on top of salads, Roasted Garlic Cauliflower Rice (page 170), or The Mama Bear Bowl: Cauli-Power Savory Steel-Cut Oatmeal (page 108). One of our favorite ways to serve this skillet is on top of my Spicy Potato Nacho Plate (page 71). Three cheers for plant-protein power! Creamy black beans mingle with sautéed jalapeño, onion, and garlic and are seasoned with fresh tomatoes, citrusy cilantro, and my sweet-and-smoky Tex-Mex Spice Blend. These saucy little black beans pack a fair amount of heat, so feel free to season them to your taste if you don't want them quite as spicy, or dollop on some of my Cashew Sour Cream (page 321) as a cooling topper. Thank you to Jennifer Houston and Ruth Tal's *Super Fresh: Super Natural, Super Vibrant Vegan Recipes* for inspiring this recipe!

1. In a large wok or skillet, heat the oil over medium heat. Stir in the onion, garlic, and jalapeño (if using), along with a pinch of salt. Sauté for 4 to 5 minutes, until softened.

2. Stir in the diced tomato and the Tex-Mex Spice Blend. Increase the heat to medium-high and sauté for 4 to 5 minutes more, until the tomato is softened. Reduce the heat, if necessary, to prevent burning.

recipe continues

recipe continued from previous page

STORAGE

Store in an airtight container in the fridge for up to 4 days, or freeze in a freezer bag with the air pressed out or in an airtight container for up to 1 month. To reheat, thaw (if frozen), then transfer to a preheated oiled skillet over medium-low heat, cover, and cook for 3 to 5 minutes, until heated through. Revive the flavors with a squeeze of lime juice and/or a pinch of Tex-Mex Spice Blend, if desired.

TIPS

* My Tex-Mex Spice Blend can be swapped out for 1 teaspoon chili powder, 1 teaspoon garlic powder, 1 teaspoon dried oregano, ¼ teaspoon cayenne pepper, and ½ teaspoon plus ⅛ teaspoon fine sea salt.

** One 14-ounce (398 mL) can of black beans is equivalent to 1½ cups cooked black beans, if you prefer to cook them from scratch.

MAKE IT KID-FRIENDLY

Omit the jalapeño and start with 1 to 2 teaspoons of the Tex-Mex Spice Blend, then add more to your child's taste.

3. Stir in the tomato paste and black beans. Cook for a few minutes more, until heated through.

4. Stir in the cilantro and cook for another minute. Taste and season with more salt, if desired.

VEGAN • GLUTEN-FREE • NUT-FREE • SOY-FREE • GRAIN-FREE • KID-FRIENDLY • FREEZER-FRIENDLY

Roasted Garlic Cauliflower Rice

Makes 3 to 3½ cups • **Active prep time** 10 minutes • **Total time** 35 minutes

5 large garlic cloves (30 g)

1 large (2½-pound/1.125 kg) head cauliflower, cut into florets

2 tablespoons extra-virgin olive oil

¾ teaspoon fine sea salt, or to taste

Freshly ground black pepper

I'm obsessed with this Roasted Garlic Cauliflower Rice! And I never thought I'd say that because, well, it's *cauliflower*, but my secret is infusing it with buttery olive oil and savory garlic. It's fantastic as a base for stews, chilis, soups, and bowls. Serve it with my Cozy Butternut Squash, Sweet Potato, and Red Lentil Stew (page 215), Sizzling Maple-Sriracha Garlic Chickpeas (page 145), and Saucy Little Black Bean Skillet (page 167). This recipe makes about 3 cups cauliflower rice; if you need more than a few servings, you can double the recipe and use two extra-large (15 by 21-inch/38 by 53 cm) baking sheets (rotating them halfway through baking in addition to flipping the rice). It's easiest to use a food processor to rice the cauliflower, but if you don't have one, you can grate a head of cauliflower on a box grater.

1. Preheat the oven to 400°F (200°C). Line an extra-large (15 by 21-inch/38 by 53 cm) rimmed baking sheet (or two large baking sheets) with parchment paper.

2. In a large food processor, process the garlic until minced.

3. Add the cauliflower to the food processor with the minced garlic. (If your processor bowl holds less than 12 cups, you may need to do this in batches.) Pulse the cauliflower (do not use the "process" button or it'll lose its texture!) 25 to 35 times, until the florets break down to resemble the size of rice. Avoid overprocessing; if any large florets remain, you can finely chop them by hand.

recipe continues

recipe continued from previous page

STORAGE

Store in an airtight container in the fridge for up to 4 days. To reheat, spread out in an even layer on a lightly oiled baking sheet and bake in a preheated 400°F (200°C) oven for 5 to 6 minutes, until heated through. You can also reheat it in an oiled skillet over medium heat, stirring occasionally, for a few minutes. Season with salt and pepper.

4. Spoon the mixture onto the prepared baking sheet in a mound. Drizzle the oil over the top and toss thoroughly to combine. Spread the mixture out into a thin layer over the pan. Sprinkle with the salt and pepper to taste.

5. Roast the cauliflower rice for 20 to 25 minutes, flipping once with a spatula halfway through roasting. When ready, the rice should look golden or charred in some spots; if not, you can cook it a bit longer. Taste and season with more salt and pepper, if desired. The cauliflower rice cools down rather quickly, so I recommend keeping it warm in the oven until you're ready to serve it.

VEGAN • GLUTEN-FREE • NUT-FREE OPTION • SOY-FREE • GRAIN-FREE • KID-FRIENDLY • ON THE GLOW

Crispy Smashed Potatoes, Endless Ways

Serves 6 (2 or 3 potatoes per serving) • **Active prep time** 15 minutes • **Total time** 1 hour 5 minutes

3 pounds (1.35 kg) small Yukon Gold potatoes (about 14)*

1 teaspoon fine sea salt, plus more as needed

Creamy Cashew or Sunflower Aioli (page 293), 24/7 Avocado-Cilantro Sauce (page 286), or pesto (pages 275, 276, 294, or 297)

2 to 3 tablespoons grapeseed oil or olive oil

Fresh herbs, such as parsley or cilantro, for serving (optional)

Adriana, at the tender age of four, saw these smashed potatoes in the oven and called them "golden eggs"! She's been obsessed with *golden eggs* ever since she found one during an Easter egg hunt as a two-year-old. These crowd-pleasing potatoes are smashed, crispy, and served with an addictive creamy sauce of your choice—Creamy Cashew or Sunflower Aioli, 24/7 Avocado-Cilantro Sauce, or one of my delicious pestos. You can change them up in endless ways! They make a killer side dish, and everyone, kids and adults alike, will inhale them faster than you can ask for seconds.

1. To a large pot, add the potatoes and the salt. Add water to cover by at least 1 inch (2.5 cm) and bring to a boil over high heat. Reduce the heat to medium-high and simmer for 20 to 30 minutes, until a fork slides easily through the centers. Be careful not to overcook the potatoes or they will begin to break down.

2. Meanwhile, preheat the oven to 450°F (230°C). Grease a large baking sheet with oil (I skip using parchment paper here because I find the potatoes get a bit crispier if roasted directly on the baking sheet).

3. Prepare the Creamy Cashew or Sunflower Aioli (or desired sauce) and set aside.

4. Drain the potatoes in a colander and let cool for 5 minutes.

recipe continues

recipe continued from previous page

STORAGE

Leftover potatoes (without any sauce) can be stored in an airtight container in the fridge for up to 4 days. Reheat them on a greased baking sheet in a preheated 400°F (200°C) oven for 10 to 15 minutes, until warmed through.

TIP

* I love the flavor of Yukon Gold potatoes, but red or new potatoes work well, too. I don't recommend using baking potatoes such as russets or fingerlings, as they are too starchy and their texture is too dry. Try to use small potatoes for this recipe, as they'll cook faster and hold together a bit better when smashed. Really, though, I'd never turn any potato away . . . and usually the broken, crispy bits are the very best part!

MAKE IT NUT-FREE

Serve the potatoes with Creamy Sunflower Aioli; 24/7 Avocado-Cilantro Sauce; or a nut-free pesto: Boom! Broccoli Pesto, Perfect Basil Pesto, Lemony Dill Protein Pesto, or Pretty Parsley-Cilantro Pepita Pesto (pepita option).

5. Place the potatoes on the prepared baking sheet. With the bottom of a large mug or metal measuring cup, press down on each potato until it's somewhat flattened, approximately ½ inch (1 cm) thick. Some potatoes might break apart a little or a lot, but that's totally normal! If the potatoes begin to stick to the bottom of the mug, you can lightly grease it with oil.

6. Drizzle each potato with 1 teaspoon of the oil (if your potatoes are very small, you can get away with ½ teaspoon), spreading it over the entire surface. Sprinkle each with a generous amount of salt.

7. Roast the potatoes for 27 to 33 minutes, until crispy, golden, and deliciously browned on the bottom. (Pro tip: They have a much better flavor and texture if you overcook them a bit!)

8. Remove the potatoes from the oven and sprinkle with more salt. Drizzle with the sauce, garnish with fresh herbs, if desired, and serve.

Game Night Crispy Potato Bruschetta

Serves 2 as a main or 6 as an appetizer • **Active prep time** 15 minutes • **Total time** 45 minutes

For the Crispy Roasted Potato Rounds

2 large russet potatoes (550 g total)

1 tablespoon grapeseed oil or olive oil

Fine sea salt

For the Avocado-Tomato Topping

2 medium garlic cloves (8 g)

½ cup lightly packed (15 g) fresh basil leaves

1 pint (300 g) grape or cherry tomatoes

1 tablespoon fresh lemon juice

1 tablespoon balsamic vinegar

¼ to ½ teaspoon fine sea salt, to taste

1 ripe large avocado (240 g)

The first time I made this recipe, Eric and I had the song "Ave Maria" playing (the Michael Bublé version . . . so hypnotizing!), and we fell into a trance as we ate crispy round after crispy round of potato bruschetta. Needless to say, we heard the angels singing, and I think you will, too! The avocado-and-tomato topping is enhanced with sweet-and-tangy balsamic vinegar, savory garlic, and aromatic basil. This recipe serves two hungry people as a main or up to six as an appetizer. The best tip I can give you before making these is to serve them directly on the baking sheet, as it keeps the rounds a bit warmer than if you transfer them to a platter. Also, be sure to top the rounds and serve them right away. If they sit for longer than 5 to 10 minutes, they'll lose their fantastic crispiness and soften considerably. Shave time off your prep by using a mandoline for the potatoes (see page 332).

1. Preheat the oven to 425°F (220°C). Line an extra-large (15 by 21-inch/38 by 53 cm) baking sheet (or two large baking sheets) with parchment paper.

2. With a sharp knife or a mandoline, slice the potatoes into ¼-inch-thick (5 mm) rounds. (Make sure they are at least ¼ inch/5 mm thick so they'll be sturdy enough to pick up with your hands and so the edges won't burn as easily during cooking.)

3. Place the rounds into the center of the prepared baking sheet in a mound. Toss with the oil until all sides of the rounds are

recipe continues

recipe continued from previous page

UP THE GLOW

Sprinkle/drizzle my Vegan Parmesan (page 317) on top.

fully coated. Spread the rounds out into a single layer, spacing them ½ inch (1 cm) apart. Sprinkle liberally with salt.

4. Roast the potatoes for 25 to 35 minutes (I do 30 minutes), until tender and golden brown in some spots, flipping once halfway through baking. I prefer these slightly overcooked so they crisp up a bit around the edges.

5. Meanwhile, prepare the Avocado-Tomato Topping: In a food processor, process the garlic and basil until finely chopped. Add the tomatoes and pulse 10 to 14 times, just until the tomatoes are chopped into almond- and pea-sized pieces. Remove the processor bowl, take out the blade, and stir in the lemon juice, vinegar, and salt. Set aside so the mixture can marinate.

6. Five minutes before the potatoes are ready, pit and dice the avocado into very small, pea-sized pieces (you should have about 1¼ cups). Fold the avocado into the tomato mixture. Taste and stir in more salt, if desired. The mixture will look quite juicy/watery, but this is normal!

7. Remove the potatoes from the oven and season with another generous sprinkle of salt. Using a fork, scoop up ½ to 1 tablespoon of the avocado-tomato mixture and strain out the juices by tapping the fork against the side of the bowl. Place the mixture in the center of a potato round. Repeat to top the rest of the rounds.

8. Serve immediately, directly from the baking sheet. If you prefer a less rustic presentation, you can transfer the rounds to a platter before adding the topping. If the potatoes sit, they will soften and lose their crispness, so I don't recommend letting them sit around for longer than 5 to 10 minutes (usually not a problem in my house!). If you have any avocado-tomato mixture left over, feel free to polish it off with some tortilla chips!

Rustic Roasted Carrot and Dill Hummus

Makes 2 cups • **Active prep time** 15 minutes • **Total time** 45 minutes

1¾ cups (240 g) diced (½-inch/1 cm pieces) peeled carrots (2 to 3 large)

3 teaspoons extra-virgin olive oil

1 to 1¼ teaspoons fine sea salt, to taste, plus more as needed

2 large garlic cloves (12 g), or to taste

3 tablespoons packed (6 g) chopped fresh dill, or more to taste

1 (14-ounce/398 mL) can chickpeas*

⅓ cup tahini

3½ to 4½ tablespoons fresh lemon juice, to taste

For garnish

Ground cumin

Ground coriander

Minced fresh dill

Olive oil (optional)

Can hummus really be a showstopper? If it's made with sweet-and-smoky roasted carrots, tangy lemon, and fresh dill, it can be! Lightly charred roasted carrots combine with fresh, bright lemon and dill to create this wonderful spring-inspired hummus. I knew I had a hit on my hands when Arlo (three years old) polished off his hummus toast, then reached for the hummus bowl and proceeded to eat it with a spoon! Happy mama. This isn't your usual beige hummus (though I love that, too!). Roasted carrots add a light sweetness and subtle orange hue and their charred bottoms add a subtle smoky flavor. All this deliciousness is enhanced by fresh dill, which makes this hummus so lively. We love to slather it on toast and crackers and dollop it onto salads, Buddha bowls, and The Mama Bear Bowl: Cauli-Power Savory Steel-Cut Oatmeal (page 108). Hummus pairs well with potatoes, too. Try it as a substitute for the broccoli pesto on my Crispy Potato Stacks (page 87). A big thank-you to Izzy at *She Likes Food* for the flavor inspo!

1. Preheat the oven to 400°F (200°C). Line a baking sheet with parchment paper.

2. Add the carrots to the prepared baking sheet. Add 1 teaspoon of the oil and toss to coat. Spread the carrots out into an even layer over the pan and sprinkle with a pinch of salt. Roast for 27 to 32 minutes, until fork-tender and golden.

3. About 5 minutes before your carrots are done, in a large food processor, process the garlic and dill until minced.

recipe continues

recipe continued from previous page

STORAGE

Store in an airtight container in the fridge for up to 5 days.

TIPS

* Aquafaba is the liquid found in a can of chickpeas. I find that using aquafaba yields a slightly creamier hummus, but feel free to use regular ol' water if you wish!

* If you are using freshly cooked chickpeas, use 1 cup rather than the 1½ cups found in a 14-ounce (398 mL) can. Using freshly cooked chickpeas makes the hummus much thicker than if you use canned chickpeas, and the texture can throw off the other flavors (you may need to adjust the amounts called for, too). You may need to add more brine or water, too. This version will also produce a slightly smaller yield.

4. Drain the chickpeas over a small bowl, reserving the liquid (aquafaba) from the can.

5. Add the chickpeas, tahini, lemon juice, 5 tablespoons of the aquafaba, the remaining 2 teaspoons oil, the salt, and roasted carrots to the food processor. Process until smooth, stopping to scrape down the side of the processor bowl as necessary. I like to let the machine run for a couple of minutes. Add more aquafaba or water, if needed, to thin the hummus to your desired consistency. Taste and adjust the flavor as desired, adding more dill, lemon juice, salt, or oil, if you like.

6. Spread the hummus over a shallow serving dish. Garnish with a sprinkle of ground cumin, coriander, and fresh dill, plus a drizzle of olive oil, if desired, and serve.

MEAL-WORTHY SALADS

Summery Chimichurri Chickpea Pasta Salad

Serves 8 (I cup per serving) • **Active prep time** 22 minutes • **Total time** 30 minutes

I batch Easy Chimichurri Sauce (page 272)

2 small or I medium zucchini (300 g)

I tablespoon grapeseed oil or extra-virgin olive oil

II ounces (3½ cups/300 g) dry chickpea fusilli pasta or pasta of choice*

I pint grape tomatoes, halved (1¾ cups/ 300 g)

3 large green onions (55 g), thinly sliced (¾ cup)

⅓ cup (65 g) oil-packed unsalted sun-dried tomatoes, drained and finely chopped

I cup (30 g) baby spinach, coarsely chopped (optional)

½ teaspoon fine sea salt, or to taste

Freshly ground black pepper

Red wine vinegar (optional)

This pasta salad comes with a warning: *Beware! You won't be able to stop eating this!* At least, we can't. Many friends and family have deemed this the best pasta salad they've tasted, and all demand the recipe. It's simply irresistible, and it's the best way to use up summer veggies like sun-ripened tomatoes, crunchy green onions, zucchini, parsley, garlic, and more (but hey, I wouldn't stop myself from making it in the dead of winter when I'm majorly craving bright summer flavors!). The Easy Chimichurri Sauce (my secret flavor weapon in this dish) can be made up to 3 days in advance, if you like, then the pasta salad comes together in just over 20 minutes! My best tip for this recipe is to have all your ducks in a row before you begin, as it moves fast and there are a few things going on all at once. You can pretend you're on an episode of *Top Chef* to make things extra dramatic.

1. Prepare the Easy Chimichurri Sauce. (If prepared in advance and refrigerated, let it sit at room temperature to soften for at least 30 minutes before using.)

2. Bring a large pot of water to a boil over high heat. Heat a grill pan (or a greased skillet, if you don't have a grill pan) over medium-high heat.

3. Trim the ends of the zucchini and slice the zucchini into long slabs ¼ to ½ inch (5 mm to I cm) thick. Brush both sides of each slab with the oil. Place the zucchini on the grill pan and

recipe continues

recipe continued from previous page

STORAGE

This pasta is best served fresh if prepared with chickpea pasta, since legume-based pastas can either get mushy or harden during storage, depending on the brand and type of legume. Traditional wheat-based pasta will keep in an airtight container in the fridge for up to 4 days.

TIP

* I love Maria's chickpea fusilli pasta in this dish. It cooks in about 6 minutes and is gluten- and grain-free. Banza chickpea pasta is also a popular brand. Be sure to see the Storage information if using chickpea pasta.

MAKE IT KID-FRIENDLY

The chimichurri sauce might have a little too much *oomph* for some kids. Set aside a kid-sized portion of the pasta and vegetables (without sauce), then stir in a small amount of the sauce or simply add their favorite pasta sauce instead.

grill for 3 to 4 minutes per side, until nicely charred and fork-tender.

4. Meanwhile, add the pasta to the boiling water and cook according to the package directions.

5. While the pasta and zucchini cook, prep the grape tomatoes, green onions, sun-dried tomatoes, and spinach (if using).

6. Allow the grilled zucchini to cool for a few minutes on a cutting board, then chop it into bite-sized pieces.

7. Drain the cooked pasta, quickly rinse, and transfer to a large bowl. Add the zucchini, grape tomatoes, green onions, sun-dried tomatoes, spinach (if using), and all the chimichurri sauce and stir well to combine. Taste and season with salt and pepper. Add a bit of red wine vinegar if you want more zing. Serve and enjoy!

Charred Broccoli Quinoa Salad with Apple Honey–Dijon Dressing

Serves 7 (I cup per serving) • **Active prep time** 17 minutes • **Total time** 35 minutes

2 large bunches broccoli (1.1 kg total)

1½ tablespoons extra-virgin olive oil

¼ teaspoon fine sea salt

¼ teaspoon freshly ground black pepper

1 cup (185 g) uncooked quinoa

1¾ cups water

1 batch Apple Honey–Dijon Dressing (page 285)

Red pepper flakes (optional)

Fresh lemon juice or lemon wedges (optional)

This unassuming little recipe could easily be overlooked if I weren't here to tell you how incredible it is! It's one of those recipes I could happily enjoy as a daily mealtime staple. It's simple but loaded with flavor, and if you're anything like me, you'll find yourself going back to the fridge to sneak bite after bite. It's light and flavorful, while packing a huge nutritional punch. The smoky flavor from the charred edges of the broccoli is complemented by the sweet, pungent Apple Honey–Dijon Dressing. We love this dish all year round and make it often, especially when we are short on time and need a quick but satisfying dish. We love to turn it into a heartier meal by adding roasted chickpeas, which are easy to roast alongside the broccoli (see Up the Glow). You can also swap out the broccoli for any veggies you have on hand or need to use up, making it truly versatile and pantry-friendly (simply cook your veggies until fork-tender, adjusting the cooking time as needed). To add a beautiful pop of color and festive touch, sprinkle on some pomegranate arils. Thanks to the lovely Alexa from the blog *Fooduzzi* for inspiring this recipe!

1. Preheat the oven to 425°F (220°C). Line an extra-large (15 by 21-inch/38 by 53 cm) baking sheet (or two large baking sheets) with parchment paper.

2. Chop the broccoli into florets, then finely chop the florets into ½-inch (1 cm) pieces (you should have 8 to 9 cups). Place the broccoli on the prepared baking sheet and drizzle the oil over the top. Thoroughly massage the oil into the broccoli until

recipe continues

recipe continued from previous page

STORAGE

Store in an airtight container in the fridge for 5 to 6 days, or freeze in a freezer bag with the air pressed out or in an airtight container for up to 1 month. Mix in fresh dressing and season with salt, black pepper, and red pepper flakes as needed to revive the flavors.

UP THE GLOW

Turn this into a satisfying meal and boost the protein by adding my Cayenne Roasted Chickpeas (see page 199)—simply pop the chickpeas in the oven 10 minutes before you add the broccoli, and they'll finish roasting at the same time!

Add a little crunch and boost the omega-3s by topping this salad with slivered almonds, roasted pepitas (see page 338), or chopped walnuts.

it's completely coated. Spread the broccoli out into a single layer over the pan. Season with the salt and pepper. Roast the broccoli, uncovered, for 20 to 24 minutes, until fork-tender and lightly charred and crispy around the edges.

3. While the broccoli roasts, in a medium pot, place the quinoa and water. Bring to a low boil over medium-high heat, then reduce the heat to medium-low, cover, and cook for 12 to 16 minutes, until the water has been absorbed and the quinoa is fluffy. You should have 2½ to 3 cups cooked quinoa. Remove from the heat, fluff with a fork, and replace the lid so the quinoa stays warm.

4. Meanwhile, prepare the Apple Honey–Dijon Dressing.

5. In a large bowl, place the warm quinoa and roasted broccoli. Shake the jar of dressing to recombine (it tends to separate quickly) and drizzle ½ cup of the dressing over the quinoa and broccoli. Toss well to combine. Taste and season with additional salt, black pepper, and red pepper flakes, if desired. Add more dressing, if you'd like, or if you'd like a bit more tanginess, add a squeeze of fresh lemon juice (or simply serve each portion with a lemon wedge on the side). Enjoy warm, adding an additional drizzle of dressing just before serving to bring out the flavors.

Pumpkin Spice and Everything Nice Salad

Makes 4 salads • **Active prep time** 20 minutes • **Total time** 50 minutes

For the Roasted Sweet Potato and Chickpeas

3 medium sweet potatoes (760 g total)

1 (14-ounce/398 mL) can chickpeas, drained and rinsed*

2 tablespoons extra-virgin olive oil

2 tablespoons pure maple syrup

2 teaspoons pumpkin pie spice, homemade (page 311) or store-bought, plus more for serving

½ teaspoon fine sea salt, plus more for serving

For the Marinated Kale Salad

1 medium bunch curly kale (265 g), stemmed and chopped (6 cups)

1 medium garlic clove (4 g), finely grated on a Microplane

1 tablespoon extra-virgin olive oil

1 teaspoon pure maple syrup, or to taste

¼ teaspoon fine sea salt

3 tablespoons fresh lemon juice

1 tablespoon runny tahini**

½ cup (80 g) roasted salted pepitas (see page 338), for garnish

This salad fills your house with the most intoxicating pumpkin spice and maple aroma—who needs to burn a pumpkin spice candle when you have this gorgeous recipe? It's quite possibly the best warm salad to dig into all fall season long. The best part? You get three recipes out of one here. In addition to making this complete salad as a hearty starter or main, both the roasted maple and pumpkin spice sweet potatoes and marinated kale salad make easy side dishes on their own. You'll want to make extra, because your neighbors are sure to knock on your door, asking where that blissful scent is coming from!

1. Prepare the Roasted Sweet Potato and Chickpeas: Preheat the oven to 400°F (200°C) Line an extra-large (15 by 21-inch/38 by 53 cm) baking sheet (or two large baking sheets) with parchment paper.

2. Peel the sweet potatoes and chop them into small 1-inch (2.5 cm) cubes (you should have about 5½ cups). Place the drained chickpeas and sweet potato on the prepared baking sheet. Drizzle with the oil and toss until thoroughly coated. Drizzle on 1 tablespoon of the maple syrup and toss again to coat. Spread the sweet potatoes and chickpeas into a single layer on the pan. Sprinkle the pumpkin pie spice and salt all over the sweet potatoes and chickpeas.

3. Roast, uncovered, for 32 to 38 minutes (I roast for 36 minutes), until the sweet potatoes are fork-tender and golden brown on the bottom and the chickpeas are a bit shriveled. I don't flip them or rotate the pan during baking.

recipe continues

recipe continued from previous page

STORAGE

Store leftover salad in an airtight container in the fridge for up to 2 days. Reheat in an oiled skillet over medium heat, stirring occasionally, for 5 to 7 minutes, until warmed through. Season with a little extra pumpkin pie spice and pure maple syrup, if desired, to revive the flavors.

TIPS

* One 14-ounce (398 mL) can of chickpeas is equivalent to 1½ cups cooked chickpeas, if you prefer to cook them from scratch.

** If you are allergic to sesame (or are simply not a fan of tahini), you can omit the tahini from the dressing. Simply increase the amount of maple syrup to 1½ to 2 teaspoons, to your taste.

4. Meanwhile, prepare the Marinated Kale Salad: Place the kale in a very large bowl. In a small bowl, whisk together the garlic, oil, maple syrup, salt, lemon juice, and tahini until smooth. Pour the dressing over the kale and massage it into the leaves with your hands until fully coated. Let the kale marinate in the dressing while the sweet potatoes and chickpeas roast.

5. When the chickpeas and sweet potatoes are finished roasting, remove the baking sheet from the oven and drizzle the remaining 1 tablespoon maple syrup over them. With a spoon, gently toss to coat. Taste and season with more pumpkin pie spice and salt, if desired (I always do!).

6. Portion the kale into bowls, top with the warm roasted sweet potatoes and chickpeas, and garnish with the roasted pepitas. Serve warm.

Glow-rious Greek Pasta with Oregano, Basil, and Lemon Zest Parmesan

Serves 8 (I cup per serving) • **Active prep time** 25 minutes • **Total time** 40 minutes

I batch Oregano, Basil, and Lemon Zest Parmesan (page 307)

Authentic-Tasting Vegan Feta Cheese (page 327; optional)

II ounces (3½ cups/300 g) dry rotini or fusilli pasta

For the Herbed Red Wine Vinaigrette

2 medium garlic cloves (8 g), minced

3 to 4 tablespoons red wine vinegar, to taste, more if needed

¼ cup extra-virgin olive oil

I teaspoon lemon zest

2 tablespoons fresh lemon juice, more if needed

I teaspoon dried basil

2 teaspoons dried oregano

¼ teaspoon fine sea salt

For the salad

½ large English cucumber (225 g), spiralized and cut into 2-inch-long (5 cm) pieces (2 heaping cups)*

I¼ cups (250 g) jarred roasted red peppers, drained and chopped

½ cup (70 g) diced red onion, rinsed and drained

This is a lovely, summery pasta dish . . . the flavors and aroma will make you feel like you're on a Greek island! I recommend enjoying it alfresco on a gorgeous summer day. I started by making a simple Greek salad flavored with a delicious herby dressing, bulked it up by adding roasted red peppers, tomatoes, red onion, and cucumber, and made it a meal by stirring in pasta and a handful of chickpeas. It's all tossed with an herby, bright, Greek-inspired lemon and red wine vinaigrette. Top it with my dreamy Oregano, Basil, and Lemon Zest Parmesan (you will fall in love with it!) and Authentic-Tasting Vegan Feta Cheese to take this pasta salad to the next level.

1. Prepare the Oregano, Basil, and Lemon Zest Parmesan and Authentic-Tasting Vegan Feta Cheese (if using). Set aside.

2. Bring a large pot of water to a boil and cook the pasta according to the package directions.

3. Meanwhile, make the Herbed Red Wine Vinaigrette: In a large bowl, whisk together the garlic, vinegar, oil, lemon zest, lemon juice, basil, oregano, and the salt. Whisk vigorously until combined.

4. Make the salad: Add the cucumber, roasted red peppers, red onion, tomatoes, chickpeas (if using), and the cooked pasta to

recipe and ingredients continue

recipe continued from previous page

I cup (I50 g) grape tomatoes, chopped

I (I4-ounce/398 mL) can chickpeas, drained and rinsed (optional)**

Fine sea salt and freshly ground black pepper

the bowl with the dressing (the pasta absorbs the dressing over time, so for the best flavor, I recommend combining it with the dressing just before serving). Toss well until thoroughly combined. Season with salt and black pepper to taste (I add about ½ teaspoon salt and lots of pepper). Taste and adjust the seasonings (you can add more lemon juice and/or vinegar if you'd like it to be tangier; if it's too tangy, add a bit more oil). Stir to combine.

5. Portion the salad onto plates. Scatter a generous handful of parmesan and feta (if using) on top of each serving. Place any leftover parmesan and feta into separate small bowls, each with a small spoon, and pass them at the table—it's nice to add more on top as you eat!

STORAGE

Store in an airtight container in the fridge for 2 to 3 days. Leftovers are delicious chilled! The flavors tend to diminish during storage, so you can bring the salad back to life by stirring in a splash of olive oil and lemon juice or red wine vinegar (and salt and pepper, if desired).

TIP

* Use a spiralizer to cut the cucumber into "noodles," if you have one. If you don't have a spiralizer, or if you want leftovers to hold up a bit better, finely chop the cucumber instead.

** One I4-ounce (398 mL) can of chickpeas is equivalent to I½ cups (375 mL) cooked chickpeas, if you prefer to cook them from scratch.

MAKE IT GLUTEN- AND GRAIN-FREE

Use a gluten- and grain-free pasta such as chickpea pasta.

MAKE IT NUT-FREE

Use the nut-free option for the Oregano, Basil, and Lemon Zest Parmesan.

UP THE GLOW

Try topping the salad with pitted kalamata olives, capers, and/or chopped sun-dried tomatoes for a salty punch!

Warm Roasted Asparagus and Baby Potato Salad with French Green Lentils

Makes 7 cups • **Active prep time** 20 minutes • **Total time** 55 minutes

For the Roasted Asparagus and Baby Potato Salad

1½ pounds (675 g) mixed baby potatoes, chopped into ½-inch (1 cm) pieces*

1½ tablespoons extra-virgin olive oil

Fine sea salt and freshly ground black pepper

2 small bunches asparagus (650 g total), ends broken off, chopped into 1-inch (2.5 cm) pieces

¾ cup (140 g) dry French green lentils (du Puy lentils)**

For the Old-Fashioned Mustard Dressing

(makes ¾ cup)

2 tablespoons old-fashioned/coarse mustard

1 tablespoon Dijon mustard

¼ cup extra-virgin olive oil

3 to 4 tablespoons fresh lemon juice, to taste

1½ teaspoons pure maple syrup, or to taste

¼ teaspoon fine sea salt

Freshly ground black pepper

Oh baby! This zesty, warm baby potato salad is absolutely addictive. I have to admit, I'm not a big asparagus fan, but when I roast it for this filling salad, I go absolutely crazy for it! This is a fantastic recipe for spring, when the weather is still on the cool side and asparagus and baby potatoes are in season. After roasting the veggies so they're buttery and crispy, I toss them in my creamy, rich, and slightly spicy Old-Fashioned Mustard Dressing along with fancy French green lentils, crunchy red onion, and fresh, herby dill. It's a delightful mix of crunchy and soft, spicy and lightly sweet. Trust me, you'll want to eat this all spring long! Serve this warm salad with my Cold-be-Gone Flavor Bomb Noodle Soup (page 213) for a cozy, flavor-packed meal. If it's not spring where you are, feel free to swap the asparagus for your favorite seasonal vegetables. Green beans are a lovely summer and early fall substitute for the asparagus.

1. Preheat the oven to 425°F (220°C). Line two large baking sheets with parchment paper.

2. Place the potatoes on one of the prepared baking sheets and toss with 1 tablespoon of the oil. Spread into an even layer and sprinkle liberally with salt and pepper. Roast for 20 minutes.

3. Meanwhile, place the chopped asparagus on the second baking sheet and toss with the remaining ½ tablespoon oil. Spread out into an even layer and sprinkle with salt and pepper.

recipe and ingredients continue

recipe continued from previous page

For serving

Fine sea salt and freshly ground black pepper

¾ cup (105 g) finely chopped red onion, rinsed and drained***

⅓ cup packed (10 g) fresh dill, minced

STORAGE

Store in an airtight container in the fridge for 4 days. Leftovers are best served chilled, straight from the fridge. Season with salt, pepper, and a squeeze of lemon juice as needed to revive the flavors. I don't recommend reheating leftovers, as the flavors diminish too much.

TIPS

* I love using a mix of purple, red, and yellow baby potatoes. The variety of colors makes this dish extra pretty! However, feel free to use just one color of baby potatoes, or even Yukon Gold potatoes.

** If you prefer to use canned lentils, you can use 1 (19-ounce/540 mL) can (drained and rinsed) or a scant 2 cups cooked lentils. If using canned, be sure to use a brand that has whole, intact lentils that are not compacted or mushy.

*** If you aren't a raw onion fan, you can reduce the amount used to suit your tastes. I like to rinse raw onion in a sieve before adding it to a dish, to cut down on the sharp flavor a bit.

After the potatoes have roasted for 20 minutes, add the pan of asparagus to the oven and roast both the potatoes and asparagus for 12 to 17 minutes, until the potatoes are golden and the asparagus is fork-tender. Be careful not to overcook the asparagus—a little resistance is great.

4. Meanwhile, in a medium pot, combine the lentils and 3 cups of water. Bring to a boil over high heat, then reduce the heat to medium and simmer, uncovered, for 25 to 35 minutes, until the lentils are tender. If necessary, add more water while cooking so the lentils don't dry out. Drain the lentils and leave them in the colander.

5. While the veggies roast, prepare the Old-Fashioned Mustard Dressing: In a small bowl, whisk together the old-fashioned mustard, Dijon mustard, oil, lemon juice (starting with 3 tablespoons), maple syrup, salt, and pepper. Whisk vigorously to combine. Taste and adjust the flavors by adding more lemon juice, maple syrup, or salt, if desired. Prepare the red onion and dill.

6. To a large bowl, add the roasted potatoes and asparagus, lentils, and red onion. Pour the dressing over the top and toss well to combine (I love adding all the dressing, but you can add it little by little, to taste, if you prefer). Season with salt and pepper. Finally, sprinkle the minced dill over the top and briefly toss just to incorporate. Serve immediately, warm.

Zesty Lime and Cayenne Roasted Chickpea and Sweet Potato Salad

Makes 4 salads • **Active prep time** 15 minutes • **Total time** 45 minutes

2 medium to large sweet potatoes (670 g total)

4 tablespoons extra-virgin olive oil

1 (14-ounce/398 mL) can chickpeas, drained and rinsed*

1/2 teaspoon fine sea salt, plus a pinch

Cayenne pepper

2 large limes

2 teaspoons pure maple syrup

1 (5-ounce/140 g) package mixed baby greens

1 large ripe avocado (240 g), pitted and diced

1/3 cup (50 g) roasted pepitas (see page 338)

This warm, bright, and flavorful salad is a wonderful weeknight option when you don't want to do a lot of fussing but are still craving a filling, protein-packed bowl. All you have to do is roast some chickpeas and sweet potatoes, and toss some greens in my easy lime dressing. This dressing lives up to its name, using just three ingredients and taking 3 minutes to prepare! The sweet potatoes and chickpeas are topped with spicy cayenne pepper to give the salad a bit of heat, which the lime and maple dressing balances with light sweetness. Everything is sprinkled with lime zest to enhance that intoxicating citrus aroma and taste.

1. Preheat the oven to 425°F (220°C). Position the oven racks in the middle of the oven. Line two large rimmed baking sheets with parchment paper.

2. Peel the sweet potatoes and chop them into small 1/2- to 1-inch (1 to 2.5 cm) chunks (you should have 4 to 4 1/2 cups chopped). Place the sweet potatoes on one of the prepared baking sheets and toss with 1 tablespoon plus 1 teaspoon of the oil until coated. Spread the potatoes out into an even layer over the pan.

3. Pat the chickpeas dry with a kitchen towel. Transfer them to the second prepared baking sheet and toss with 2 teaspoons of the oil. Spread out into an even layer over the pan. Sprinkle the sweet potatoes and the chickpeas with 1/4 teaspoon of the salt

recipe continues

recipe continued from previous page

STORAGE

Store the sweet potatoes, chickpeas, and dressing in separate airtight containers in the fridge for up to 3 days. The dressed salad greens don't keep very long, so I don't recommend storing leftovers in the fridge. Instead of dressing all the greens at once, you can build a single salad at a time to ensure everything stays fresh.

TIP

* One 14-ounce (398 mL) can of chickpeas is equivalent to 1½ cups cooked chickpeas, if you prefer to cook them from scratch.

UP THE GLOW

For an extra-creamy salad, try drizzling your favorite tahini over the top!

each and season them with a bit of cayenne pepper (start with a small amount, as it's intense—you can add more after roasting, if desired).

4. Roast the potatoes and chickpeas for 25 to 35 minutes (I roast for 30 minutes), until the sweet potatoes are fork-tender and the chickpeas are golden and crunchy and look a bit shriveled. There's no need to flip them halfway through roasting (score!).

5. Meanwhile, to make the dressing, zest and juice the limes; set aside the zest for later. In a large bowl, whisk together the remaining 2 tablespoons oil, 3 tablespoons of the lime juice, the maple syrup, and a pinch of salt. Transfer 2 tablespoons of the dressing to a small bowl and set aside for topping the salads just before serving.

6. Add the mixed greens to the bowl with the dressing and toss until fully coated.

7. Portion the dressed greens into four shallow bowls. Divide the sweet potatoes, chickpeas, avocado, and pepitas (about 4 teaspoons per bowl) equally among the bowls.

8. Top each salad with 1½ teaspoons of the reserved dressing and a sprinkling of the lime zest. Serve warm.

Cauliflower "Potato" Salad

Serves 5 (1 cup per serving) • Active prep time 15 minutes • Total time 35 minutes

½ large head cauliflower (1¼ pounds/ 565 g), cut into ½-inch (1 cm) florets and pieces (4 heaping cups)

2 medium celery stalks (105 g), finely chopped (¾ cup)

4 large green onions (75 g), thinly sliced (1 cup)

½ cup (75 g) finely chopped red bell pepper

⅓ cup (65 g) finely chopped dill pickle, or more to taste

1 large garlic clove (6 g), minced

1½ teaspoons yellow mustard, or more to taste

1 heaping tablespoon minced fresh dill, plus more for serving

6 tablespoons vegan mayo

1 to 1½ tablespoons fresh lemon juice, or to taste

¼ to ½ teaspoon fine sea salt, to taste

Freshly ground black pepper

Garlic powder

Toasted bread, crackers, wraps, or lettuce cups, for serving (optional)

MAKE IT AHEAD

This salad can be fully assembled 24 hours in advance and stored in an airtight container in the fridge. Stir before serving, and refresh the flavors by adding a little more lemon juice, dill, and salt.

MAKE IT SOY-FREE

Use soy-free vegan mayo (Vegenaise makes a great version!).

We make this Cauliflower "Potato" Salad all the time as a quick side dish for veggie burgers—try it with Bruschetta Veggie Burgers (page 49), Rebellious Battered Broc-Cauli Burgers with Sriracha Aioli (page 113), or Smoky Black Bean and Brown Rice Veggie Burgers (page 131) with OSG House Sauce (page 331). It's a great addition to a picnic or potluck spread—it's the perfect sneaky (and lighter!) alternative to potatoes, and everyone is always surprised that cauliflower can be so flavorful and addictive. Feeling brave? Add a drizzle of sriracha or your favorite hot sauce for a kick of heat! If you're serving several people, this recipe doubles beautifully.

1. In a medium pot, bring a few inches of water to a simmer over medium-high heat and place a steamer basket on top (or simply use a countertop steamer appliance). Place the cauliflower in the steamer, cover, and steam for 7 to 12 minutes, until *just* fork-tender. Be careful not to overcook the cauliflower, as you don't want it to get mushy.

2. Meanwhile, in a large bowl, combine the celery, green onions, bell pepper, dill pickle, garlic, mustard, and fresh dill. Set aside.

3. After steaming, let the cauliflower cool for about 5 minutes, then transfer it to the fridge to cool for another 10 to 15 minutes, until no longer warm.

4. Add the mayo to the raw veggie mixture in the large bowl and stir in the cooled cauliflower. Season with the lemon juice, salt, and pepper. Sprinkle on additional minced dill, if desired, and garlic powder to taste. Serve as desired.

STORAGE

Store leftovers in an airtight container in the fridge for up to 3 days.

Mega Crunch Sun-Dried Tomato–Pepita Taco Salad

Makes 4 large salads • **Active prep time** 25 minutes • **Total time** 25 minutes

For the Pepita and Sun-Dried Tomato Taco Crumble
(makes 2 packed cups)

2 medium garlic cloves (8 g), or to taste

6 tablespoons (74 g) oil-packed unsalted sun-dried tomatoes, drained

1½ cups (160 g) roasted pepitas (see page 338)

2 to 3 teaspoons chili powder, to taste, plus more for serving

1½ teaspoons ground cumin, plus more for serving

¾ to 1 teaspoon red pepper flakes, to taste

1½ tablespoons extra-virgin olive oil

3 tablespoons salsa*

Fine sea salt, for serving

For the Easy Lime Dressing
(makes ⅔ cup)

6 tablespoons fresh lime juice (from 2 or 3 large limes)

¼ cup extra-virgin olive oil

2 to 4 teaspoons pure maple syrup, to taste

Fine sea salt and freshly ground black pepper

This salad is one I love to make whenever I'm hosting a few girlfriends for a laid-back dinner—everyone goes wild for it. It's one of those fun build-your-own bowls that can be customized to each person's likes and dislikes. The nutty flavor of roasted pepitas and lightly salty, umami-rich tang of sun-dried tomatoes are pure heaven, especially when served over crisp lettuce and drizzled with tangy, sweet Easy Lime Dressing. This dish is hearty, while still feeling light and energizing (just the way I like it). Cashew Sour Cream is lovely on top, but it's totally optional; if you're looking for a nut-free swap, hummus and 24/7 Avocado-Cilantro Sauce (page 286) are great options. To round out the meal, I love pairing these salads with a side of tortilla chips, leftover salsa, Vegan Cheese Sauce 2.0 (page 290), and more Cashew Sour Cream! The best part? All the components can be made in advance and stored in the fridge. This keeps the kitchen clean on the big day, and I'm not wasting precious time cooking during my friends' visit. I like to chop the lettuce and avocado just before everyone arrives, and within minutes, we are sitting around the table, building our bowls and swapping stories!

1. Prepare the Pepita and Sun-Dried Tomato Taco Crumble: In a food processor, place the garlic and sun-dried tomatoes and process until minced. Add the pepitas, chili powder, cumin, red pepper flakes, oil, and salsa. Pulse until coarsely chopped, about 25 times. Avoid overprocessing the pepitas; you want to stop pulsing just as the mixture starts to come together so

recipe and ingredients continue

recipe continued from previous page

For the salad

1 large head iceberg lettuce (700 g), chopped

1 pint grape or cherry tomatoes, halved (300 g)

2 ripe medium avocados (400 g total), pitted and chopped

¾ cup (105 g) diced red onion, rinsed and drained

½ cup (11 g) fresh cilantro, minced, or more to taste

½ cup Cashew Sour Cream (page 321; optional)

¼ cup pickled jalapeños, drained (optional)

there is some texture remaining. Taste the mixture and season with salt. Set aside.

2. Prepare the Easy Lime Dressing: In a small jar, combine the lime juice, oil, maple syrup (starting with 2 teaspoons), and salt and pepper to taste. Secure the lid and shake the jar vigorously for 10 seconds or so to combine. (If you don't have a jar, vigorously whisk the dressing in a medium bowl until combined.)

3. To make each salad, put a couple big handfuls of lettuce in each bowl and top with ½ cup of the tomatoes, one-quarter of the avocado, 3 tablespoons of the red onion, 1 tablespoon of the cilantro, ½ cup packed taco crumble, 2½ to 3 tablespoons of the dressing, 2 tablespoons of the Cashew Sour Cream (if using), and 1 tablespoon of the pickled jalapeños (if using). Add a small sprinkling of chili powder, cumin, and salt on top, to taste, and enjoy.

STORAGE

Store the components in separate airtight containers in the fridge for up to 4 days. Alternatively, you can assemble one large salad in an airtight container, using all the components except the avocado and dressing, and store it in the fridge for up to 4 days. When ready to serve, add the dressing and chop the avocado fresh. The taco crumble can be frozen in a freezer bag with the air pressed out or in an airtight container for up to 2 months.

TIP

* The spice level of the salsa you use is an easy way to change up this taco crumble! I like to use medium or hot salsa for a gentle amount of heat.

MAKE IT KID-FRIENDLY

Crumble some tortilla chips on top of their salad. Kids love crunch! Use a mild salsa.

UP THE GLOW

Sprinkle some hemp hearts onto each salad for a protein boost!

Cilantro-Speckled Green Rice and Avocado Stack

Serves 4 (¾ cup per serving) • **Active prep time** 17 minutes • **Total time** 35 minutes

1½ tablespoons extra-virgin olive oil

1½ cups (210 g) diced sweet or yellow onion

6 large garlic cloves (36 g), minced (3 tablespoons)

1½ cups packed (53 g) fresh cilantro leaves

½ cup packed (10 g) fresh parsley leaves (optional)

3 medium jalapeños (125 g), finely chopped (⅔ cup)*

1½ teaspoons ground cumin

1 cup (180 g) uncooked white basmati rice**

1½ cups plus 2 tablespoons low-sodium vegetable broth

½ teaspoon fine sea salt, or to taste

Freshly ground black pepper

Pretty Parsley-Cilantro Pepita Pesto (page 275)

Fresh lemon juice

2 ripe large avocados (480 g total), pitted and halved or sliced

Red pepper flakes (optional)

Smoked paprika (optional)

This dish is my plant-based spin on traditional Peruvian-style *arroz con pollo*. Served over avocado, it's so full of complex texture and flavor—fluffy, creamy, savory, and fresh, with a touch of gentle heat. It's healthy comfort food, and such a quick dish to whip up. Dollop with my Pretty Parsley-Cilantro Pepita Pesto to create a variation that is out of this world! Or spoon some of the rice, sliced avocado, and pesto into a wrap for *on the glow* family burritos.

1. In a medium (3-quart/3 L) pot, heat the oil over medium heat. Add the onion and garlic and stir to coat with the oil. Sauté for 4 to 6 minutes, until the onion is softened.

2. Meanwhile, mince the cilantro and parsley (if using) and set aside. Add the jalapeños and cook, stirring, for 3 to 4 minutes, until softened.

3. Stir in the cumin and cook for a minute, until fragrant.

4. Add the cilantro and parsley (if using), rice, broth, salt, and pepper, to taste, and stir to combine. Increase the heat to high and bring to a boil. Immediately reduce the heat to medium-low, stir again, and cover with a tight-fitting lid. Cook for 12 to 16 minutes, until the water has been absorbed and the rice is tender.

5. Meanwhile, prepare the Pretty Parsley-Cilantro Pepita Pesto. Set aside.

recipe continues

recipe continued from previous page

TIPS

* Use mild jalapeños for a very mild dish or "hot" jalapeños for a moderate-to-high spice level. Jalapeños are typically mild, but their heat level varies with age. The older the jalapeño is, the spicier it will be (well, hey, I get spicier the older I get, too!). You can tell if a jalapeño is older because it'll have raised white lines along the skin of the pepper. Younger jalapeños will have smooth skin and will be much milder. Also note that if you leave the inner white membranes in the jalapeños, they'll be spicier; if you remove them, they'll be milder.

** It's important to use white basmati rice in this recipe, as it cooks quickly and has a fluffy texture and mild flavor. The ingredient measurements and cooking times in this recipe are accurate only for white basmati rice. The hearty flavor of brown rice is too overpowering for this dish and it has a much longer cooking time than white.

UP THE GLOW

Top with hemp hearts and roasted pepitas (see page 338) for added protein and healthy fats! Add a sprinkle of cayenne pepper for a spicy kick of antioxidant power. Stir in some cooked corn kernels or crunchy red bell pepper for a pop of flavor and veggie power.

6. Remove the rice from the heat and let stand, covered, for 3 to 5 minutes. Taste and season with more salt and pepper, to taste, and a squeeze of fresh lemon juice, until the flavors pop!

7. Arrange the avocados on four serving plates. Season with salt and pepper. Stack a generous spoonful of rice on top of the avocado. Garnish with a sprinkle of red pepper flakes and smoked paprika, if desired, top with a generous dollop of pesto, and serve.

STORAGE

Store in an airtight container in the fridge for up to 4 days, or freeze in a freezer bag with the air pressed out or in an airtight container for up to 1 month. Reheat the rice in a pot, covered, over medium-low heat, with a little veggie broth added to moisten.

HEARTY SOUPS *and* STEWS

Cold-Be-Gone Flavor Bomb Noodle Soup

Serves 8 (I cup per serving) • **Active prep time** 20 minutes • **Total time** 35 to 40 minutes

2 tablespoons extra-virgin olive oil

2 cups (280 g) diced sweet or yellow onion (I large)

6 large garlic cloves (36 g), minced (3 tablespoons)

3 medium carrots (220 g), peeled

3 medium stalks celery (160 g)

2½ teaspoons grated fresh ginger (I use a Microplane)*

¾ teaspoon dried thyme leaves

¾ teaspoon ground sage

2 tablespoons tomato paste

6 cups (1.4 L) vegetable broth

5 ounces (1½ cups/140 g) dry pasta of choice (I used rotini)**

¾ cup packed (15 g) fresh parsley leaves, minced

I teaspoon fresh lemon juice, or more to taste

⅛ teaspoon cayenne pepper (optional)

Fine sea salt and freshly ground black pepper

I don't know about you, but I'm not down with bland, boring soups. Give me a rich soup with a ton of flavor! I want herbs, I want spice, I want a kick of tang and a rich broth with umami. Thanks to all the immune-boosting ingredients like fresh garlic, warming ginger, lemony thyme, fresh parsley, and tangy lemon juice, this is a fantastic soup to whip up when you have a cold coming on (but it's also handy when you're not sick, simply to keep your immune system humming along!). The pasta adds heartiness that will make this a well-loved dinner for fall, winter, or spring. For even more staying power, add 1½ cups cooked chickpeas or white beans, or add 2 cups of stemmed and finely chopped kale! To amp up the flavors even more, I love this soup served with a hefty sprinkle of Italian Herb Parmesan (page 301) or a swirl of one of my homemade pestos (pages 275, 276, 294, and 297). Serve it with my Pumpkin Spice and Everything Nice Salad (page 191) for an even heartier meal.

1. In a large pot, stir together the oil, onion, and garlic to combine. Sauté over medium heat for 5 to 6 minutes, until the onion is softened.

2. Meanwhile, dice the carrot and celery into ¼- to ½-inch (5 mm to I cm) pieces. This will help them cook faster. You should have 1½ cups carrot and 1⅓ cups celery. Add the carrot and celery to the pot and stir to combine. Sauté for a couple of minutes.

recipe continues

recipe continued from previous page

STORAGE

This soup is best served fresh, due to the pasta's tendency to soften during storage, but you can store it in an airtight container in the fridge for up to 3 days. Some types of noodles will soak up the broth as the soup sits, so you may want to add a bit more broth when reheating, seasoning again to taste. I don't recommend freezing this soup with the pasta in it, as the pasta can soften too much upon thawing. However, you can freeze the soup *without* the pasta and add freshly cooked pasta when reheating.

TIPS

* Using 2½ teaspoons grated fresh ginger results in a spicy soup, especially after sitting overnight. If you prefer a less intense broth, start with 1 teaspoon ginger and add more to taste.

** Read the directions for your pasta carefully. Pasta that requires only 5 minutes to cook and requires a cold rinse, such as chickpea pasta and some other gluten-free versions, will not work in this recipe because it will become mushy. You'll want to cook these types of pasta on the side, in their own pot. Store the cooked pasta separately, and add it to individual bowls when serving.

MAKE IT GLUTEN- AND/OR GRAIN-FREE

Swap the pasta for a 14-ounce (398 mL) can of chickpeas (drained and rinsed) or 1½ cups cooked chickpeas, or use gluten-free (and grain-free, if needed) pasta. If using gluten-free pasta, please see the Tip above.

3. Stir in the ginger and sauté for 1 minute.

4. Add the thyme, sage, tomato paste, and broth. Increase the heat to high and bring to a boil, then reduce the heat to medium-high, cover, and simmer for 5 minutes, or until al dente (still a bit firm).

5. Add the pasta and cook, uncovered, stirring occasionally, until al dente, following the timing guidelines on the pasta package. Check on the pasta frequently while it's cooking, as you don't want to overcook it.

6. Once the pasta is al dente, remove the pot from the heat and stir in the parsley, lemon juice, cayenne pepper (if using), and salt and black pepper to taste. Serve immediately.

Cozy Butternut Squash, Sweet Potato, and Red Lentil Stew

Serves 10 (1 cup per serving) • **Active prep time** 20 minutes • **Total time** 40 minutes

2 tablespoons extra-virgin olive oil

1 large sweet or yellow onion (280 g), diced (2 cups)

4 large garlic cloves (24 g), minced (2 tablespoons)

3 cups (400 g) diced (½-inch/1 cm pieces) butternut squash

2½ cups (340 g) diced peeled sweet potato (1 large)

½ teaspoon fine sea salt, plus more as needed

3 cups low-sodium vegetable broth

1 (14-ounce/398 mL) can diced tomatoes, with their juices

1 (14-ounce/398 mL) can light coconut milk

½ cup (100 g) dried red lentils, rinsed and drained*

3 tablespoons tomato paste

1½ teaspoons ground turmeric

1½ teaspoons ground cumin

½ teaspoon chili powder

¼ teaspoon cayenne pepper, or to taste

Freshly ground black pepper

1 tablespoon apple cider vinegar, or more to taste

1 small bunch chard (450 g), stemmed, leaves finely chopped**

Butternut squash, red lentils, and sweet potato are wrapped in a lightly sweet, creamy coconut-and-tomato broth accented with the smoky, spicy notes of turmeric, cumin, chili powder, and cayenne. Apple cider vinegar provides a tangy brightness to bring everything together. It's both cozy *and* energizing (my favorite combo!). While it tastes absolutely delicious once it's cooked, it tastes even better the next day, after the flavors have had a chance to mingle. Serve it with crusty bread, over cooked rice or my Roasted Garlic Cauliflower Rice (page 170), or all on its own. A special thanks to Ella from *Deliciously Ella* for inspiring this recipe!

1. In a large pot, heat the oil over medium heat. Add the onion and garlic and stir to coat with the oil. Sauté for 4 to 6 minutes, until the onion is softened.

2. Add the squash and sweet potato and stir to combine. Add a pinch of salt and sauté for a few minutes longer.

3. Add the broth, diced tomatoes with their juices, coconut milk, lentils, tomato paste, turmeric, cumin, chili powder, cayenne pepper, salt, and black pepper to taste. Stir well to combine.

4. Increase the heat to high and bring to a boil. Immediately reduce the heat to medium and stir again, scraping any lentils off the bottom of the pot if they start to stick. Simmer, uncovered, stirring occasionally, for 28 to 40 minutes, until the squash and potato are fork-tender. Reduce the heat if necessary.

recipe and ingredients continue

recipe continued from previous page

For serving (optional)

Cooked rice

Minced fresh cilantro or parsley

Garlic powder

Chili powder

5. Add the vinegar. Taste and season with more salt and pepper, and more of the other spices, if desired.

6. Stir in the chard, reduce the heat to medium-low, and cook, uncovered, for a couple of minutes more, until the chard is wilted.

7. To serve, scoop some cooked rice into each serving bowl, if desired, then ladle the stew over the top. Garnish with minced cilantro and a good dusting of garlic powder and chili powder, if desired.

STORAGE

Store in an airtight container in the fridge for up to 5 days, or freeze in an airtight container for up to 2 months.

TIPS

* You can swap out the red lentils for 1 (14-ounce/398 mL) can chickpeas (drained and rinsed) or 1½ cups cooked chickpeas.

** You can swap out the chard for 5 ounces (140 g) baby spinach (coarsely chopped) or a small bunch of kale (stemmed and coarsely chopped).

Green Goddess Gazpacho

Serves 5 (I cup plus 2 tablespoons per serving) • **Active prep time** 10 minutes • **Total time** 10 minutes

I½ cups water

I½ cups (235 g) ripe avocado (from 2 large)

2 cups (380 g) sliced English cucumber (⅔ large)

3 large garlic cloves (18 g)

¼ cup (30 g) diced red onion

2½ tablespoons fresh lime juice, or to taste

2 tablespoons apple cider vinegar, or to taste

I tablespoon extra-virgin olive oil

2 to 3 teaspoons sriracha, to taste*

¾ to I teaspoon fine sea salt, or to taste

6 large ice cubes (I heaping cup), or as needed

Topping ideas

Roasted salted pepitas (see page 338)

Sliced green onion

Chopped avocado or cucumber

Croutons

STORAGE

Refrigerate leftovers in an airtight container for 3 days.

TIP

* The sriracha really makes the flavors come together, so I don't recommend skipping it.

I'm always sad when soup season comes to an end (note: This is *not* the same as being sad about cold weather ending!), but gazpacho makes parting with my favorite warming soups much less painful. I'm so grateful for recipes like this—especially when I'm not feeling much like a goddess—because they make me glow from the inside out and give me balanced energy levels. It's absolutely refreshing when enjoyed post-workout, and you can even pop leftovers into a thermos and bring them for an energizing lunch. I have a feeling this creamy, lively gazpacho with a mild kick of heat is going to be your new go-to this summer. The reason I love it so much, in addition to how nutritious it is, is that it feels so rich and satiating compared to a traditional tomato-based gazpacho. If you aren't a big fan of acidic, tangy flavors, you may want to add a bit less lime juice and vinegar than called for, adding more to taste after the first blend. And because the soup is blended, a rough (nonperfect) chop is all you need when prepping the ingredients. Make this soup goddess-worthy (yes, that's you!) by topping it with roasted pepitas, chopped cucumber, cubed avocado, and a pretty drizzle of olive oil. Round out the meal with toasted buttery garlic bread for dipping . . . mmm, yes.

I. To a high-speed blender, add the water, avocado, cucumber, garlic, red onion, lime juice, vinegar, oil, sriracha, salt, and ice. Blend on high until silky smooth.

2. Taste and adjust the seasoning with more salt, sriracha, or lime juice/vinegar, if needed, and blend again to combine.

3. Pour the gazpacho into small bowls and add your desired toppings.

Immune-Boosting Hungarian Mushroom and Wild Rice Stew

Serves 6 (1 cup per serving) • **Active prep time** 25 minutes • **Total time** 40 minutes

¾ cup (140 g) uncooked wild rice blend

2 tablespoons extra-virgin olive oil

2 cups (280 g) finely chopped yellow onion (1 large)

5 or 6 large garlic cloves (30 to 36 g), minced (3 tablespoons)

16 ounces (455 g) cremini mushrooms, thinly sliced

4 teaspoons dried dill

1 tablespoon paprika

1½ teaspoons smoked paprika

2 teaspoons arrowroot starch

1 cup unsweetened plain cashew or oat milk*

2 cups water

¾ to 1 teaspoon fine sea salt

Freshly ground black pepper

2 to 3 teaspoons apple cider vinegar or fresh lemon juice, to taste

Cayenne pepper (optional)

This is my vegan spin on classic Hungarian mushroom soup. The traditional robust dill and paprika flavors pair so well with umami-packed mushrooms, wild rice, and rich, creamy broth. My version uses both smoked and regular paprika for added depth and toasty flavor. It's the ultimate warming-on-a-chilly-night bowl. It also helps boost the immune system, thanks to the powerful antioxidants found in mushrooms, garlic, and cayenne. If you don't have any fresh bread on hand, try serving it with my Sneaky Protein-Packed Mashed Potatoes (page 164) for a creamy, ultra-comforting duo. It's also irresistible with a bit of Cashew Sour Cream (page 321) swirled in, and minced fresh dill on top! For added nutrition, serve it over a base of my Roasted Garlic Cauliflower Rice (page 170).

1. Cook the wild rice according to the directions on the package. Be sure not to overcook the rice, as it'll get mushy in the soup (you'll be cooking it for 5 minutes more at the end). It's a good idea to check on the rice occasionally to see if you need to add more water or if the rice is tender before the suggested cook time. You should have 2 cups cooked rice.

2. Meanwhile, in a large pot, heat the oil over medium heat. Add the onion and garlic and stir to coat with the oil. Sauté for 4 to 5 minutes, until the onion is softened.

3. Add the mushrooms, raise the heat to medium-high, and sauté, uncovered, stirring occasionally, for 9 to 11 minutes, until

recipe continues

recipe continued from previous page

STORAGE

Store in an airtight container in the fridge for up to 5 days, or freeze in a freezer bag with the air pressed out or in an airtight container for up to 2 months.

TIP

* Don't have cashew or oat milk? Simply combine ⅓ cup (48 g) raw cashews and I cup plus 2 tablespoons water in a high-speed blender and blend for about 30 seconds on high. Strain through a fine-mesh sieve and measure out I cup to use in this recipe.

MAKE IT NUT-FREE

Use the oat milk option.

the mushrooms have softened. There may be some liquid in the pot—this is normal!

4. Stir in the dried dill, paprika, and smoked paprika and sauté for I minute, until fragrant.

5. In a medium bowl, whisk together the arrowroot starch and milk.

6. Add the milk mixture and the water to the pot with the mushrooms. Season with salt and black pepper and stir to combine. Bring to a boil, then reduce the heat to medium and simmer, uncovered, for 10 minutes. During the last 5 minutes of cooking, stir in the cooked wild rice.

7. Add the vinegar a teaspoon at a time, until the flavors pop. Taste and add more salt and black pepper to your liking. If you like a spicy kick, add a small sprinkle of cayenne pepper to your bowl. Serve and enjoy!

Heavenly Chili-Spiced Jalapeño and Garlic Veggie Stew

Serves 8 (1 cup per serving) • **Soak time** 1 hour or up to overnight
Active prep time 20 minutes • **Total time** 45 minutes

For the Creamy Cashew Stock
⅔ cup (100 g) raw cashews

5 cups (1.2 L) vegetable broth*

For the stew
2 tablespoons extra-virgin olive oil

1½ cups (210 g) diced yellow or sweet onion (1 medium)

1 cup (105 g) diced celery (2 large stalks)

6 large garlic cloves (36 g), minced (3 tablespoons)

3 large or 4 medium mild jalapeños (180 g total), seeded and minced (1 heaping cup)**

1 cup (180 g) diced fresh tomato (1 large or 2 medium)

2 cups (270 g) diced (¼-inch/5 mm pieces) peeled sweet potato (1 medium)

2½ teaspoons dried oregano

2½ teaspoons ground cumin

2½ teaspoons chili powder

3 tablespoons tomato paste

Fine sea salt and freshly ground black pepper

3 cups packed (90 g) chopped baby spinach or stemmed kale leaves (optional)

2 to 3 teaspoons white wine vinegar, to taste

This soup has a lot of lovely flavors. It's made with a rich cashew-based stock, enticing and aromatic chili spices, oodles of garlic and jalapeño, and a healthy dose of veggies. It's so rich and flavorful right out of the pot, but just wait until you taste it the next day—the broth thickens into a robust stew and the flavors deepen in the best way. Serve it with a sprinkle of smoked paprika and garlic powder for a savory topping that brings everything together. You can turn it into an even heartier meal by serving it with my Mediterranean Smashed Chickpea Salad with Tzatziki Aioli (page 119) stuffed into wraps or pitas alongside.

1. Prepare the cashew stock: Place the cashews in a small bowl and add boiling water to cover. Soak for 1 hour, then drain. (Alternatively, soak the cashews in room-temperature water to cover for at least 8 hours or up to overnight, then drain.)

2. Transfer the drained cashews to a high-speed blender and add the broth. Blend on high until super smooth. Set aside.

3. Make the stew: In a large pot, heat the oil over medium heat. Add the onion, celery, garlic, and jalapeños (in that order) and stir to coat with the oil. Sauté, stirring occasionally, for 6 to 7 minutes, until softened.

4. Add the tomatoes, sweet potato, oregano, cumin, and chili powder. Stir to combine and cook for a few minutes more, until fragrant.

recipe and ingredients continue

recipe continued from previous page

Garlic powder, for garnish

Smoked paprika, for garnish

1 teaspoon sriracha, for serving (optional)

TIPS

* If you're a little short on veggie broth, you can swap in water to replace up to 1 cup of the broth.

** This soup's spice level will vary depending on the jalapeños you use: The older the jalapeño is, the spicier it will be (well, hey, I get spicier the older I get, too!). You can tell if a jalapeño is older because it'll have raised white lines along the skin of the pepper. Younger jalapeños will have smooth skin and will be much milder. Also, if you leave the inner white membranes in the jalapeños, they'll be spicier; if you remove them, they'll be milder. After cooking, if you'd like the soup to be spicier, add a bit of cayenne pepper.

5. Add the cashew stock, tomato paste, and salt and pepper to taste and stir to combine. It will look foamy at this stage, but this is normal. Raise the heat to high and bring to a boil. Reduce the heat to medium and stir again. Cover and gently simmer, stirring occasionally, for 16 to 20 minutes, until the veggies are fork-tender.

6. During the last 5 minutes of cooking, add the chopped greens (if using) and stir until combined.

7. Remove from the heat and stir in the vinegar, to taste, along with more salt and pepper, if desired. Serve in bowls, with a sprinkle of garlic powder and smoked paprika, if you like (they bring all the flavors together so well). If you'd like a spicy kick, stir in a bit of sriracha.

STORAGE

Store in an airtight container in the fridge for up to 4 days. (This stew is even better the next day!) This stew separates after freezing and thawing due to the combo of cashew stock and vinegar, so freezing is not recommended.

MAKE IT KID-FRIENDLY

Reduce the jalapeño or chili powder if your child is spice shy. Serve with toasted bread cut into rectangles for dipping.

UP THE GLOW

Add 1 (14-ounce/398 mL) can chickpeas or white beans (drained and rinsed) or 1½ cups cooked chickpeas or white beans to boost the protein and fiber. For a spicy kick, add cayenne pepper.

Glowing Spiced Lentil Soup

Serves 7 (I cup per serving) • **Active prep time** 15 minutes • **Total time** 30 to 35 minutes

1½ tablespoons extra-virgin olive oil

2 cups (280 g) diced sweet or yellow onion (I large)

3 large garlic cloves (18 g), minced (1½ tablespoons)

½ to ¾ teaspoon fine sea salt, to taste

2 teaspoons minced fresh ginger

2 teaspoons ground turmeric

1½ teaspoons ground cumin

½ teaspoon ground cinnamon

¼ teaspoon ground cardamom

I (14-ounce/398 mL) can diced tomatoes, with their juices

I (14-ounce/398 mL) can full-fat coconut milk*

¾ cup (140 g) dried red lentils

3½ cups low-sodium vegetable broth

I (5-ounce/140 g) package baby spinach, coarsely chopped

2 to 3 teaspoons fresh lime juice, or to taste

Freshly ground black pepper

STORAGE

Refrigerate in an airtight container for up to I week or freeze for up to 2 months.

TIP

* Full-fat coconut milk makes this broth luxuriously creamy, but light coconut milk can be used in a pinch.

This is a quintessential "pantry soup," so I find myself making it a lot during the long winter months. There aren't many vegetables to chop for this soup, and it relies mostly on pantry staples, so it takes just 15 minutes of prep time and is hands-off while it cooks, which makes it handy for weeknights. It's powered by anti-inflammatory ingredients like turmeric, ginger, cinnamon, and garlic. Feel free to change up the baby spinach for other greens like chopped stemmed kale or chard leaves. Like most soups, it's great served with some crusty bread on the side (if you have some on hand, slather it with my 5-Ingredient Vegan Butter, page 318!). If you like a kick of heat like I do, try adding a bit of red pepper flakes or cayenne pepper for some spice.

I. In a large pot, heat the oil over medium heat. Add the onion, garlic, and a pinch of salt and stir to combine. Sauté for 4 to 5 minutes, until the onion softens. Stir in the ginger and sauté for I minute more.

2. Stir in the turmeric, cumin, cinnamon, and cardamom until combined and cook for about I minute, until fragrant.

3. Add the diced tomatoes with their juices, coconut milk, red lentils, and broth. Stir to combine.

4. Increase the heat to high and bring to a low boil. Immediately reduce the heat to medium-high and stir well, scraping up any lentils stuck to the bottom of the pot. Simmer, uncovered, stirring occasionally, for 17 to 22 minutes, until the lentils are fluffy and tender.

5. Turn off the heat and stir in the spinach until wilted. Stir in the lime juice, to taste, and season with salt and pepper.

VEGAN • GLUTEN-FREE • NUT-FREE • SOY-FREE • GRAIN-FREE • KID-FRIENDLY
FREEZER-FRIENDLY • ON THE GLOW • ONE POT

Hunky Heartbeet Cabbage Soup

Serves 9 (1 cup per serving) • **Active prep time** 20 minutes • **Total time** 1 hour 40 minutes

2 tablespoons coconut oil

2 cups (280 g) diced red onion (1 large)

5 cups (540 g) diced red cabbage
(½ medium)

4 cups (500 g) diced (¼-inch/5 mm
pieces) peeled raw beets (about
3 extra-large/4 or 5 medium-large)*

5 cups marinara sauce**

3 cups water

Fine sea salt or Herbamare and freshly
ground black pepper

Cashew Sour Cream (page 321),
for serving (optional)

Chopped fresh dill, for garnish
(optional)

STORAGE

Store in an airtight container in the
fridge for up to 1 week, or freeze in a
freezer bag with the air pressed out
or in an airtight container for up to
2 months.

TIPS

* To prevent the beets from staining
your hands, wear disposable gloves
while peeling and dicing the beets.

** It's important that you use a great-
tasting marinara sauce in this recipe,
since it forms the base of the soup.
I love Victoria brand's White Linen
Collection marinara sauce, or try my
Fail-Proof Marinara Sauce from *Oh
She Glows Every Day* (page 175).

From its gorgeous shades of plum and violet during the prep stage
to its final bold crimson, this might be the most beautiful soup
I've ever made. It brightens up any chilly autumn or winter day,
that's for sure! A bright and acidic tomato base is balanced with
sweet beets and a swirl of Cashew Sour Cream. This soup takes
an hour and change to cook, thanks to the raw beets, so be sure to
give yourself enough time; the bonus is that you can cover it and
walk away as it simmers! To ensure the shortest cooking time,
be sure to chop the beets into tiny, pea-sized pieces, as this will
help them cook faster. A big thanks to my lovely aunt Elizabeth for
inspiring this tempting twist on traditional borscht!

1. In a large pot, melt the coconut oil over medium heat. Add the
onion and sauté for 4 to 6 minutes, until softened.

2. Stir in the cabbage, followed by the beets, and sauté for 7 to
8 minutes.

3. Stir in the marinara sauce and water to combine. Increase the
heat to high and bring the soup to a boil. Immediately reduce
the heat to medium, cover, and simmer for 1 hour 20 minutes
to 1 hour 45 minutes, until the beets are fork-tender. After the
1-hour mark, I like to reduce the heat just a smidge to medium-
low. Your cook time will depend on the freshness and size of the
chopped beets. (If it's your first time cooking the soup, you may
want to check on it a few times during cooking to stir and make
sure it's not sticking to the bottom of the pot.)

4. Carefully taste, and season with salt and pepper.

5. Ladle into bowls and serve with a spoonful or swirl of
Cashew Sour Cream and fresh dill if desired.

TREATS
and DRINKS

O Canada! Spiced Maple Cream Torte with Warm and Gooey Apple Pie Compote

Makes one 9-inch (23 cm) torte (serves 10) • Soak time 1 hour or up to overnight
Active prep time 35 minutes • Chill time 4 hours or up to overnight • Total time 6 hours

1½ cups (225 g) raw cashews

Coconut Whipped Cream (page 322; optional)

For the Pecan-Oat Crust

2 cups (200 g) gluten-free rolled oats

¾ cup (90 g) raw pecans

¼ teaspoon fine sea salt

¼ cup coconut oil, melted

3 tablespoons pure maple syrup

For the Spiced Maple Cream

½ cup coconut oil, melted

½ cup plus 2 tablespoons pure maple syrup

4 to 5 teaspoons fresh lemon juice, to taste

2 tablespoons plain or vanilla almond milk

1½ teaspoons apple pie spice, homemade (page 308) or store-bought

1 teaspoon pure vanilla extract

¼ teaspoon fine sea salt

For serving

1 batch Warm and Gooey Apple Pie Compote (page 235)

Whipped cream (optional)

Chopped pecans (optional)

Step aside, nanaimo bars—this creamy torte is worthy of being famous, too. A chilled spiced maple cream filling is topped with my favorite Warm and Gooey Apple Pie Compote, and the contrast of temperatures is just heavenly! The addictive rich and buttery pecan crust provides a crunchy, nutty contrast to the creamy maple filling and gooey apple compote. This torte is also fantastic served with my Coconut Whipped Cream or Easy Sea Salt Vanilla Caramel (page 325). Since this torte stores so well in the freezer, it's the perfect dessert for making any night of the week a special one. While it has a few components, each one can be made ahead if you'd like to break up the prep work. One spring day, after trying this torte, Eric said, "I know what you can get me for Father's Day . . . this torte!" (Spoiler alert: I now make it for him every Father's Day.)

1. Place the cashews in a small bowl and add boiling water to cover. Soak for 1 hour, then drain. (Alternatively, soak the cashews in room-temperature water to cover for at least 8 hours or up to overnight, then drain.)

2. Prepare the Coconut Whipped Cream (if using). Cover and refrigerate until serving.

3. Prepare the Pecan-Oat Crust: Preheat the oven to 350°F (180°C). Oil a 9-inch (23 cm) glass pie dish and line the bottom with a circle of parchment paper cut to fit.

recipe continues

recipe continued from previous page

STORAGE

Store the torte in an airtight container in the fridge for up to 1 week or in the freezer for up to 2 months. The refrigerated torte will have a semifirm, cheesecake-like texture; frozen, the torte will have a solid, very firm texture. If serving from the freezer, allow the torte to sit at room temperature for 20 to 30 minutes, or until soft enough to slice, before serving.

TIP

For the torte shown in the photo, I used a 7-inch (1.5 L) springform pan for added height.

MAKE IT AHEAD

You can prepare any or all of the components in advance, saving you time and effort on the day you'd like to serve the torte. Assemble the Pecan-Oat Crust (without baking), then wrap it in plastic wrap and refrigerate for up to 24 hours. Let sit at room temperature for 30 minutes (baking it chilled could impact the baking time), then bake as directed. The Spiced Maple Cream can be prepared and refrigerated in an airtight container for up to 48 hours. Let sit at room temperature for 30 to 60 minutes to soften before using.

4. To a food processor, add the oats, pecans, and salt and process for 15 to 20 seconds, into a coarse flour. Add the melted coconut oil and maple syrup and process for 10 to 15 seconds, until the mixture comes together into a heavy dough and sticks together easily when pressed between your fingers. If it feels a bit dry, add water, a teaspoon at a time, and briefly process to combine until it holds together.

5. Spoon the dough into the prepared pie dish and spread it evenly over the bottom. Lightly wet your fingers. Starting at the center of the dish, press down on the dough until you have formed an even crust over the bottom and up the sides of the dish. Use your fingers to level the crust along the top. Using a fork, poke 10 to 12 holes into the dough.

6. Bake the crust for 10 to 12 minutes, until semifirm along the edge but still soft on the bottom. Let the crust cool on a cooling rack for at least 20 minutes (it will firm up as it cools).

7. Prepare the Spiced Maple Cream: To a high-speed blender, add the drained cashews, melted coconut oil, maple syrup, lemon juice (starting with 4 teaspoons), milk, apple pie spice, vanilla, and salt. Blend on high speed until the mixture is super smooth. If your blender has a tamper, use it to help push down on the mixture to ease blending. Taste and add a touch more lemon juice and apple pie spice, if desired.

8. Spoon the filling into the cooled crust and spread it evenly with a spatula. Place on a level surface in the freezer, uncovered, and chill for at least 4 hours or until frozen throughout.

9. About 30 minutes before you plan to serve the torte, prepare the Warm and Gooey Apple Pie Compote.

10. Slice the torte, and plate each slice. (If it's too firm to slice, let it sit on the counter for 15 to 20 minutes before slicing.) Top each slice with a scoop of hot apple pie compote (it cools down quickly, so make sure the compote is nearly bubbling hot when served). If desired, add a dollop of whipped cream (pro tip: If you place the whipped cream away from the warm compote, it won't melt as fast), garnish with a sprinkle of chopped pecans, if desired, and serve.

Warm and Gooey Apple Pie Compote

Makes 3 generous cups • **Active prep time** 12 minutes • **Total time** 30 minutes

1 to 1½ teaspoons apple pie spice, homemade (page 308) or store-bought, to taste

4 large sweet apples (865 g), peeled, cored, and chopped into ¼- to ½-inch (5 mm to 1 cm) cubes (6 cups)*

1 cup plus 2 tablespoons water, plus more if needed

⅔ cup lightly packed (120 g) brown sugar or coconut sugar

Dash or two of fine sea salt

2 teaspoons arrowroot starch, plus more if needed

Would you believe you can satisfy your apple pie craving in just a half hour? My lightly sweet autumn-spiced compote can do just that! I first created this compote as a topping for my O Canada! Spiced Maple Cream Torte (page 233), but I quickly discovered that it's delicious all on its own—served warm or cold. In late summer and fall months, we can be found spooning it over bowls of overnight oats and vegan vanilla ice cream (pro tip: Heat up the compote in the fall for a cozy cold-hot temperature contrast with the ice cream) or the maple cream torte. In colder months, we love it on top of pancakes, waffles, and oatmeal. I bet you can find at least five delicious ways to enjoy it, too . . .

1. Make the Apple Pie Spice Mix (if not using store-bought apple pie spice).

2. To a large pot, add the apples, 1 cup of the water, the brown sugar, apple pie spice (starting with 1 teaspoon), and salt. Stir well to combine.

3. Bring the mixture to a simmer over high heat, then reduce the heat to medium-high and simmer, uncovered, for 13 to 18 minutes, until the apple pieces are fork-tender and glazed with the brown sugar syrup. Remove from the heat.

4. In a small bowl, whisk together the remaining 2 tablespoons water and the arrowroot starch until smooth. Spoon the arrowroot slurry into the apple mixture and stir well to

recipe continues

recipe continued from previous page

STORAGE

Store in an airtight container in the fridge for up to 1 week or in the freezer for up to 1 month. To reheat, thaw (if frozen), then transfer to a pot, cover, and heat over medium-low heat for 3 to 5 minutes, until warmed through.

TIP

* Gala or Honeycrisp apples are delicious in this, and it's nice to use a mix of apple varieties, too. If your apples are on the smaller side, you may need to use as many as 7 apples. As long as you have 6 cups (1.5 L/650 g) once they're peeled and chopped, the recipe will work perfectly!

MAKE IT AHEAD

The Warm Apple Pie Compote can be prepared and refrigerated in an airtight container for up to 4 days ahead of when you plan to enjoy it or it can be frozen for up to 1 month. See Storage tip for reheating instructions.

combine. The liquid will thicken slightly after a minute of sitting. Taste and stir in additional apple pie spice, to taste, if desired. If for some reason your compote is still too thin and watery, you can stir in more arrowroot slurry as needed (starting with 1 teaspoon arrowroot starch mixed with a couple teaspoons of water).

5. Serve with my O Canada! Spiced Maple Cream Torte, or see the headnote for other fun serving ideas.

Fastest No-Bake Jammy Oat Crumble Squares

Makes 10 squares • **Active prep time** 10 minutes
Chill time 20 minutes • **Total time** 35 minutes (if using store-bought jam)

½ cup plus 2 tablespoons Chia Seed Jam, homemade (page 279) or store-bought

½ cup packed (125 g) pitted Medjool dates*

⅓ cup coconut oil, at room temperature**

2 cups (200 g) gluten-free rolled oats

Small pinch of fine sea salt, or to taste

2 to 3 tablespoons water, as needed

My whole family is obsessed with my Strawberry Oat Crumble Bars from *Oh She Glows Every Day* (page 45), but they take quite a long time to bake and cool, and it's hard for my kids (okay, okay, for me, too) to wait that long! I came up with this super-speedy no-bake version that we all absolutely adore. During the high heat of summer, I'm happy not to turn on the oven. Though I have made them many, many times, I still can't believe just how quick and easy these are to pull together, especially when I use pre-made jam. With my Chia Seed Jam, these squares are light enough for a nutritious breakfast or midday snack. If you use store-bought jam (which tends to be much sweeter), they can pass for dessert, especially with a scoop of ice cream on the side! If you're looking for a larger yield, this recipe doubles beautifully using a 9-inch (2.5 L) square pan.

1. Prepare the Chia Seed Jam, if using homemade jam, and chill until cooled.

2. Line a 9 by 5-inch (2 L) loaf pan with a piece of parchment paper cut to fit the width of the pan, with a few inches of overhang on each side (for easier lifting later!).

3. In a heavy-duty food processor, process the dates and coconut oil until the dates are finely chopped, about 15 seconds.

recipe continues

recipe continued from previous page

STORAGE

Store leftovers in an airtight container in the fridge for up to 1 week or in the freezer for up to 6 weeks. I also like to wrap and freeze individual squares, so I can grab one and go when the craving hits or tuck them into lunch boxes. If frozen, let the squares sit on the counter to soften a bit before serving.

TIPS

* Use soft, fresh Medjool dates for best results. If your dates are dry, soak them in hot water for 30 minutes, then drain them well before using. If you soak your dates, you may need to use less water than called for in the recipe.

** If you don't enjoy the subtle coconut flavor that virgin coconut oil imparts, use refined coconut oil.

UP THE GLOW

Turn these into "PB and Jammy" squares: Place 2 tablespoons peanut butter in a small zip-top bag, snip off a corner, and pipe the peanut butter over the jam layer, then proceed with the recipe as written. Sunflower seed butter is a delicious option, too!

MAKE IT NO-BAKE

Use store-bought jam instead of Chia Seed Jam.

4. Add the oats, salt, and 2 tablespoons of the water to the food processor with the dates and coconut oil. Process for 8 to 15 seconds, until the mixture is coarsely chopped and easily sticks together when pressed between your fingers. If the dough is still a bit dry, add the remaining 1 tablespoon water and process briefly to combine.

5. Scatter 1⅓ cups of the oat crumble mixture over the bottom of the prepared pan. Spread it out evenly and press it down firmly with your fingers to form a level crust.

6. Pour the jam over the crust, spreading it out evenly to cover the surface. Scatter the remaining crumble over the top (it'll fully cover the surface of the jam) and gently press it into the jam so it adheres a bit. (If you find yourself with a bit too much crumble topping, you can shape it into energy cookies for an easy snack . . . my kids love these chilled in the fridge, where they firm up a bit.)

7. Transfer the pan to the freezer to chill for 20 to 25 minutes so the slab can firm up (do not freeze it for much longer than this, or the jam itself will start to harden), or chill in the fridge for an hour or two if preferred.

8. Using the overhanging parchment, lift the slab out of the pan and place it on a cutting board. Slice into squares—they'll be crumbly, but trust me, no one will care!—and serve each one on a plate with a fork, as they're a bit easier to eat this way.

Brainchild Cherry-Lemon Coconut Cream Pops

Makes 5 medium or 20 mini pops • **Active prep time** 7 minutes
Freeze time 3 to 5 hours • **Total time** 3 to 5 hours

1 (14-ounce/398 mL) can full-fat coconut milk

1 medium to large ripe (not overripe) banana (180 g)

Slightly heaping ½ cup (80 g) frozen sweet cherries*

3 tablespoons fresh lemon juice (1 large)

2 tablespoons pure maple syrup, or 3 large Medjool dates, pitted**

1 teaspoon pure vanilla extract

Fruit-flavored plant-based DHA oil (optional)

This is one of those family-pleasing recipes that I've memorized because I've made it so many times. During one hot summer, my kids asked for these cream pops almost every single day! The base is made with coconut cream, which adds a luxurious creamy texture. Sweet cherries provide a boost of antioxidants and summertime flavor, while banana and pure maple syrup sweeten the pops naturally. Lemon juice adds a kick of immune-boosting vitamin C and acts as a tangy contrast to the sweet base. I love to stir in a bit of plant-based DHA oil as a fun way of sneaking in healthy fats that are great for little ones' brain development (us old farts could use a little brain tune-up now and then, too!), but you can totally skip it if you prefer. I find these taste best when I use a perfectly yellow banana that isn't very spotty, because the banana flavor is very pronounced when you use an overripe banana. When I asked then-four-year-old Annie if I should put this ice pop in the cookbook, her eyes got wide and she nodded her head enthusiastically, with pink ice pop covering half her face. Then, right after, I asked then-two-year-old Arlo if I should put it in the cookbook, and he said adamantly, "NO!!!! It'll get messy!" . . . with pink ice pop all over his mouth. Out of the mouths of babes, indeed! Be sure to see Kitchen Tools and Appliances (page 332) for my favorite kid-sized ice pop mold recommendation.

1. Chill the can of coconut milk in the fridge for 24 hours, or until solid, if necessary.

recipe continues

recipe continued from previous page

TIPS

* You can change up the flavor by swapping in frozen blueberries or other mixed berries for the cherries (however, cherry will always be my favorite fruit to use in this recipe!). Fresh berries work, too! Always add the sweetener to taste to ensure a delicious end result.

** If you don't have a high-speed blender, use the maple syrup option. If your banana isn't that ripe, add another 1½ teaspoons pure maple syrup, or as needed.

STORAGE

Store pops in the freezer for up to 2 weeks.

UP THE GLOW

Zest the lemon before juicing it and add 1 teaspoon of the zest to the mix.

2. Open the can of coconut milk and scoop the solid white cream from the top into a high-speed blender (you should have 1 scant cup). Do not add the coconut water (the clearish liquid left in the can)—store it in the fridge for another use, such as a smoothie or coconut water ice cubes.

3. Add the banana, cherries, lemon juice, maple syrup, and vanilla to the blender. Blend on high until smooth. Taste and add more sweetener, if necessary. You'll have about 2 cups.

4. If you are using the DHA oil, fill each ice pop mold halfway with the ice pop mixture, then add ⅛ to ¼ teaspoon DHA oil to each mold and mix well until thoroughly combined. Fill the molds with more ice pop mixture until it reaches the top. (If you are not using the DHA oil, simply fill the molds with the ice pop mixture.)

5. Insert sticks and freeze for 3 to 5 hours (depending on the size of your molds), until solid. When ready to enjoy, run the molds under hot water until you're able to remove each pop.

Kombucha Strawberry-Lime Granita

Serves 8 (½ cup per serving) • **Active prep time** 10 minutes
Chill time 3 to 5 hours • **Total time** 10 minutes plus freezing

I pound (450 g) fresh strawberries, hulled, or frozen strawberries, thawed and drained

5 tablespoons fresh lime juice, or to taste

⅓ cup plus I tablespoon vegan honey or agave nectar, at room temperature, or to taste*

½ cup berry-flavored or plain kombucha**

Coconut Whipped Cream (page 322), for serving (optional)

STORAGE

Cover and freeze for up to I week. Let sit at room temperature for 7 to 10 minutes, until slightly softened, before serving.

TIP

* I use Bee Free Honee, which is an apple-based honey substitute.

** If you are serving this to your kids, you can easily swap out the kombucha for coconut water or just plain water.

Sweet, with a slightly tangy punch, this is a downright refreshing treat on a hot day. My version of granita is given a lift by using gut-friendly kombucha for a probiotic boost. Feel free to experiment with the recipe by changing up the fruit—try raspberries, blueberries, cherries, etc. (adjust the sweetener as needed). Lemon juice can easily be swapped in for the lime juice, too. Not to worry if you don't have a food processor—you can easily make this in a blender instead. Blend on medium speed to avoid the mixture getting too frothy.

I. In a large food processor, place the strawberries, lime juice, and honey. Process until smooth.

2. Add the kombucha and process for only a couple of seconds, just enough to combine the ingredients. Taste and add more lime juice or honey, if desired.

3. Pour the mixture into an 8-inch (2 L) square glass dish or similar-sized dish. Place on a level surface in the freezer and chill, uncovered, for I hour. After an hour, stir the mixture with a fork to break up any frozen chunks and run the fork along the edge to release any frozen bits stuck to the sides of the dish. Return the dish to the freezer and chill for another hour. Repeat this process hourly for 3 to 4½ hours, until the texture of the granita is to your liking. For a soft, sorbet-like texture, freeze for 3 to 3½ hours total. For a firmer texture, freeze for 4 to 5 hours.

4. Using an ice cream scoop, scoop the granita into parfait glasses or small bowls and top with a spoonful of Coconut Whipped Cream, if desired. The granita is delightful when it melts just a touch . . . it gets so gooey and delicious!

Peppermint Crunch Ice Cream

Serves 8 (½ cup per serving) • **Chill time** Overnight for the ice cream maker bowl, 2 hours for ice cream
Active prep time 20 minutes • **Total time** 45 minutes (plus freezing)

I batch Chewy Double-Chocolate Sunflower Cookies (page 249)

2 (14-ounce/398 mL) cans full-fat coconut milk

½ cup (110 g) natural cane sugar

1¼ teaspoons peppermint extract, or to taste

I teaspoon pure vanilla extract

⅛ teaspoon fine sea salt

3 tablespoons raw cacao nibs, for garnish

Fresh mint leaves, for garnish (optional)

"This is one of the best vegan ice creams I have ever tasted! We're dying over it!" This was the dramatic email I sent my recipe tester, Nicole, immediately after my family devoured my first trial of this ice cream. I knew I had hit the jackpot on something very special and that this recipe would be one I make all summer long (and it sure was!). It's refreshing, creamy, crunchy, chewy, chocolaty, and minty, all at the same time . . . you really need to experience this on a hot summer day. It also makes a fun dessert option for my Father's Day Lunch menu (see page 35). Serve it in bowls, or try it in ice cream cookie sandwiches, too. One thing is for sure: Your friends and family will be requesting this vegan ice cream on the regular.

1. Chill the ice cream maker bowl in the freezer overnight or for at least 12 hours.

2. Prepare the Chewy Double-Chocolate Sunflower Cookies. When you pop the cookies into the oven, start making the ice cream.

3. In a high-speed blender, place the coconut milk, sugar, peppermint extract, vanilla, and salt and blend for about 10 seconds, until smooth.

4. Place the frozen ice cream bowl into the ice cream maker, insert the churning arm, cover with the lid, and turn on the machine (if the instructions for your ice cream maker are different, please follow the directions that came with your machine). Slowly pour the coconut milk mixture into the chilled

recipe continues

recipe continued from previous page

STORAGE

Store leftovers in an airtight container in the freezer for up to 3 weeks. Let the ice cream rest on the counter for 20 to 30 minutes to soften before scooping. Since there aren't any gums in this ice cream, it can get icy in the freezer, so I prefer it when freshly made (though I wouldn't pass it up from the freezer!). You can also press a piece of plastic wrap directly against the surface of the ice cream before sealing the container to help prevent freezer burn.

TIPS

My churning time is an estimate only; you may find you need more or less time with your machine. Always follow the manufacturer's directions for your ice cream maker, as there may be slight variations.

For a fun serving idea, instead of scooping the ice cream into bowls and garnishing with the leftover cookies, use the cookies to make ice cream sandwiches!

bowl of the ice cream maker and follow the manufacturer's instructions to churn for 30 to 35 minutes, until the mixture has thickened to a soft serve–like texture.

5. Meanwhile, remove the cookies from the oven and let cool on the baking sheet for 10 to 15 minutes, then transfer to a plate and chill in the freezer.

6. When the ice cream is nearly finished churning, chop 6 of the frozen cookies into small, almond-sized pieces (keep the remaining cookies in the freezer).

7. When the ice cream has churned for 30 to 35 minutes, with the ice cream maker still churning, slowly add the chopped cookies (I like to use a fork or spoon to help push them down into the ice cream). Churn for 3 to 7 minutes more, until the ice cream is creamy and thick, then serve immediately. For a firmer texture, transfer to an airtight container and freeze for 2 hours before serving.

8. To serve, scoop into bowls and top with one of the remaining cookies, a couple teaspoons of cacao nibs, and fresh mint leaves, if desired.

Chewy Double-Chocolate Sunflower Cookies

Makes 12 cookies • **Active prep time** 10 minutes • **Total time** 30 minutes

1 tablespoon ground flaxseed*

3 tablespoons water

¼ cup plus 1 tablespoon unsweetened shredded coconut

2 tablespoons unsweetened cocoa powder

½ cup (50 g) gluten-free rolled oats

½ cup packed (110 g) brown sugar

1 teaspoon baking powder

½ teaspoon fine sea salt

¼ cup (45 g) vegan mini chocolate chips

½ cup smooth natural sunflower seed butter**

1 teaspoon pure vanilla extract

2 tablespoons pure maple syrup

Meet your new favorite chewy double-chocolate cookies (and they're nut-free, to boot)! Doubly chocolaty from the cocoa powder and mini chocolate chips, chewy from the sunflower seed butter, with a hint of coconut macaroon flavor . . . these are snack perfection. Unlike traditional baked cookies, these taste better and better as they chill (I actually love them best straight from the fridge). That's probably why I created them especially for my Peppermint Crunch Ice Cream (page 246) . . . what a delicious, chilly duo! But rest assured, they are fabulous all on their own, too.

1. Preheat the oven to 350°F (180°C) and position an oven rack in the middle of the oven. Line a large baking sheet with parchment paper.

2. In a medium bowl, whisk together the ground flaxseed and water and set aside.

3. In a large bowl, whisk together the shredded coconut, cocoa powder, oats, brown sugar, baking powder, salt, and chocolate chips. Add the sunflower seed butter, vanilla, and maple syrup. Stir until thoroughly combined. The mixture will be very thick.

4. Using a spatula (this helps you to scoop up every last bit), scoop the wet ingredients into the dry ingredients and stir until thoroughly combined. The dough will seem too dry at first, but keep mixing and it'll come together (I like to get in there with my hands and knead the dough to help it come together). The dough will be very sticky and dense.

recipe continues

recipe continued from previous page

STORAGE

Store in an airtight container in the fridge for up to 5 days, or freeze in a freezer bag with the air pressed out or in an airtight container for up to 1 month.

TIPS

* You can swap out the 1 tablespoon ground flaxseed for 1 *teaspoon* ground chia seed, if desired. Ground chia seed absorbs more water than ground flaxseed, which is why you need to use less.

** Be sure to use natural sunflower seed butter for this recipe. I love organic SunButter (with only sunflower seeds on the ingredient list). Stir it well before measuring, and avoid using the super-dry sunflower seed butter that tends to form on the bottom of the jar. You can also swap natural peanut or almond butter for the sunflower seed butter.

5. Lightly wet your hands (shaking off excess water) and form the dough into 12 golf ball–sized balls, placing them 2 to 3 inches (5 to 8 cm) apart on the prepared baking sheet as you go. Gently press down on each ball to flatten slightly. If you have any loose chocolate chips remaining at the bottom of the bowl, scoop them up and press them into the cookies.

6. Bake for 12 to 14 minutes. Let the cookies cool on the baking sheet for 10 minutes, then carefully transfer to a cooling rack and let cool completely (or better yet, pop them in the fridge to chill, which, to me, is the best way to enjoy these cookies). The cookies will be very soft and delicate coming out of the oven, but will firm up as they cool. If you're making these cookies for my Peppermint Crunch Ice Cream (page 246), the cooling directions differ slightly, so be sure to follow the instructions in that recipe.

6-Ingredient Chocolate Peanut Butter Oat Crumble Squares

Makes 15 small squares • **Active prep time** 15 minutes • **Total time** 55 minutes

For the Oat Crumble

½ cup packed (113 g) pitted Medjool dates*

⅓ cup coconut oil, at room temperature**

2 cups (200 g) gluten-free rolled oats

Fine sea salt

2 to 3 tablespoons water, as needed

For the PB Drizzle

1 tablespoon virgin coconut oil

2 tablespoons smooth natural peanut butter

1 tablespoon plus 2 teaspoons pure maple syrup

Pinch of fine sea salt (optional)

For the Chocolate–Peanut Butter Sauce

¼ cup pure maple syrup

¼ cup coconut oil**

5 tablespoons (25 g) unsweetened cocoa powder

1½ tablespoons smooth natural peanut butter

Pinch of fine sea salt (optional)

Melt-in-your-mouth homemade peanut butter–infused chocolate is sandwiched between a date-sweetened oat-and-coconut-oil crumble. I still can't believe just how quick and easy these are to whip up—just 15 minutes to prep! When I feel like transforming the squares into a lavish dessert, I like to add a dollop of my Coconut Whipped Cream (page 322) and drizzle on a little Easy Sea Salt Vanilla Caramel (page 325). Oh my word . . . that's next-level. Their versatility doesn't stop there, though: The PB Drizzle and Chocolate–Peanut Butter Sauce also make an incredible freezer fudge. Simply prepare them as directed, layer them in a silicone muffin mold, and freeze. Once firm, pop the fudge out of the molds and refrigerate or freeze in an airtight container for up to 6 weeks. You'll thank me later!

1. Line a 9 by 5-inch (2 L) loaf pan with a piece of parchment paper cut to fit the width of the pan, with a few inches of overhang on each side.

2. Prepare the Oat Crumble: To a heavy-duty food processor, add the dates and coconut oil and process until finely chopped, 15 to 20 seconds. Add the oats, ⅛ teaspoon salt, and 2 tablespoons of the water. Process for 8 to 10 seconds, just until the mixture is coarsely chopped and easily sticks together when pressed between your fingers. If your dough is a bit dry, add the remaining 1 tablespoon water and process until just combined.

recipe continues

recipe continued from previous page

STORAGE

Store the squares in an airtight container in the fridge for up to 1 week or in the freezer for up to 6 weeks. If necessary, let the frozen squares sit at room temperature for 5 to 10 minutes to soften slightly before serving. I love them best served straight from the fridge.

TIPS

* Use soft, fresh Medjool dates for best results. If your dates are dry, soak them in hot water for 30 minutes, then drain them well before using. If you soak your dates, you may need to use less water than called for in the recipe.

** If you aren't a fan of the subtle coconut flavor imparted by virgin coconut oil, use refined coconut oil.

MAKE IT NUT-FREE

Swap out the peanut butter for unsweetened natural sunflower seed butter.

3. Scatter 1⅓ cups of the oat mixture over the bottom of the prepared pan. Spread it out evenly and press it down firmly with your fingers to form a level crust. Set aside the remaining oat mixture.

4. Prepare the PB Drizzle: In a small pot, melt the coconut oil over low heat. Transfer the melted oil to a small bowl and whisk in the peanut butter and maple syrup until smooth. Add a tiny pinch of salt, to taste, if desired, and whisk to combine. The drizzle will be very runny and liquidy (if your peanut butter is on the thick side, however, the mixture will be thicker). Set aside.

5. Prepare the Chocolate–Peanut Butter Sauce: In the same pot you used for the drizzle (no need to clean it out!), combine the maple syrup and coconut oil and heat over low heat until the coconut oil has melted. Whisk in the cocoa powder until smooth, then add the peanut butter and whisk until smooth. Add a pinch of salt, to taste, and whisk to combine. The chocolate sauce will look a bit gooey, oily, and a bit thicker than the PB Drizzle, but this is normal.

6. Pour the chocolate–peanut butter sauce over the crust, and spread it out evenly until it covers the entire surface.

7. Slowly pour the drizzle over the chocolate sauce in a zigzag pattern (don't worry, it doesn't have to cover the chocolate sauce completely!). If you have any big chocolate patches without any drizzle, you can use a spoon to gently spread the chocolate sauce to cover them.

8. Crumble the remaining oat mixture over the top, gently pressing it into the drizzle so it adheres.

9. Transfer the pan to a level surface in the freezer and chill for at least 40 minutes and up to 2 hours, until the squares firm up. Using the overhanging parchment, lift the slab from the pan and set it on a cutting board. Slice into squares and serve.

One-Bowl Vegan Banana Bread

Makes one 9 by 5-inch (2 L) loaf (serves 9) • **Active prep time** 10 minutes • **Total time** 1 hour

Wet ingredients

1⅓ cups (320 g) mashed overripe bananas (about 4 medium or 3 large)*

2 tablespoons ground flaxseed

⅓ cup vanilla almond milk

⅓ cup coconut oil, melted

2 tablespoons pure maple syrup**

2 teaspoons pure vanilla extract

Dry ingredients

6 tablespoons (60 g) coconut sugar

½ cup (50 g) rolled oats

1 teaspoon baking soda

½ teaspoon baking powder

½ teaspoon fine sea salt

1½ cups (210 g) light/white spelt flour or whole-grain spelt flour***

Optional toppings

Sliced banana

Chopped walnuts

Vegan chocolate chips

Seriously, what's not to love about banana bread? The refined white flour and sugar, you say? Well, you'll love everything about *this* loaf, with its whole-grain flour, natural sweetener, and quick prep time! This vegan banana bread recipe quickly became the most popular recipe on my blog. I've received messages from readers all over the world telling me it was the best banana bread they had ever made, vegan or not. I was honored when some told me it even beat their heirloom family recipes! I don't think I've ever made it exactly the same way twice: Sometimes I swirl cinnamon and nutmeg into the batter, other times I add chocolate chips or chunks. And sometimes I top the batter with chopped walnuts, pecans, or even sliced bananas (which enhance the banana flavor). I've loved every variation! I go wild for a slice spread with my 5-Ingredient Vegan Butter (page 318), coconut oil, or Chia Seed Jam (page 279) and peanut butter. Be sure to use the ripest bananas possible, like those black ones you forgot about on the counter, or at minimum heavily spotted bananas, to ensure the best possible banana flavor and sweetness. You can use cane sugar as a swap for the coconut sugar, but coconut sugar will give it a wonderful, light caramel taste. Also, be sure to see my flour measuring tip on page 41 for best results!

1. Preheat the oven to 350°F (180°C). Lightly spray a 9 by 5-inch (2 L) loaf pan with oil.

2. In a large bowl, stir together the wet ingredients—the mashed banana, ground flaxseed, milk, melted coconut oil, maple syrup, and vanilla—until combined.

recipe continues

recipe continued from previous page

STORAGE

Tightly wrap the remaining loaf or individual slices in aluminum foil or plastic wrap and store in the fridge for up to 4 days or in the freezer for up to 6 weeks. If freezing, place the wrapped loaf or individual slices into a large zip-top bag for extra protection.

TIPS

* If you have any extra mashed banana, you can freeze it for a smoothie.

** If you don't have any maple syrup on hand, feel free to substitute an additional 2 tablespoons coconut sugar. The loaf won't be quite as moist, but it'll still work.

*** I like using light/white spelt flour because it lends a great flavor while still feeling quite light in texture. You can also use whole-grain spelt flour—it is heartier and denser in texture (and cracks more on the top of the loaf), but it's still delicious! If your whole-grain spelt flour is very coarse, I recommend sifting it prior to use for the best results. I don't recommend using all-purpose flour—it doesn't have the complex, nutty flavor that spelt flour does.

3. Stir the dry ingredients into the wet ingredients, one by one, in the following order: sugar, oats, baking soda, baking powder, salt, and flour. Be careful not to overmix the batter—stop stirring when there are no flour patches at the bottom of the bowl.

4. Spoon the batter into the prepared loaf pan and spread it out evenly. Add any desired toppings in a single layer and gently press them into the surface of the batter to adhere.

5. Bake, uncovered, for 45 to 55 minutes, until lightly golden and firm on top and a toothpick inserted into the center of the loaf comes out clean; the top of the loaf should slowly spring back when touched with a fingertip. Be careful not to underbake the banana bread.

6. Let the banana bread cool in the pan on a cooling rack for 30 minutes, then slide a knife around the loaf to loosen it and gently remove it from the pan. Set the loaf on the rack and let completely cool (or, to hasten the cooling process, transfer the loaf to a plate and chill in the fridge for 45 minutes).

7. Slice the loaf into 1-inch-thick (2.5 cm) slices and serve.

VEGAN • GLUTEN-FREE • NUT-FREE OPTION • SOY-FREE • RAW/NO BAKE
KID-FRIENDLY • FREEZER-FRIENDLY • ONE BOWL

Always Hangry PB&J Protein Snacking Bites

Makes about 21 bites • **Active prep time** 7 minutes • **Chill time** 20 minutes • **Total time** 27 minutes

⅔ cup packed (103 g) dried sweet cherries

½ cup packed (113 g) pitted fresh Medjool dates

1 cup (100 g) gluten-free rolled oats

½ cup (70 g) hemp hearts

¼ cup natural peanut butter*

2 tablespoons virgin coconut oil, at room temperature

½ teaspoon ground cinnamon, or to taste

Pinch of fine sea salt, to taste

1 to 2 tablespoons water

Kid hanger is a real thing. I don't know at what age your hunger meter starts working, but it doesn't seem to function optimally in toddlerhood. There's no middle ground—they are either full and happy (the best version of their sweet toddler selves) or savage beasts falling to the ground crying because they needed to eat 45 minutes ago (and somehow forgot to tell you). I've learned to have emergency snacks on hand to tide my kids over until mealtime (they come in handy for us adults, too). Plus, these peanut butter and "jam" protein bites couldn't be easier to whip up, and they're packed with protein-rich hemp hearts and peanut butter to squash that hanger monster in all of us. A nice dose of cinnamon helps balance blood sugar levels, Medjool dates and dried cherries sweeten the mix (cherries also provide that lovely sweet-tart "jam" flavor), and coconut oil lends immune-boosting benefits as well as antibacterial and antifungal properties. My kids love these unadorned, but for adults and older kids, you can drizzle on melted dark chocolate before chilling or even add mini chocolate chips to the dough for a satisfying crunch.

1. Line an 8 by 4-inch (1.5 L) or 9 by 5-inch (2 L) loaf pan with a piece of parchment paper cut to fit the length of the pan, with a few inches of overhang on each side.

2. To a large heavy-duty food processor, add the dried cherries and the dates and process until finely chopped and the mixture comes together in a ball. Add the oats, hemp hearts, peanut

recipe continues

recipe continued from previous page

STORAGE

Store leftovers in an airtight container in the fridge for up to 10 days or in the freezer for up to 2 months. I prefer their texture straight from the fridge because they soften a great deal at room temperature. If frozen, allow them to sit on the counter for 5 to 10 minutes before serving.

TIP

* If your peanut butter is salted, you may not need to add any salt.

MAKE IT NUT-FREE

Swap out the peanut butter for sunflower seed butter.

butter, coconut oil, cinnamon, and salt. Process until the mixture is very finely chopped. The mixture will stick to the sides and bottom of the bowl, so stop to scrape it down as frequently as needed.

3. Add 1 tablespoon of the water and process again. The dough should easily stick together when pressed between your fingers. If it doesn't, add more water, a teaspoon at a time, and process again until the dough holds together.

4. Spoon the dough into the prepared pan. With your hands (wet them lightly first, if needed, to prevent sticking), press down on the dough until it's firmly and evenly packed into the pan.

5. Freeze for about 20 minutes, until firm enough to slice. Using the overhanging parchment, remove the dough from the pan and set it on a cutting board. Slice into small bites and enjoy.

Mint-Ginger Simple Syrup

Makes 1 cup plus 3 tablespoons • **Active prep time** 10 minutes
Steep time 1 hour 30 minutes to 2 hours • **Total time** 1 hour 40 minutes

1 cup water

1 cup (220 g) natural cane sugar

2 cups packed (38 g) fresh mint leaves
(1 very large or 2 small bunches)

2 tablespoons grated fresh ginger*

STORAGE

Store in the jar or airtight container in the fridge for up to 1 month, or freeze in a freezer bag with the air pressed out or in an airtight container for up to 2 months. You can also pour the syrup into a silicone ice cube tray and freeze until solid, then transfer the frozen cubes to a freezer bag or airtight container to store in the freezer for quick and easy single-serving drinks!

TIP

* I peel the ginger using a Y-peeler and then grate it on a Microplane (to ensure a strong infusion).

Looking for a delightful fresh twist on simple syrup? You've come to the right place! The mint here is just right, not sickeningly overpowering, and the slight heat coming through from the ginger is absolute perfection. As an added bonus, this syrup doubles as a natural house freshener, filling your house with a peppy ginger-and-mint aroma as it simmers. This syrup is fantastic in my Mint, Ginger, and Lemon Sparkling Sipper (page 268), or if it's winter where you are, try it in my Soothing Mint and Ginger Green Tea (page 267)—they're both so soothing for the stomach, and they make mealtimes feel extra special! This concentrated syrup has a modest amount of heat from the fresh ginger, but don't worry—this dissipates once the syrup is mixed into drinks.

1. In a medium pot, stir together the water, sugar, mint, and ginger. Bring to a boil over high heat, then immediately reduce the heat to medium-high. Simmer gently, uncovered, stirring every now and then, for 3 minutes. Remove from the heat, and let the mixture steep in the pot, uncovered, for 1 hour 30 minutes to 2 hours.

2. Strain the syrup through a sieve into a wide-mouth jar or airtight container. Using a spoon, gently press down on the solids to push all that syrupy goodness into the jar below. (Compost the solids or, if you are a tea person, transfer them to a small separate container and store them in the fridge for up to 3 days. I like to put a spoonful of the solids into my tea steeper along with some loose-leaf green tea for a delicious twist on green tea.) Secure the lid and refrigerate the syrup to use as needed. Stir the syrup before each use.

Immunity Glo Shot

Serves 10 (2 tablespoons per serving) • **Active prep time** 10 minutes • **Total time** 10 minutes

I cup fresh lemon juice (from 4 to 5 large)

5 medium garlic cloves (20 g), to taste*

1¾ ounces (50 g) fresh ginger (one 5-inch-long/12 cm piece), peeled

¼ cup apple cider vinegar

Pure maple syrup (optional)

Elderberry or echinacea tincture drops (optional)**

STORAGE

Store in an airtight container in the fridge for up to 5 days or in the freezer for 1 to 2 months. I like to freeze leftover juice in silicone ice cube trays. This way, I have single servings on hand whenever I feel a cold coming on! Pop a frozen cube into a mug and cover it with hot water (it'll melt fast), then enjoy.

TIPS

* If you're not a fan of raw garlic, you can leave it out.

** How many drops of echinacea or elderberry tincture should you add? I recommend following the guidelines on the product label, as they'll provide an estimate for a single serving. I like to fill my silicone ice cube tray with the strained liquid and then add the echinacea and elderberry drops to each individual cavity.

Introducing my very first Glo Shot! These are a far cry from the "shots" of my university days *<insert teeth-gritting emoji>*, but they leave me feeling much better, to say the least. I've faced some health challenges in recent years, and for a while I was getting hit with one cold after another. One day, I decided to battle early cold symptoms by combining all my favorite "cold remedies" in my Vitamix and blending away. It was such a boost to my immune system, I decided to name them Glo Shots. I find they work best when taken at the immediate onset of cold symptoms, but you can enjoy them regularly throughout the fall and winter seasons to give your immune system a boost. I like adding elderberry and echinacea tinctures to mine, but please follow the medical advice of your own physician. For the ultimate powerhouse nutritious meal, enjoy one of these Glo Shots alongside a steaming bowl of Cold-Be-Gone Flavor Bomb Noodle Soup (page 213).

1. To a blender, add the lemon juice, garlic, and ginger. Blend on high until smooth.

2. Place a fine-mesh sieve over a bowl (preferably a bowl with a pour spout). Strain the mixture through the sieve and use a spoon to press down on the solids to ensure all the juice comes out. Compost or discard the solids in the sieve.

3. Stir in the vinegar and maple syrup (if using) to taste. Add elderberry and/or echinacea tincture, if desired.

4. Fill a shot glass with the liquid and drink up! Or, if you prefer, add a shot of the liquid to a mug of warm or cold water and drink with a straw (to protect your tooth enamel).

Solid Gold Pumpkin Pie Spice Coconut Latte

Serves 3 (1¼ cups per serving) • **Active prep time** 10 minutes • **Total time** 10 minutes

2 cups hot strong brewed coffee*

1 (14-ounce/398 mL) can light coconut milk

⅓ cup (50 g) coconut sugar, or to taste

Pumpkin pie spice, homemade (see page 311) or store-bought, to taste

1 teaspoon pure vanilla extract

Tiny pinch of fine sea salt

TIPS

* To make my coffee, I use a French press with ⅓ cup ground beans and 2½ cups water (I use a bit more water, as the grounds will soak up some of it while brewing, then I measure out the 2 cups needed for the recipe). I brew the coffee in the press for about an hour. Using a coffee machine or other brewing method also works; just be sure to make the coffee a bit stronger than usual (if that floats your boat!). Or feel free to use decaf, if you prefer.

Only need a single serving? Prepare the recipe as directed, but use ¾ cup coffee, ⅔ cup coconut milk, 1½ to 2 tablespoons coconut sugar (to taste), pumpkin pie spice (to taste), ¼ teaspoon vanilla extract, and a dash of fine sea salt.

There is "Uncaffeinated Ange" and "Caffeinated Ange," and I greatly prefer the latter. My group of girlfriends and I all adore this drink, and they now request it for our get-togethers. This latte is lovely served chilled after a summer dinner alfresco, or warm, following a cozy wintertime meal indoors. This nut-free coconut latte couldn't be easier, and it satisfies my craving for creamy lattes during pumpkin spice season (which for me can last year-round). Since it's coconut-based, it's also great for those who can't have soy-, almond-, or cashew-based lattes.

1. Prepare the coffee. In a medium pot, stir together the coconut milk and coconut sugar. Bring to a simmer over medium-high heat, then remove from the heat. Stir again.

2. In a blender, place the hot coffee, the warmed coconut mixture, pumpkin pie spice (I use about ¾ teaspoon), vanilla, and salt. (Depending on the size of your blender, you may have to blend this in a couple of batches.) Blend on low, gradually increasing the speed to medium, for 10 to 15 seconds, until combined and a bit frothy.

3. Serve immediately, with a sprinkle of pumpkin pie spice on top!

STORAGE

Store leftovers in an airtight container in the fridge for up to 3 days. Simply stir and drink chilled, or reheat in a small pot until warmed through. If the latte separates when chilled, you can throw it into the blender and blend until smooth and recombined before serving.

VEGAN • GLUTEN-FREE • NUT-FREE • SOY-FREE • GRAIN-FREE • OIL-FREE
ADVANCE PREP REQUIRED • ON THE GLOW

Soothing Mint and Ginger Green Tea

Serves 1 • **Active prep time** 2 minutes (not including simple syrup) • **Total time** 7 minutes

1½ cups water

1 bag green tea

1 to 3 teaspoons Mint-Ginger Simple Syrup (page 261), to taste

This is a fun way to use my Mint-Ginger Simple Syrup during the colder winter months! A few teaspoons of the syrup stirred into green tea imparts a lovely fresh flavor while removing the characteristic bitterness of green tea. It's such a relaxing yet invigorating tea, and you'll often find me with my hands wrapped around a steaming mug after a meal to help aid digestion.

1. Bring the water to a boil. Remove from the heat and let sit for 30 to 60 seconds.

2. Place the tea bag in a large mug. Pour the hot water over the top and steep for about 5 minutes.

3. Remove the tea bag and stir in the simple syrup, to taste, 1 teaspoon at a time. Enjoy!

STORAGE

This tea is best served fresh.

Mint, Ginger, and Lemon Sparkling Sipper

Serves I • **Active prep time** 5 minutes • **Total time** 5 minutes

4 large ice cubes

½ cup sparkling water, chilled

2 tablespoons fresh lemon juice, or to taste

5 to 6 teaspoons Mint-Ginger Simple Syrup (page 261), to taste, chilled

These sparkling sippers are the perfect thirst quenchers on a hot summer day, and they use my delectable Mint-Ginger Simple Syrup. The cooling mint is the perfect partner for the warming ginger. The bright lemon and bubbly sparkling water bring it all together in an ideal stomach-soothing and refreshing summer beverage! Whip up this sparkling sipper to make any warm-weather dinner feel extra special.

1. Put the ice cubes in an 8-ounce lowball glass.

2. Add the sparkling water, lemon juice, and simple syrup. Stir well. Taste and add more lemon juice or simple syrup, if desired. Enjoy immediately.

STORAGE

This drink is best served fresh due to the carbonation.

TIP

To increase the yield to serve a small group, prepare the drink in a pitcher using the following amounts: 12 to 24 large ice cubes, I (26 ounces/750 mL) bottle sparkling water (chilled), ¾ cup fresh lemon juice (or to taste), and ¾ cup Mint-Ginger Simple Syrup. Add fresh mint leaves for garnish, pour into lowball glasses, and serve. This makes six ¾-cup servings.

SAUCES, DRESSINGS, SPICES, *and* MORE

VEGAN • GLUTEN-FREE • NUT-FREE • SOY-FREE • GRAIN-FREE • RAW/NO BAKE
FREEZER-FRIENDLY • ON THE GLOW • ONE BOWL

Easy Chimichurri Sauce

Makes I scant cup • **Active prep time** 7 minutes • **Total time** 7 minutes

4 medium garlic cloves (16 g)

I medium/large red chile (15 g), seeded and coarsely chopped*

¾ cup packed (18 g) fresh flat-leaf parsley (thick stems removed)

I tablespoon dried oregano

½ cup extra-virgin olive oil

¼ cup red wine vinegar

¼ to ½ teaspoon fine sea salt, to taste

Have you heard of chimichurri? It's a thin, herby, piquant sauce native to Argentina and it adds a vivacious kick to many different dishes. Tangy and robust from the fresh parsley, red wine vinegar, and sharp garlic, boy, does this sauce add vibrancy to almost any dish. You must try this sauce in my Summery Chimichurri Chickpea Pasta Salad (page 185) and my Flavor Bomb Chimichurri Guacamole (page 163)—yes, that's another order in this book (I'm getting bossy, sheesh)! It's also lovely drizzled over roasted or grilled veggies, cooked grains, avocado toast, or veggie burgers. The sky is the limit, my friends.

To a food processor or blender, add the garlic and chile and process until minced. Scrape down the sides of the bowl. Add the parsley, oregano, oil, vinegar, and salt to the food processor or blender. Process or blend until smooth, 30 to 60 seconds. The sauce will be very thin and liquidy, but this is normal.

STORAGE

Store in an airtight container in the fridge for up to 5 days, or freeze in a freezer bag with the air pressed out or in an airtight container for up to 2 months.

TIP

* If you don't have a red chile on hand, feel free to omit it. You can add some red pepper flakes or cayenne pepper, to taste, or use ½ green serrano pepper, if you'd like. Leaving the chile's white inner membrane intact will yield a slightly spicier sauce.

Pretty Parsley-Cilantro Pepita Pesto

Makes scant 1 cup • **Active prep time** 8 minutes • **Total time** 8 minutes

1 large garlic clove (6 g)

½ cup (80 g) roasted pepitas
(see page 338) or raw cashews

1 cup lightly packed (20 g) fresh parsley
leaves

1 cup lightly packed (22 g) fresh cilantro
leaves

¼ cup extra-virgin olive oil

2 tablespoons water

2 tablespoons fresh lemon juice,
or to taste

1 tablespoon nutritional yeast

¼ teaspoon fine sea salt, plus more
to taste

Double-Batch Pretty Parsley-Cilantro Pepita Pesto

2 large garlic cloves (12 g), 1 cup (150 g)
toasted pepitas or raw cashews,
1½ cups lightly packed (30 g) fresh
parsley leaves, 1½ cups lightly packed
(33 g) fresh cilantro leaves, ½ cup
extra-virgin olive oil, ¼ cup water,
¼ cup fresh lemon juice,
2 tablespoons nutritional yeast,
½ teaspoon fine sea salt or more to
taste. This makes 1¾ cups plus
2 tablespoons pesto.

STORAGE

Store leftovers in an airtight container
in the fridge for up to 1 week. The
pesto will firm up when chilled but
will soften at room temperature.

Dairy-free pestos are one of the unsung heroes of plant-based diets because they can literally transform a meal from so-so to *mind-blowing*. Due to allergies, I went through a time when I had to avoid nuts completely, and this pesto is another nut-free delight I came up with during a phase of creative desperation. The best part is, I don't feel like I'm missing out at all, and I don't think you will, either. Here's another big win: Pepitas are much less expensive than cashews, which tend to be go-tos for vegan pestos. I love to use roasted salted pepitas in this pesto (I buy huge bags from Costco at a great price)—they're a great source of zinc and an amazing snack all on their own. This lively, zippy recipe is adored by parsley and cilantro lovers alike, and like my other pesto recipes, this one is handy to make weekly so you have a batch on hand for Crispy Potato Stacks (page 87), cooked pasta (such as my Glow Green 30-Minute Pesto Pasta, page 55), The Mama Bear Bowl: Cauli-Power Savory Steel-Cut Oatmeal (page 108), sandwiches/wraps, hummus, School Night Tofu Scramble with Roasted Red Pepper and Walnut Dip (page 78), and more. And, of course, it's the perfect solution during the summer if you have these fresh herbs growing in the backyard and need to use them up before they bolt! Now go on and bolt to the kitchen to whip this up! Bad joke, I know.

1. In a food processor, process the garlic until minced.

2. Add the pepitas and process into fine crumbs.

3. Add the parsley, cilantro, oil, water, lemon juice, nutritional yeast, and salt and process until super smooth, stopping to scrape down the bowl if necessary. Taste and adjust the seasoning with more lemon juice, salt, oil, or nutritional yeast if desired.

Boom! Broccoli Pesto

Makes 1¾ cups • **Active prep time** 15 minutes • **Total time** 17 minutes

5 medium garlic cloves (20 g)

1½ tablespoons (18 g) chopped oil-packed unsalted sun-dried tomatoes, drained, plus 1½ tablespoons oil from the jar*

½ cup packed (12 g) fresh parsley, or more to taste

5 tablespoons (50 g) roasted pepitas (see page 338)

5 tablespoons fresh lemon juice, or to taste**

2 tablespoons nutritional yeast

½ teaspoon sea salt, or to taste, plus more for boiling water

¼ teaspoon freshly ground black pepper

2 heaping cups packed (160 g) broccoli florets (1-inch/2.5 cm florets)

5 tablespoons extra-virgin olive oil

I just love how a great pesto can transform a whole meal—it adds a vibrant twist to pasta, roasted veggies, bowls, sandwiches, wraps, and more. As the basil season wraps up near the end of September, I like to switch over to this zippy broccoli pesto with bold lemon and garlic flavors. Sun-dried tomatoes add an anchoring umami, while the bright, in-season freshness of the lightly blanched broccoli lights up the dish and packs in mega nutrition. Looking for serving inspiration? We love this pesto on my Crispy Potato Stacks (page 87) or Green Powerhouse Roasted Protein Bowl (page 61), stirred into cooked pasta, spread onto crackers or crostini, used as a dip for raw veggies, spread on sandwiches or wraps, alongside roasted veggies, or swirled into soup. Boom!

1. Bring a medium pot of water to a rolling boil over high heat.

2. Meanwhile, to a food processor, add the garlic and process until minced.

3. Add the sun-dried tomatoes, sun-dried tomato oil, parsley, pepitas, lemon juice, nutritional yeast, salt, and pepper to the food processor, but don't turn on the processor yet.

4. When the water comes to a boil, add 2 teaspoons salt and the broccoli. Cover the pot and blanch the broccoli for 90 seconds. Drain, then immediately run the broccoli under cold water to stop the cooking. Drain well.

recipe continues

recipe continued from previous page

STORAGE

Store leftovers in an airtight container in the fridge for 5 to 6 days, or freeze in a freezer bag with the air pressed out or in an airtight container for up to 1 month. After thawing, taste and adjust the seasonings, if needed.

TIPS

* You can use rehydrated sun-dried tomatoes instead of oil-packed ones; just replace the sun-dried tomato oil with extra-virgin olive oil.

** If you aren't a big lemon fan, start with a bit less than 5 tablespoons, and add more, a little bit at a time, to taste.

5. Add the drained broccoli to the food processor with the sun-dried tomato mixture and process for 10 seconds, then stop and scrape down the sides of the bowl. With the food processor running, stream in the olive oil and then let the machine run for a good minute or so. If the pesto is too thick for your liking, add a bit of water or oil, a tablespoon at a time, and process again. Taste and check the flavors, adding additional lemon juice, garlic, salt, etc., if desired.

6. Serve immediately. For a bolder pesto, transfer to a jar and refrigerate for a few hours or up to overnight before serving. The flavor will grow stronger as it chills (I love it best after a few hours of chilling).

Chia Seed Jam

Makes 1 to 1¼ cups • **Active prep time** 5 minutes • **Total time** 20 minutes (does not include chilling)

3 slightly heaping cups (400 g) frozen fruit*

3 tablespoons pure maple syrup, or to taste**

2 tablespoons chia seeds

1 teaspoon pure vanilla extract

The different flavor variations of chia seed jam are endless! I especially love that you can change it up depending on which frozen or fresh fruit you have on hand. Tart-and-sweet combos of strawberry, cherry, blueberry, peach . . . there are options aplenty. My go-to flavor is strawberry-vanilla . . . it tastes a bit like the strawberry Fruit Roll-Ups of my youth, and it's absolute perfection sandwiched inside my Fastest No-Bake Jammy Oat Crumble Squares (page 239). My family also loves it stirred into hot oatmeal and overnight oats, or for healthier peanut butter and "jelly" sandwiches (my kids are obsessed). I've played around with all different kinds of cooked and no-cook "raw" chia jams, but I always come back to this method—simmering the fruit on the stovetop brings out the fruit's deep, sweet flavors and also cooks off the water, resulting in an incredibly flavorful thick, rich jam. If you are serving a larger crowd (or simply want to make extra for the freezer), this recipe doubles beautifully. The cook time will likely double and you may need to increase the heat a bit to simmer the larger volume of fruit.

1. In a medium pot, stir together the frozen fruit and maple syrup to combine. Bring to a simmer over medium-high heat, then reduce the heat to medium-low and gently simmer, uncovered, stirring frequently, for 5 to 8 minutes, until the fruit is thawed and fork-tender.

2. Transfer the fruit to a food processor (I use my 4-cup/1 L mini processor) and process until mostly smooth.

recipe continues

recipe continued from previous page

STORAGE

Store the jam in the jar in the fridge for up to 1 week. Chia Seed Jam also freezes beautifully! I love to freeze it in single servings. I simply divide the jam among the cavities of a silicone mini-muffin mold and freeze them until solid, then transfer the frozen "pucks" of jam into a freezer-safe container with a piece of parchment paper between each layer to prevent sticking. Frozen this way, the jam will keep for up to 6 weeks.

TIPS

* You can also use fresh fruit in this recipe. One pound (450 g) fresh strawberries, hulled and diced, gives you a scant 3 cups, which is perfect for this recipe.

** Different fruits will require slightly different amounts of sweetener. Add the maple syrup to taste, and you can't go wrong. If the jam isn't sweet enough after chilling, you can always stir in a bit more maple syrup.

If you don't have a food processor, you can use a potato masher. The jam will have a chunkier consistency. You could also blend the fruit directly in the pot using an immersion blender.

This is a one-pot recipe if the fruit is mashed directly in the pot as opposed to using a food processor.

UP THE GLOW

Get fancy and add a little lemon, lime, or orange zest, vanilla bean powder, or warm spices such as cinnamon and ginger.

3. Spoon the fruit mixture back into the pot and stir in the chia seeds until combined. Gently simmer over medium-low heat, stirring frequently, for 4 to 5 minutes, until the jam has thickened slightly. Remove from the heat and stir in the vanilla.

4. Transfer to a jar and let cool, uncovered, in the fridge, then use as desired or secure the lid and store. For faster cooling, transfer the jam to the freezer for 30 to 60 minutes, until cold, then secure the lid and transfer to the fridge for longer storage.

Strawberry-Vanilla Chia Seed Jam

Use 3 slightly heaping cups (450 g) frozen strawberries and follow the recipe as written. This is my favorite flavor!

Garlic Cashew Cheese Sauce

Makes 4 cups plus 2 tablespoons • **Soak time** I hour or up to overnight
Active prep time 7 minutes • **Total time** 7 minutes

I cup (150 g) raw cashews

1½ cups water

¾ cup (60 g) nutritional yeast

¾ cup grapeseed oil

¼ cup fresh lemon juice

¼ cup white wine vinegar

8 medium garlic cloves (32 g)

1¼ teaspoons fine sea salt

I tablespoon sriracha (optional, but recommended)

TIP

This sauce is spectacular on pasta! For a quick, simple weeknight pasta dish, cook 3 cups (10 ounces/250 g) dry pasta as directed on the package, adding a handful of frozen peas during the last minute of cooking, if desired. Drain the pasta, return it to the pot, and stir in 1½ cups Garlic Cashew Cheese Sauce. Cover and let sit over low heat for a few minutes so the pasta can absorb the sauce's lovely, tangy flavors. Taste and season with salt and pepper, if desired. Serve on its own or topped with Vegan Parmesan (page 317).

This Garlic Cashew Cheese Sauce is my secret weapon to take scalloped potatoes to the next level. It is brimming with garlicky, cheesy goodness that cooks perfectly into the sliced potatoes, creating a beautifully tangy, creamy, salt-and-vinegar-flavored dish. You can also mix it into cooked pasta for a fresh spin on pasta sauce (see Tip).

I. Place the cashews in a small bowl and add boiling water to cover. Soak for I hour, then drain. (Alternatively, soak the cashews in room-temperature water to cover for at least 8 hours or up to overnight, then drain.)

2. Transfer the drained cashews to a high-speed blender and add the water, nutritional yeast, oil, lemon juice, vinegar, garlic, salt, and sriracha (if using). Blend for I to 2 minutes, until very smooth. The sauce will be very bubbly and thin, but this is normal. Don't be alarmed if the sauce tastes a bit tangy; it'll mellow once baked into the potatoes!

STORAGE

Store in an airtight container in the fridge for up to 5 days, or freeze in a freezer bag with the air pressed out or in an airtight container for up to I month. Allow the sauce to sit at room temperature for an hour before using to ensure it's spreadable.

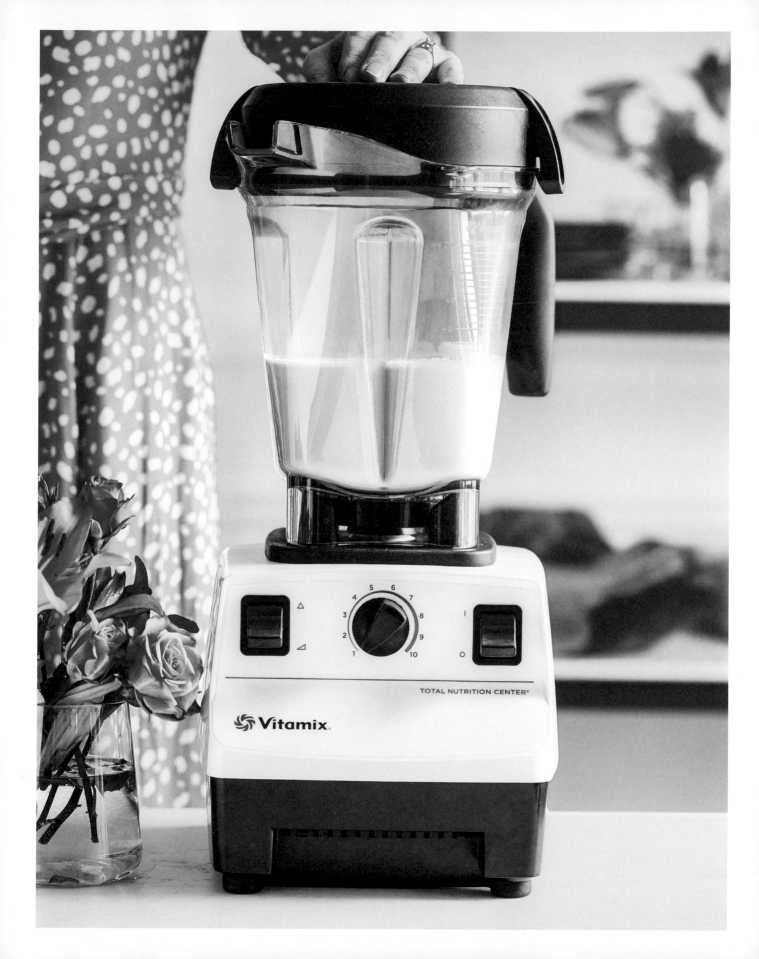

Apple Honey–Dijon Dressing

Makes 1 cup • **Active prep time** 5 minutes • **Total time** 5 minutes

1 large garlic clove (6 g), minced

½ cup extra-virgin olive oil

¼ cup fresh lemon juice

2 tablespoons plus 2 teaspoons apple honey, at room temperature*

2 tablespoons Dijon mustard

¼ to ½ teaspoon fine sea salt, to taste**

TIPS

* I love Bee Free Honee, which is an apple-based honey substitute. Use any honey you like, though!

** When making this dressing for my Charred Broccoli Quinoa Salad, I use ½ teaspoon salt, since it needs more salt when it's added to the quinoa and broccoli. When making this as a salad dressing, I tend to use only ¼ teaspoon salt.

Apple Honey–Dijon Mixed Greens: Toss the dressing with mixed greens for a nutritious and simple side option.

This simple dressing is so fast and easy, and it quickly became a family favorite as the perfect pairing for my Charred Broccoli Quinoa Salad (page 187). Lightly sweet from the apple-based vegan honey and tangy from the pungent Dijon mustard and fresh lemon juice, the flavors balance so nicely. It'll keep well in the fridge for a couple of weeks, too, so it's a great one to have on hand for topping salads, sautéed greens, or roasted veggies, and for drizzling over my Crispy Brussels Sprouts in Garlic Oil (page 151). This dressing is also lovely tossed with mixed field greens for a simple (yet delicious) side salad! Try topping this simple salad with your favorite toasted nuts or seeds for a bit of crunch.

Add the garlic, oil, lemon juice, honey, Dijon, and salt to a small mason jar. Shake vigorously to combine. The honey has a tendency to settle on the bottom of the jar, so I like to give it a good stir with a spoon, scraping the honey off the bottom, as needed. Taste and adjust the flavor as desired.

STORAGE

Refrigerate in the jar for up to 2 weeks. If the dressing solidifies somewhat in the fridge, let it sit at room temperature before using. Shake well before each use.

24/7 Avocado-Cilantro Sauce

Makes ¾ cup • **Active prep time** 5 minutes • **Total time** 5 minutes

1 medium garlic clove (4 g)

¼ cup lightly packed (6 g) fresh cilantro or parsley*

1 ripe medium avocado (200 g), pitted

2 tablespoons fresh lime juice, or to taste

¼ cup vegan mayo

¼ to ½ teaspoon fine sea salt, to taste

STORAGE

Store in a jar in the fridge for up to 3 days. Stir before use.

TIP

* I slightly prefer the cilantro version of this sauce, but the parsley option is lovely!

MAKE IT SOY-FREE

Use soy-free vegan mayo.

This sauce is so creamy and flavorful, we find ourselves wanting to eat it 24/7! Rich and decadent from the mayonnaise, creamy from the avocado, and citrusy from the fresh cilantro (or parsley, if you prefer) and lime, it's vibrant and fresh when dolloped on my Fast Family Fajitas (page 53), Kitchen Sink Sheet Pan Buddha Bowl (page 125), Crispy Smashed Potatoes, Endless Ways (page 173), Saucy Little Black Bean Skillet (page 167), roasted veggies, or burrito bowls, or spread on hearty wraps.

1. In a food processor, process the garlic and cilantro until minced.

2. Add the avocado flesh (you should have about ¾ cup), lime juice (starting with 1½ tablespoons), vegan mayo, and salt to the food processor with the garlic and cilantro. Process until smooth, stopping to scrape the bowl if necessary. Taste and add more lime juice and salt, if desired.

Double-Batch 24/7 Avocado-Cilantro Sauce

2 medium garlic cloves (8 g), ½ cup packed (12 g) fresh cilantro or parsley, 2 ripe medium avocados (400 g total, pitted), ¼ cup fresh lime juice (or to taste), ½ cup vegan mayo, ½ teaspoon fine sea salt (or to taste). This makes 1½ cups sauce.

Sriracha Aioli

Makes ¾ cup • **Active prep time** 3 minutes • **Total time** 3 minutes

4 to 5 medium garlic cloves (16 to 20 g), to taste

¾ cup vegan mayo

3 to 6 teaspoons sriracha, to taste

STORAGE

Store in an airtight container in the fridge for up to 1 week.

MAKE IT SOY-FREE

Be sure to buy a soy-free vegan mayo. I love Vegenaise brand.

MAKE IT KID-FRIENDLY

Reduce the sriracha to 1 to 2 teaspoons (or less, if desired) and reduce the garlic, if desired.

UP THE GLOW

Add a tiny squeeze of fresh lemon juice for a pop of tangy brightness (so good!).

My Sriracha Aioli has a decadent creaminess, immune-boosting nutrition from the raw garlic, and a fiery *ka-pow* from the sriracha! Not to worry if you aren't a spice fan, though—you can easily adjust the amount to suit your tastes, starting with 1 teaspoon and adding more little by little, if you'd like. I love how something as simple as this three-ingredient aioli can transform the flavors of so many dishes. Serve this punchy aioli on my Rebellious Battered Broc-Cauli Burgers (page 113), Seasoned Crispy Baked Potato Wedges (page 159), Spicy Potato Nacho Plate (page 71), Crispy Brussels Sprouts in Garlic Oil (page 151), and Savory Herb and Veggie Chickpea Pancakes (page 116). But you don't have to wait until you're making one of these delicious recipes to whip up this aioli—it's a versatile condiment you'll want to keep handy in your fridge! I love a generous dollop on top of avocado toast (you really need to try this combo!) or on a fluffy baked potato . . . mmm.

1. Grate the garlic on a Microplane (or simply mince it with a knife).

2. In a small bowl, stir together the grated garlic, mayo, and 3 teaspoons of the sriracha. Stir to combine. Taste and add more sriracha, if desired. (I use about 5 teaspoons total sriracha, sometimes 6 teaspoons if I'm feeling wild, for a nice kick of heat.)

Vegan Cheese Sauce 2.0

Makes 2¼ cups • **Soak time** 1 hour or up to overnight • **Active prep time** 10 minutes • **Total time** 25 minutes

6 tablespoons (55 g) raw cashews

1¾ cups (270 g) diced peeled yellow or red potatoes

¾ cup (110 g) diced peeled carrots

3 tablespoons grapeseed oil or refined coconut oil*

¼ cup water

4 teaspoons fresh lemon juice

¾ teaspoon fine sea salt, or to taste

3 medium garlic cloves (12 g)

4½ to 5 tablespoons (23 to 25 g) nutritional yeast, to taste

½ to 1 teaspoon white wine vinegar, to taste

UP THE GLOW

For a spicy kick, add sriracha or other hot sauce, to taste.

TIPS

* If you don't have grapeseed or refined coconut oil on hand, a light-tasting olive oil should do the trick.

If you don't have a high-speed blender, a heavy-duty food processor will work, but you may have to process the mixture for a few minutes and the sauce will be more textured.

MAKE IT NUT-FREE

Simply omit the cashews.

This vegan cheese sauce is a rich, creamy topping for my Cheesy Lentil Bolognese Casserole (page 59) and my Weeknight Tex-Mex Quinoa with Cashew Sour Cream (page 75), and it's scrumptious heated up and served as a nacho dip with salsa, guacamole, or refried beans. It's also fantastic drizzled over roasted or steamed broccoli or cauliflower (that's a fun way to get kids excited about veggies, too!) or as a dip for celery sticks. Or stir this sauce into cooked pasta (mac and cheese, anyone?) and throw in any veggies you have on hand (think peas or roasted veggies). A big thanks to Jennifer Houston and Ruth Tal's *Super Fresh* cookbook for inspiring this recipe.

1. Place the cashews in a small bowl and add boiling water to cover. Soak for 1 hour, then drain. (Alternatively, soak the cashews in room-temperature water to cover for at least 8 hours or up to overnight, then drain.)

2. To a small pot, add the potatoes and carrots and add water to cover. Bring to a boil, reduce the heat to medium, and simmer for 10 to 15 minutes, until fork-tender. Drain. (Alternatively, you can steam the veggies until fork-tender.)

3. To a high-speed blender, add the drained cashews, potatoes, carrots, oil, water, lemon juice, salt, garlic, nutritional yeast, and vinegar and blend until smooth. If the mixture is too thick or won't blend well, a splash of water or oil can help it along. Taste the sauce and adjust the seasonings as desired.

STORAGE

Store in an airtight container in the fridge for up to 1 week. Not suited for freezing.

Creamy Cashew or Sunflower Aioli

Makes 1 cup • **Soak time** 1 hour or up to overnight • **Active prep time** 5 minutes • **Total time** 5 minutes

½ cup (80 g) raw cashews or sunflower seeds

6 tablespoons water

2 or 3 medium garlic cloves (8 to 12 g), to taste

3 tablespoons plus 1 teaspoon fresh lemon juice, or to taste

¼ to ½ teaspoon fine sea salt, to taste

2 tablespoons nutritional yeast

2 tablespoons vegan mayo

STORAGE

Store in an airtight container in the fridge for 5 to 6 days.

MAKE IT NUT-FREE

Use the sunflower seed option.

MAKE IT SOY-FREE

Use soy-free vegan mayo.

MAKE IT KID-FRIENDLY

Use a little less garlic and lemon juice for a more subtle flavor.

This luscious aioli is an essential complement to so many dishes. I've served it stirred into cooked lentils, poured it over Buddha bowls, and dolloped it on top of my Crispy Smashed Potatoes, Endless Ways (page 173), Italian One-Pot Buttery Tomato, White Beans, and Farro (page 96), and Rebellious Battered Broc-Cauli Burgers (page 113). The fresh garlic and lemon juice make this aioli sing, while the nutritional yeast and vegan mayo lend a lush, creamy texture. If you are a garlic lover, go ahead and use the higher end of the garlic range . . . that's what I do, and I love the flavor punch! If you're not as big of a fan, the lower end of the range will give a subtle yet zippy aioli.

1. Place the cashews in a small bowl and add boiling water to cover. Soak for 1 hour, then drain. (Alternatively, soak the cashews in room-temperature water to cover for at least 8 hours or up to overnight, then drain.)

2. To a high-speed blender, add the drained cashews, water, garlic (start with 2 cloves, or less, if you are sensitive to garlic), lemon juice, salt, nutritional yeast, and mayo. Blend on high until smooth, adding a bit more water, only if needed, for a smooth result. Taste and adjust the salt, garlic, and lemon juice to taste, if desired, until the flavors pop. Transfer to an airtight container or glass jar.

Perfect Basil Pesto

Makes scant 1 cup • **Active prep time** 5 minutes • **Total time** 5 minutes

1 large garlic clove (6 g)

½ cup (80 g) roasted pepitas
(see page 338)*

2 cups packed (50 g) fresh basil leaves

¼ cup extra-virgin olive oil

2 tablespoons water

2 to 3 tablespoons fresh lemon juice

1½ teaspoons nutritional yeast
(optional)

¼ to ½ teaspoon fine sea salt, to taste

This is a tasty pesto to make weekly so you have a batch on hand for using on avocado toast or stirring into pasta, tofu scrambles (such as my School Night Tofu Scramble with Roasted Red Pepper and Walnut Dip, page 78), or The Mama Bear Bowl: Cauli-Power Savory Steel-Cut Oatmeal (page 108). Or try it spread on sandwiches or wraps, or as a seasonal swap for my Crispy Potato Stacks (page 87).

1. In a food processor, process the garlic until minced.

2. Add the pepitas to the food processor with the garlic and process into fine crumbs.

3. Add the basil, oil, water, lemon juice, nutritional yeast, and salt and process until mostly smooth, stopping to scrape down the bowl if necessary. Taste and add more lemon juice, if you'd like more of a lemony kick, and process again.

STORAGE

Store leftovers in an airtight container in the fridge for 1 to 2 weeks, or freeze in a freezer bag with the air pressed out or in an airtight container for up to 6 weeks. The pesto will firm up in the fridge but will soften at room temperature.

TIP

* You can swap out the roasted pepitas for raw cashews. The pesto will be a bit sweeter and will no longer be nut-free.

Lemony Dill Protein Pesto

Makes generous 1 cup • **Active prep time** 10 minutes • **Total time** 10 minutes

3 large garlic cloves (18 g)*

1½ cups lightly packed (40 g) fresh dill (thick stems removed)

⅔ cup (100 g) hemp hearts

¼ cup extra-virgin olive oil

5 tablespoons fresh lemon juice, or to taste

2 tablespoons nutritional yeast

¼ teaspoon plus ⅛ teaspoon fine sea salt, or to taste

TIP

* This is a garlicky pesto. If you aren't a fan of raw garlic, start with 1 clove and add more from there, if desired.

TO MAKE A CASHEW VERSION

Omit the hemp hearts and use ⅔ cup (100 g) raw cashews instead. The pesto will be slightly sweeter and less tangy than the hemp hearts version, and will no longer be nut-free; taste and adjust the flavor with more lemon juice or dill if desired.

MAKE IT KID-FRIENDLY

Use less lemon juice and garlic, depending on your child's tastes.

Three cheers for protein-rich pesto! Using hemp hearts as the base of this zippy, bold pesto adds not only creaminess but also loads of protein, healthy fats, fiber, zinc, iron, and more. It's healthy and flavorful, with a strong lemony punch . . . just the way I like it. Serve this pesto along with Rustic Roasted Carrot and Dill Hummus (page 179) and some raw veggies or crackers for a light yet filling summer meal (and it's a great way to use up the fresh dill). It also adds zing to baked potatoes or home fries (try it as a swap on my Crispy Potato Stacks, page 87) and roasted vegetables. Want to change it into something totally new? You can stir this pesto into vegan mayo to create a delicious dill aioli to use on sandwiches and veggie burgers or as a dip.

1. In a food processor, process the garlic and dill until minced.

2. Add the hemp hearts, oil, lemon juice, nutritional yeast, and salt to the food processor with the garlic and dill and process until super smooth, stopping to scrape down the bowl if the dill and garlic stick to the sides. Let the machine run for a minute or two to break down the hemp hearts and allow the mixture to get super creamy.

3. Taste the pesto and adjust the flavor as desired with additional lemon juice, nutritional yeast, oil, or salt.

STORAGE

Store leftovers in an airtight container in the fridge for up to 5 days, or freeze in a freezer bag with the air pressed out or in an airtight container for up to 6 weeks. The pesto will firm up in the fridge but will soften at room temperature.

Roasted Red Pepper and Walnut Dip

Makes 1 cup • **Active prep time** 5 minutes • **Total time** 5 minutes

1 large garlic clove (6 g)

⅔ cup (70 g) walnut halves

1 cup (175 g) jarred roasted red peppers, drained

1 tablespoon fresh lemon juice, or to taste

1 tablespoon tahini

½ teaspoon ground cumin

½ teaspoon red pepper flakes

¼ teaspoon plus ⅛ teaspoon fine sea salt, or to taste

Freshly ground black pepper

MAKE IT NUT-FREE

Omit the walnuts and substitute ⅔ cup (100 g) roasted pepitas (see page 338).

MAKE IT KID-FRIENDLY

If your child doesn't like dip, try stirring this into pasta.

I created this muhammara-inspired spread one weekend to top a crunchy, fresh-out-of-the-oven crostini, but I soon realized it's incredibly versatile. You can use it as a dip for veggies and crackers, stir it into pasta or stir-fries for an instant flavor pop, or use it as a sweet-and-savory topper for Buddha bowls, roasted veggies, Crispy Smashed Potatoes, Endless Ways (page 173), and my delicious School Night Tofu Scramble (page 78). *Whew*, inspired yet? You can also use it as a swap for the pesto in my Crispy Potato Stacks (page 87). It also keeps well in the fridge, freezes beautifully, uses one bowl, and is ready in 5 minutes. Don't worry if you can't have walnuts—the nut-free version is absolutely delicious as well.

1. In a food processor, process the garlic until minced.

2. Add the walnuts, roasted red peppers, lemon juice, tahini, cumin, red pepper flakes, salt, and black pepper to taste and process until mostly smooth, scraping down the sides of the bowl if needed. Taste and adjust the seasonings, adding more lemon juice, salt, black pepper, or red pepper flakes, if desired, until the flavors pop.

STORAGE

Store in an airtight container in the fridge for up to 3 days. Add a squeeze of lemon juice and a sprinkle of salt to revive the flavors, if desired, to taste. Freeze in a freezer bag with the extra air pressed out or in an airtight container for up to 1 month. Thaw overnight in the refrigerator or on the counter for a few hours.

Italian Herb Parmesan

Makes 1 cup • **Active prep time** 8 minutes • **Total time** 8 minutes

1 to 2 medium garlic cloves (4 to 8 g), to taste

1 tablespoon fresh thyme leaves

1 tablespoon fresh rosemary leaves

1 cup (160 g) roasted pepitas (see page 338) or raw cashews*

2 tablespoons nutritional yeast

1 tablespoon extra-virgin olive oil

1 to 2 teaspoons sherry vinegar, to taste**

¼ teaspoon fine sea salt, or more to taste

TIPS

* If making the raw cashew version, omit the oil, since the cashews naturally release more oil than pepitas do while processing, and using oil in the cashew version results in a sticky consistency.

** Sherry vinegar is my preference in this parmesan (2 teaspoons for a bright pop!), but red wine vinegar will work in a pinch.

Do you have leftover fresh thyme and rosemary? Why not make my Festive Bread-Free Stuffing Balls (page 105) or Portobello Boats with Rosemary-Lentil Crumble and Balsamic-Apple Glaze (page 47)?

MAKE IT NUT-FREE

Use roasted pepitas.

This recipe is an absolute game-changer! I love to experiment with fresh herbs in my vegan parmesan recipes, and when I hit on this combo, I was swept away to my honeymoon stop in Italy. Lemony fresh thyme and peppery, woody fresh rosemary add lovely green, bright notes to this Italian Herb Parmesan. A touch of sherry vinegar makes it all pop. Trust me when I say that you're going to want to eat this one straight from the processor bowl. It really is a flavor bomb topping. Use it with abandon on my Italian Herb Parmesan–Crusted Portobellos with Sneaky Protein-Packed Mashed Potatoes (page 72), Cheesy Lentil Bolognese Casserole (page 59), Humble Creamy Mushrooms and Toast (page 122), Italian One-Pot Buttery Tomato, White Beans, and Farro (page 96), Summery Chimichurri Chickpea Pasta Salad (page 185), Cilantro-Speckled Green Rice and Avocado Stack (page 207), avocado or hummus toast, baked potatoes, salads, and more.

1. In a food processor, process the garlic, thyme, and rosemary until finely chopped.

2. Add the pepitas, nutritional yeast, oil, vinegar, and salt to the food processor with the garlic and herbs and process until coarsely chopped, only 5 to 10 seconds. The parm will be a bit "wet" in texture due to the moisture from the oil and vinegar. Taste and adjust seasonings, if desired.

STORAGE

Store in an airtight container in the fridge for up to 5 days, or freeze in a freezer bag with the air pressed for up to 2 months. There is a slight flavor loss after freezing, so I like to refresh the thawed parm by stirring in a touch of sherry vinegar, salt, and olive oil, to taste.

Pretty Quick-Pickled Red Onions

Makes 2 cups (with brine) • **Active prep time** 5 minutes • **Soak time** I hour • **Total time** I hour 5 minutes

I medium red onion (200 g)

I cup water

¼ cup distilled white vinegar

¼ cup apple cider vinegar

I½ tablespoons natural cane sugar

I½ teaspoons fine sea salt

STORAGE

Store in the jar or in another airtight container in the fridge for up to 3 weeks. Be sure to use a clean utensil, not your fingers, to remove onions from the jar to prevent spoilage.

The first time I "quick pickled" anything, I was truly amazed by how fast and easy it was. I don't quite have the patience to get into canning at this stage in my life (maybe someday, though), so quick-pickling things is perfect for my "I need this done *yesterday*" state of mind. These pickled red onions are a delicious, tangy, crunchy topping for my Sloppy Glows (page 90), Spicy Potato Nacho Plate (page 71), Mega Crunch Sun-Dried Tomato– Pepita Taco Salad (page 204), Bruschetta Veggie Burgers (page 49), Smoky Black Bean and Brown Rice Veggie Burgers (page 131), and Rebellious Battered Broc-Cauli Burgers (page 113). They're pretty, too; the vibrant purple shade of the onion subtly infuses the liquid and looks so gorgeous—I like to set the jar on the table when I have friends over to impress them with my mad quick-pickling skills! For the fastest prep time possible (we're talking mere seconds to slice an onion, here), be sure to use a mandoline (see page 332).

1. Using a mandoline, thinly slice the red onion and transfer 2 cups (130 g) to a heat-safe I- to I½-pint (500 to 750 mL) jar with a lid; reserve any extra onion for another use. Set aside.

2. In a small pot, combine the water, distilled white vinegar, apple cider vinegar, sugar, and salt. Bring to a boil over high heat, then remove from the heat and stir until the sugar and salt have dissolved.

3. Carefully pour the hot liquid into the jar over the onion. Use a spoon to gently push the onion downward into the liquid until fully submerged.

4. Let the jar sit on the counter, uncovered, for I hour. After an hour, you can enjoy the pickled onions right away, or secure the lid and store them in the fridge.

Rosemary and Thyme Mushroom Gravy

Makes 3 cups • **Active prep time** 15 minutes • **Total time** 25 minutes

2 tablespoons extra-virgin olive oil

1 cup (140 g) diced onion

5 or 6 medium garlic cloves (20 to 24 g), minced (2 tablespoons)

8 ounces (225 g) cremini mushrooms

Fine sea salt

2 cups low-sodium vegetable broth, more if needed

6 tablespoons (52 g) light/white spelt flour, more if needed*

2 tablespoons nutritional yeast

½ teaspoon freshly ground black pepper, or to taste

2 teaspoons packed fresh thyme leaves

1½ teaspoons minced fresh rosemary

1 to 1½ teaspoons white wine vinegar, to taste

This is a hearty, rich, and nutritious mushroom gravy accented with aromatic fresh rosemary and thyme. Using umami-rich mushrooms and lively herbs gives the gravy a bright, savory flavor, as well as immune-boosting nutrients. Serve it over my Sneaky Protein-Packed Mashed Potatoes (page 164), Festive Bread-Free Stuffing Balls (page 105), Crispy Smashed Potatoes, Endless Ways (page 173), or a winter-friendly comfort-food power bowl made up of cooked grains, sautéed greens, and roasted or steamed veggies.

1. In a large pot or skillet, heat the oil over medium heat. Add the onions and garlic and stir to coat with the oil. Sauté for 5 to 6 minutes, until softened.

2. Meanwhile, thinly slice the mushrooms (no thicker than 1/16 inch/2 mm) or finely chop them into pea-sized pieces.

3. Add the mushrooms and a small pinch of salt to the pot with the onion and garlic. Stir to combine. Raise the heat to medium-high and sauté, uncovered, for 6 to 8 minutes, until most of the water from the mushrooms cooks off and the mushrooms are tender.

4. Meanwhile, pour the broth into a medium bowl and whisk in all the flour until no lumps remain. Add the nutritional yeast and pepper and whisk to combine.

5. Add the thyme and rosemary to the pot, stir, and sauté for a minute, until fragrant.

Leftover gravy can be stored in an airtight container in the fridge for a few days. It will thicken as it cools. To reheat, gently warm it in a small pot over medium-low heat for 3 to 5 minutes. Add a little broth to the gravy to thin it, if needed.

TIP

* You can use 2 tablespoons all-purpose flour in place of the light/white spelt flour, if you prefer.

MAKE IT GLUTEN-FREE

Swap the spelt flour for 2 tablespoons plus 2 teaspoons Bob's Red Mill Gluten-Free 1 to 1 Baking Flour.

6. Pour the broth mixture into the pot and stir until combined. Simmer, uncovered, whisking frequently, until the gravy thickens, about 3 minutes. Reduce the heat, if necessary, to prevent the mixture from sticking to the pot.

7. Add the vinegar and salt to taste and stir to combine. If the gravy is too thin, you can whisk another tablespoon of light/white spelt flour (or 1 teaspoon white all-purpose flour, if using) with 1 tablespoon water in a small bowl, then whisk this mixture into the gravy until smooth. If the gravy is too thick, you can stir in a splash of broth to thin it.

Oregano, Basil, and Lemon Zest Parmesan

Makes 1½ cups • **Active prep time** 7 minutes • **Total time** 7 minutes

2 medium garlic cloves (8 g)

⅓ cup lightly packed (9 g) fresh basil leaves

2 tablespoons fresh oregano leaves, or 1 teaspoon dried

1 cup (150 g) raw cashews

2 tablespoons nutritional yeast

1 tablespoon extra-virgin olive oil

1 teaspoon lemon zest

1 teaspoon fresh lemon juice

¼ teaspoon plus ⅛ teaspoon fine sea salt, or to taste

STORAGE

Store in an airtight container in the fridge for up to 5 days, or freeze in a freezer bag with the air pressed out or in an airtight container for up to 1 month.

MAKE IT NUT-FREE

Swap the cashews for a mixture of ½ cup (80 g) roasted pepitas (see page 338) and ½ cup (75 g) raw hulled sunflower seeds. I prefer the sweeter flavor of the cashew version, but this is a great nut-free option!

After being a cashew parmesan devotee for years, I've fallen in love with experimenting with herbs and seasonings. This unique Greek-inspired vegan parmesan uses richly scented fresh oregano, basil, and lemon zest to lend so much Mediterranean flavor. Thanks to a touch of olive oil, the texture is moister than traditional cashew parmesan, which gives it a bit of a feta texture—enjoy it on my Glow-rious Greek Pasta (page 193). Even though I created this recipe specifically for the Greek pasta, it's also a fantastic topper for salads, roasted veggies, avocado toast, and more. I hope you have fun with it, customizing the amounts of fresh herbs and garlic to your own taste and using it on, well, everything!

1. To a food processor, add the garlic, basil, and oregano and process until minced.

2. Add the cashews, nutritional yeast, oil, lemon zest, lemon juice, and salt to the food processor. Process for 7 to 15 seconds, until the cashews are coarsely chopped and have the texture of parmesan cheese. Avoid overprocessing, as the mixture will turn into a paste quite quickly. The texture of this parmesan is moist, thanks to the olive oil and fresh herbs, not dry like my other versions.

Apple Pie Spice Mix

Makes 2 tablespoons plus 2 teaspoons • **Active prep time** 3 minutes • **Total time** 3 minutes

2 tablespoons ground cinnamon

¾ teaspoon ground nutmeg

½ to ¾ teaspoon ground cardamom, to taste*

¼ teaspoon ground ginger

¼ teaspoon ground allspice

Apple pie spice can be tricky to locate, depending on the grocery store and time of year, so this recipe comes in handy if you want to mix up your own batch! If you're using store-bought, I've found that the ingredients can differ quite a bit from brand to brand, but the most important thing is that you add the spice mix little by little to suit your own taste. Try this spice mix in my Warm and Gooey Apple Pie Compote (page 235) or sprinkled over vegan vanilla ice cream for a lovely autumn flavor kick. A special thanks to Jamie from *My Baking Addiction* for inspiring this flavorful mix!

Add the cinnamon, nutmeg, cardamom, ginger, and allspice to a small jar. Secure the lid and shake to combine.

STORAGE

Store in the jar in a cupboard for up to 6 months. Shake the jar before each use.

TIP

* Some people are sensitive to the robust flavor of cardamom, so I recommend starting with ½ teaspoon and adding more to taste.

Opposite, left to right: Apple Pie Spice (page 308), Tex-Mex Spice (page 313), Italian Seasoning (page 312), Pumpkin Pie Spice (page 311)

VEGAN • GLUTEN-FREE • NUT-FREE • SOY-FREE • GRAIN-FREE • OIL-FREE
RAW/NO BAKE • KID-FRIENDLY • ONE BOWL

Pumpkin Pie Spice Mix

Makes 6 tablespoons • **Active prep time** 3 minutes • **Total time** 3 minutes

2 tablespoons plus 2 teaspoons ground cinnamon

1 tablespoon plus 1 teaspoon ground ginger

2 teaspoons packed freshly grated nutmeg

2 teaspoons ground allspice

1 teaspoon ground cloves

Use this delightful pumpkin pie spice in my Solid Gold Pumpkin Pie Spice Coconut Latte (page 264) and Pumpkin Spice and Everything Nice Salad (page 191). It really is the most delicious thing sprinkled on roasted sweet potatoes with sea salt and a drizzle of pure maple syrup. You can even add it to Coconut Whipped Cream (see page 322) to make an autumn-friendly flavored version! I like to keep a large batch on hand because I find myself using it in (and on) just about everything throughout the fall and winter seasons . . . cakes, cookies, bars, oatmeal, smoothies, lattes, chia seed pudding, and more. It's sure to perk up any gloomy-weather day! And if you're looking for a last-minute host or hostess gift, look no further. Simply assemble the spice mix in a small glass jar (feel free to double the recipe, if need be), pop a tag and ribbon on it, and you have a lovely edible gift that'll keep on giving all season long! Thanks to Nicole Axworthy and Lisa Pitman's cookbook, *DIY Vegan*, for inspiring this recipe.

Add the cinnamon, ginger, nutmeg, allspice, and cloves to a small jar. Secure the lid and shake well to combine.

STORAGE
Store in the jar in a cupboard for up to 6 months. Shake the jar before each use.

Italian Seasoning

Makes ¼ cup • **Active prep time** 5 minutes • **Total time** 5 minutes

1 tablespoon dried oregano

2 teaspoons dried marjoram

2 teaspoons dried thyme

2 teaspoons dried basil

1 teaspoon dried rosemary

1 teaspoon dried sage

I use this handy Italian Seasoning in many of my recipes. It's a great one to make ahead and keep on hand in your spice rack! I created this spice mix to be salt-free, so you have control over the sodium content of your recipe. This recipe can easily be doubled or tripled, if you think you'll use it often. Try it in my Humble Creamy Mushrooms and Toast (page 122), Italian One-Pot Buttery Tomato, White Beans, and Farro (page 96), or Cheesy Lentil Bolognese Casserole (page 59). I love the Simply Organics brand of Italian seasoning (after which this recipe was modeled!), so feel free to substitute that if you're running short on your homemade mix (or time).

Add the oregano, marjoram, thyme, basil, rosemary, and sage to a small jar. Secure the lid and shake to combine.

STORAGE

Store in the jar in a cupboard for up to 6 months. Shake the jar before each use.

TIP

For this seasoning mix, be sure to use whole-leaf dried herbs, not ground. Ground versions of herbs like sage and rosemary will be much more potent, and their flavor could be overpowering.

Tex-Mex Spice Blend

Makes 2 tablespoons plus 1¼ teaspoons • **Active prep time** 2 minutes • **Total time** 2 minutes

1 tablespoon chili powder

1½ teaspoons ground cumin

1 teaspoon smoked sweet paprika, or
½ teaspoon paprika

¼ teaspoon cayenne pepper

¾ teaspoon fine sea salt*

¼ teaspoon ground coriander

Use this spice mix in my Tex-Mex Flavor Bombs (page 314) or Weeknight Tex-Mex Quinoa with Cashew Sour Cream (page 75), or simply as a seasoning for power bowls, tofu, roasted chickpeas, and my 20-Minute Sweet Potato Noodle Bowl with Sesame, Cilantro, Lime, and Avocado (page 102) for the quickest flavor kick. One of my pals, Katie, calls it "the best Tex-Mex flavoring ever!" and I'd have to agree! I hope it will be a hit at your house, too.

Add the chili powder, cumin, paprika, cayenne, salt, and coriander to a small jar. Secure the lid and shake to combine.

Double-Batch Tex-Mex Spice Blend

2 tablespoons chili powder, 1 tablespoon ground cumin, 2 teaspoons smoked sweet paprika (or 1 teaspoon paprika), ½ teaspoon cayenne pepper, 1½ teaspoons fine sea salt*, ½ teaspoon ground coriander. This makes ¼ cup plus 2½ teaspoons.

STORAGE

Store in the jar in a cupboard for up to 6 months. Shake the jar before each use.

TIP

* If you are sensitive to salt, you can use a bit less than what is called for.

Tex-Mex Flavor Bombs

Makes 9 (2-tablespoon) bombs • **Active prep time** 15 minutes • **Total time** 15 minutes

4 large garlic cloves (24 g)

I medium jalapeño (50 g), seeded and coarsely chopped (⅓ cup)*

I small red bell pepper (180 g), coarsely chopped (I cup)

2 medium green onions (35 g), coarsely chopped (heaping ⅓ cup)

I teaspoon garlic powder

I teaspoon dried oregano

½ to I teaspoon sriracha, to taste

¼ cup Tex-Mex Spice Blend (page 313)

¼ cup tomato paste

2 teaspoons fresh lime juice

TIPS

* I recommend using a mild jalapeño, not a hot one. Jalapeños are typically mild, but the older the jalapeño is, the spicier it will be. You can tell if a jalapeño is older because it'll have raised white lines along the skin of the pepper. Younger jalapeños will have smooth skin and will be much milder.

If you don't have a silicone muffin mold or ice cube tray, spoon the mixture into paper muffin liners.

MAKE IT KID-FRIENDLY

Swap out the jalapeño for more chopped red bell pepper, and use ½ teaspoon sriracha.

Most days, I love to take my time with a recipe, adding herbs and spices to get the dish just right. Often, though, the time just isn't there. Recently, I found myself craving fast, simple meals where I could throw a few ingredients into a pot and be done. These smoky, lightly spicy Tex-Mex Flavor Bombs are the solution to this dilemma. Make a batch to have on hand for meals like my Fast Family Fajitas (page 53), or to add to cooked grains or simple stir-fries for a lightning-fast Tex-Mex-inspired meal.

1. In a food processor, process the garlic until minced.

2. Add the jalapeño, bell pepper, green onions, garlic powder, oregano, ½ teaspoon of the sriracha, the Tex-Mex Spice Blend, tomato paste, and lime juice to the food processor with the garlic. Process for about I minute, until smooth, stopping to scrape down the bowl as needed. Taste and add more sriracha, if desired. (Keep in mind that this is concentrated flavor and it's not supposed to taste that good in its undiluted form! So don't worry if you don't love the taste straight out of the processor; once it's mixed into fajitas, it'll be fantastic!)

3. You can use the Tex-Mex Flavor Bombs right away or freeze for later use. To freeze, spoon 2 tablespoons of the mixture into each cavity of a silicone muffin mold or ice cube tray (you should have about 9 "bombs"). Once the bombs are solid, transfer them to a freezer bag with the air pressed out or in an airtight container and freeze until needed.

STORAGE

Store the mixture in an airtight container in the fridge for up to 5 days, or freeze as directed above for up to 2 months.

Vegan Parmesan

Makes ½ cup plus 3 tablespoons • **Active prep time** 3 minutes • **Total time** 3 minutes

1 medium garlic clove (4 g)*

½ cup (80 g) raw cashews or pepitas (see page 338)

2 tablespoons nutritional yeast

¼ to ½ teaspoon fine sea salt, to taste

STORAGE

Store in an airtight container in the fridge for up to 2 weeks, or freeze in a freezer bag with the air pressed out or in an airtight container for up to 2 months.

TIP

* You can swap out the garlic clove for ¼ teaspoon garlic powder—just add it when you add the salt. Fresh garlic tastes so much better, though, so do try to use fresh whenever you can!

MAKE IT NUT-FREE

Use the pepita option.

Vegan Parmesan is a little trick I like to keep handy in my fridge or freezer. When a dish needs a little jazzing up or when I'm serving a dish to someone I want to impress, I pull out this Vegan Parmesan and scatter a little (or a lot!) on top of the meal. It works like magic to add a savory, slightly cheesy flavor and subtle crunch. From the simplest avocado toast to more involved casseroles, its subtly sweet, garlicky notes enhance a variety of recipes and dishes. In this recipe, I provide the original "cheesy" cashew version as well as a nut-free pepita version . . . both are enchanting atop dishes like my Ultimate Creamy Salt-and-Vinegar Scalloped Potatoes (page 147), Game Night Crispy Potato Bruschetta (page 176), or Italian One-Pot Buttery Tomato, White Beans, and Farro (page 96). One of the easiest ways to serve it is scattered all over a simple marinated kale salad, such as my Pumpkin Spice and Everything Nice Salad (page 191).

1. In a food processor, process the garlic until minced.

2. Add the cashews, nutritional yeast, and salt to the food processor with the garlic. Process into a coarse meal, 10 to 15 seconds.

5-Ingredient Vegan Butter

Makes 9 tablespoons • **Active prep time** 5 minutes • **Chill time** 2 to 4 hours • **Total time** 2 to 4 hours

3 tablespoons aquafaba (canned chickpea brine)*

¼ teaspoon fine sea salt

¼ teaspoon apple cider vinegar

¼ cup plus 3 tablespoons refined coconut oil**

1 tablespoon plus 1 teaspoon extra-virgin olive oil

Ground turmeric, for color (optional)

This rich vegan butter can be stirred into hot savory oats (like my Mama Bear Bowl: Cauli-Power Savory Steel-Cut Oatmeal, page 108), pasta, and even my Easy Sea Salt Vanilla Caramel (page 325). You can also use it in my Balsamic Roasted Root Vegetable Medley with Thyme and Cayenne (page 139), Sneaky Protein-Packed Mashed Potatoes (page 164), or Italian One-Pot Buttery Tomato, White Beans, and Farro (page 96). I absolutely love slathering a generous layer on a slice of my One-Bowl Vegan Banana Bread (page 255), fresh out of the oven. The only caveat is that this base recipe isn't very *spreadable*, but I've included a variation that'll give you butter with a spreadable consistency similar to store-bought vegan butter! This recipe is lightly adapted from Nina's Game Changing Vegan Butter with Aquafaba on her blog, *PlantePusherne*—thanks for the inspiration, Nina!

1. In a tall narrow container (I use the one that came with my immersion blender), place the aquafaba, salt, and vinegar (make sure it's only ¼ teaspoon!). Set aside.

2. In a small pot, melt the coconut oil over low heat. Once two-thirds of the oil has melted, remove it from the heat and stir until fully melted. Stir the olive oil into the melted coconut oil.

3. Place the immersion blender into the container with the aquafaba mixture and turn it on. (Since there's so little liquid, I like to tilt the container and blender at a bit of an angle to help it along.) Blend for 1 minute, until the aquafaba is white and frothy.

recipe continues

recipe continued from previous page

STORAGE

Store in an airtight container in the fridge for up to 2 weeks, or freeze in a freezer bag with the air pressed out or in an airtight container for up to 1 month. If frozen, thaw in the fridge before using. The refrigerated butter will be very firm; let it stand on the counter at room temperature to soften. (A bit of condensation will form on its surface—this is totally normal! Simply pour it off the butter before use.) I like to portion my vegan butter into a silicone mini ice cube mold so I can pop out handy single servings to soften on the counter as needed.

TIPS

* Aquafaba (canned chickpea brine) is the liquid found in a can of chickpeas. The next time you open a can of chickpeas, simply drain them over a bowl and store the liquid in an airtight container in the fridge for up to 3 days to use in recipes that call for aquafaba.

** It's important to use refined coconut oil so it doesn't impart any coconut flavor (unless you don't mind that, in which case, by all means use virgin coconut oil).

4. Add a sprinkle or two of turmeric (if using) to the mixture and blend for a few seconds to combine.

5. With the blender running, slowly stream the melted oil mixture into the aquafaba mixture, about a teaspoon at a time, to emulsify the oil. This will take a couple of minutes or so. The butter mixture will look white, silky, and similar in appearance to mayonnaise (but a bit thinner).

6. Transfer the butter mixture to a small airtight container and chill in the fridge, uncovered, for 2 to 4 hours, until completely solid. If for some reason your butter doesn't firm in the fridge (this can happen occasionally), transfer it to the freezer and chill until solid, then store it in the fridge.

Spreadable Vegan Butter

Are you looking for a spreadable consistency? Simply add ¼ teaspoon liquid sunflower lecithin and ⅟₁₆ teaspoon xanthan gum to the container with the aquafaba, salt, and vinegar in step 1 of the recipe and continue as directed. Allow the refrigerated butter to sit on the counter for 15 to 25 minutes before using, to soften to a spreadable texture.

Cashew Sour Cream

Makes 2 cups • **Soak time** 1 hour or up to overnight • **Active prep time** 5 minutes • **Total time** 5 minutes

1½ cups (225 g) raw cashews

¾ cup water

2 tablespoons fresh lemon juice

2 teaspoons apple cider vinegar

½ teaspoon fine sea salt, or to taste

STORAGE

Store in an airtight container in the fridge for up to 1 week, or freeze in a freezer bag with the air pressed out or in an airtight container for up to 6 weeks. I like to freeze the Cashew Sour Cream in a silicone mini-muffin mold so I always have individual portions on hand, ready to go! Simply divide it among the cavities of the mold and freeze until solid, then pop them out of the mold, transfer to a freezer bag or airtight container, and freeze until ready to use.

TIP

Looking for a nut-free option? Try my Sunflower Aioli (see page 293) instead. While it's not an exact swap for Cashew Sour Cream, it's delicious and creamy in its own right!

This multipurpose Cashew Sour Cream can be used in a variety of dishes, such as my Creamy Mushroom, Green Bean, and Wild Rice Casserole (page 153), Spicy Potato Nacho Plate (page 71), Fast Family Fajitas (page 53), and Weeknight Tex-Mex Quinoa (page 75), to name a few. And it's an absolute dream swirled into my Sloppy Glows (page 90)! You can also use Cashew Sour Cream on sandwiches, wraps, or vegan nachos, or stir it into salad dressings, chili, soup, savory oatmeal, and more. The recipe makes a generous amount, but it freezes and thaws beautifully. I love to freeze my leftover sour cream in a silicone mini-muffin mold. That way, I can thaw individual servings on a whim. How's that for easy?

1. Place the cashews in a small bowl and add boiling water to cover. Soak for 1 hour, then drain. (Alternatively, soak the cashews in room-temperature water to cover for at least 8 hours or up to overnight, then drain.)

2. Transfer the drained cashews to a high-speed blender and add the water, lemon juice, vinegar, and salt. Blend on high until smooth, stopping to scrape down the sides of the blender if necessary. You can add a splash more water if needed to help it along.

3. Use immediately or transfer to an airtight container and store for later use.

Half-Batch Cashew Sour Cream (makes 1 cup)

¾ cup (115 g) raw cashews (soaked as directed), 6 tablespoons water (plus more if needed), 1 tablespoon fresh lemon juice, 1 teaspoon apple cider vinegar, ¼ teaspoon fine sea salt, or more to taste.

Coconut Whipped Cream

Makes ¾ to 1 cup • **Chill time** 24 hours • **Active prep time** 5 minutes • **Total time** 5 minutes

1 (14-ounce/398 mL) can full-fat coconut milk, chilled for 24 hours*

1 to 2 tablespoons sweetener (maple syrup, vegan confectioners' sugar, cane sugar, etc.), to taste

1 vanilla bean, split lengthwise and seeds scraped, or ½ teaspoon pure vanilla extract

With as little as three ingredients and 5 minutes of work, you can have your lucky self a bowl of lightly sweet, fluffy, dreamy coconut whipped cream! I like to dollop it on top of my O Canada! Spiced Maple Cream Torte with Warm and Gooey Apple Pie Compote (page 233) and 6-Ingredient Chocolate Peanut Butter Oat Crumble Squares (page 252). It's a quick, simple "dress up" for humble bowls of sliced fruit at a special occasion breakfast, and adds a light, summery feel to a fruit crisp. The options are endless! You'll want to chill the can of coconut milk for at least 24 hours before you begin to ensure that the white coconut cream solidifies and separates from the coconut water in the can. However, if your room-temperature can doesn't make a "sloshing" sound when it's shaken, this is a good sign that your coconut cream is already solid and scoopable.

1. Chill the can of coconut milk in the fridge for 24 hours.

2. About 1 hour before making the coconut whipped cream, place a large bowl or the bowl of a stand mixer in the freezer to chill (this helps the cream stay cold while you beat it).

3. Open the chilled can of coconut milk and scoop the solid white cream from the top into the chilled bowl (you should have ¾ to 1 cup). Do not add the coconut water (the clearish liquid left in the can)—store it in the fridge for another use, such as a smoothie or coconut water ice cubes.

Store in an airtight container in the fridge for up to 1 week, or freeze in a freezer bag with the air pressed out or in an airtight container for up to 1 month. After storing in the fridge or freezer, allow it to sit at room temperature until it softens slightly, then rewhip it if needed.

TIP

* Some brands of canned coconut milk are better than others for making Coconut Whipped Cream. I find these brands give the most consistent results: Native Forest, Trader Joe's Organic Coconut Cream, and Earth's Choice. Be sure to select full-fat coconut milk, not anything labeled "light."

4. Using a handheld mixer or a stand mixer fitted with the whisk attachment, beat the cream until fluffy and smooth, 15 to 30 seconds.

5. Add the sweetener, to taste, and the vanilla seeds and beat until smooth, 10 to 15 seconds more. Be careful not to overwhip the cream. As soon as your coconut cream reaches an airy, whipped texture, stop whipping. Overwhipping can result in the whipped cream getting too hot and returning to its "nonwhipped" state.

6. Cover the bowl and refrigerate the whipped cream until ready to use.

Pumpkin Spice Coconut Whipped Cream

Add ½ to 1 teaspoon pumpkin pie spice, homemade (page 311) or store-bought, to taste. Mmm!

Easy Sea Salt Vanilla Caramel

Makes scant 1 cup • **Active prep time** 3 minutes • **Chill time** 24 hours • **Total time** 12 minutes

1 (14-ounce/398 mL) can full-fat coconut milk*

¾ cup (120 g) coconut sugar**

¼ to ½ teaspoon fine sea salt, to taste

1 teaspoon pure vanilla extract

With just four ingredients, you can whip up a decadent salted vegan caramel sauce in only 12 minutes. This caramel adds dreamy luxury to so many recipes . . . where do I even begin? Enjoy it drizzled over my vegan ice cream, 6-Ingredient Chocolate Peanut Butter Oat Crumble Squares (page 252), O Canada! Spiced Maple Cream Torte with Warm and Gooey Apple Pie Compote (page 233), Warm and Gooey Apple Pie Compote (page 235), stirred into my Solid Gold Pumpkin Pie Spice Coconut Latte (page 264) for a special occasion, or as a dip for sliced apples. Just keep in mind that it's very important that you use coconut sugar or Sucanat for this caramel to work (see Tip).

1. Chill the can of coconut milk in the fridge for 24 hours.

2. Open the chilled can of coconut milk and scoop the solid white cream from the top into a medium pot (ideally, you should have 1 cup cream, but ¾ cup works in a pinch). Do not add the coconut water (the clearish liquid left in the can)— store it in the fridge for another use, such as a smoothie or coconut water ice cubes.

3. Set the pot over low heat and allow the coconut cream to melt.

4. Stir the sugar and salt into the melted coconut cream until combined. Increase the heat to medium and bring the mixture to a simmer, stirring a few times. Reduce the heat to medium-low and *gently* simmer (there should be a gentle bubble), uncovered, for 8 to 10 minutes, until golden brown and slightly

recipe continues

recipe continued from previous page

STORAGE

Store in the jar or in an airtight container in the fridge for 7 to 10 days, or freeze in a freezer bag with the air pressed out or in an airtight container for up to 1 month. It will thicken when chilled. Return the caramel to a liquid state by scooping it into a pot and warming it gently over low heat.

TIPS

* Chilling the can of full-fat coconut milk solidifies the coconut cream so it separates from the coconut water, making the coconut cream easy to scoop out to use in recipes. But if the coconut cream in your can of coconut milk is already solid, you don't need to chill it beforehand. Shake the can—if you don't hear or feel any liquid sloshing around inside, it's solid. If you hear a lot of sloshing when you shake the can, be sure to chill it as directed in the recipe.

** I prefer the flavor of coconut sugar, but Sucanat works, too (the flavor just isn't as "caramel-like," in my humble opinion). Unfortunately, natural cane sugar and processed white sugar *do not* work in this recipe, so please don't swap those in or you will cry, and then I will cry, and nobody wants that.

UP THE GLOW

If you have any of my 5-Ingredient Vegan Butter (page 318) on hand, stir a few teaspoons into the caramel when you add the vanilla for an even more luxurious treat.

thickened (there's no need to stir it during this time, but reduce the heat as necessary to prevent burning).

5. Remove from the heat and stir in the vanilla. Transfer the caramel to a heat-safe jar and let it sit on the counter for about 20 minutes to cool slightly, then serve immediately or cover and refrigerate until ready to use.

Authentic-Tasting Vegan Feta Cheese

Makes 3 to 4 cups • **Active prep time** 10 minutes
Chill time 1 hour 30 minutes • **Total time** 1 hour 40 minutes

1 (12-ounce/350 g) block extra-firm or firm tofu

½ cup refined coconut oil*

2 tablespoons plus 2 teaspoons fresh lemon juice, or more to taste

1½ tablespoons apple cider vinegar, or more to taste

1¼ to 1¾ teaspoons fine sea salt, to taste

2 to 3 teaspoons dried oregano, for garnish

In my early twenties, I had a bit of a feta obsession (I say "a bit," but in fact, I rarely ate a salad without it), and it is something I've missed dearly since committing to a plant-based diet. I'll be the first to admit that tofu-based feta doesn't sound very appealing, but you'll just have to trust me on this one . . . this really does taste eerily similar to dairy-based feta! This tofu feta features protein, B vitamins, omega-3 fatty acids, and more, and it's tangy, salty, and addictive. It's my new favorite topper! It's absolutely delicious served with my Bruschetta Veggie Burgers (page 49), Glow-rious Greek Pasta with Oregano, Basil, and Lemon Zest Parmesan (page 193), and Humble Creamy Mushrooms and Toast (page 122). Try crumbling it over a traditional Greek salad, or even avocado toast with a little sliced cucumber and tomato (out of this world). You can make this feta as mild- or powerful-tasting as you please. If you follow the recipe as written, the flavor will be similar to that of "traditional" feta, but if you prefer a sharper, more intense feta, feel free to add more lemon juice, apple cider vinegar, and salt to suit your taste. Due to the refined coconut oil, this feta will melt when heated, so it's not to be cooked with. When serving it with warm food, I suggest adding it as a garnish right before serving so it doesn't soften too much. A huge thanks to Rob, Ben, and Alex from Virtuous Pie, a popular Canadian vegan restaurant, for inspiring this recipe!

recipe continues

recipe continued from previous page

STORAGE

Store in an airtight container in the fridge for up to 1 week or in the freezer for up to 2 weeks. I like to cube it before freezing, and thaw as many cubes as I need by setting them on the counter for 30 to 45 minutes.

TIP

* Using refined coconut oil ensures there will be no detectable coconut flavor in the feta.

1. Using a tofu press, press the tofu for 30 minutes. If you don't have a tofu press, wrap the tofu block in a couple of absorbent kitchen towels, place it on a large plate or cutting board, set another plate on top of the tofu, and stack several heavy books on top of the plate.

2. Line an 8- or 9-inch (2 or 2.5 L) square pan with two pieces of parchment paper placed perpendicular to each other, cut to fit the width of the pan with a few inches of overhang on each side.

3. In a small pot, melt the coconut oil over low heat.

4. Break the pressed tofu into 6 to 8 chunks and put them in a food processor. Add the melted coconut oil, lemon juice (starting with 2 tablespoons plus 1 teaspoon), vinegar, and salt (starting with 1¼ teaspoons). Process until very smooth, about 45 seconds. The mixture will be thick.

5. Taste and add more lemon juice and salt, if desired. (I like to add a bit more lemon juice and vinegar than called for and around 1¾ teaspoons salt.) The feta mixture should taste tangy and salty. Process again to combine.

6. Using a spatula, spoon the feta mixture into the prepared pan. Gently spread it to cover the bottom of the pan. Sprinkle the oregano over the top and press down lightly to adhere.

7. Refrigerate, uncovered, for 1 hour 30 minutes to 2 hours, until firm to the touch. After chilling, it will be semifirm but still slightly soft. Using the overhanging parchment, remove the feta from the pan. Break up the feta and crumble it with your hands, or simply chop it into tiny cubes.

Dreamy Peanut Butter Sauce with Ginger and Lime

Makes ¾ cup • **Active prep time** 7 minutes • **Total time** 7 minutes

1 large garlic clove (6 g)

1 teaspoon grated fresh ginger
(I use a Microplane)

3 to 4 tablespoons water

6 tablespoons smooth natural peanut butter

2 tablespoons plus 1 teaspoon fresh lime juice

2 tablespoons grapeseed oil

1 tablespoon low-sodium tamari

2 teaspoons pure maple syrup, or to taste

1 teaspoon sriracha, or to taste

¼ teaspoon fine sea salt, or to taste

STORAGE

Store in an airtight container in the fridge for up to 4 days.

MAKE IT SOY-FREE

Swap the low-sodium tamari for 1 tablespoon coconut aminos (soy-free seasoning sauce).

Hello, dreamboat (am I the only one who talks to my food this way?). This sauce is rich and nutty from the peanut butter, tangy from the lime, warming thanks to the fresh ginger and sriracha, and garlicky, all at once. A touch of sweetener balances it all out into a sauce you won't be able to stop eating. Drizzle it generously over my Dreamy Peanut Butter Crunch Veggie Noodle Bowls (page 127). It also makes a quick, flavorful dressing (with a bit of protein from the peanut butter) for salads, noodles, cooked veggies, or crispy tofu (drizzle it over my Cast-Iron Tofu from *Oh She Glows Every Day*, page 137!). For convenience and a simple cleanup, I use my small 4-cup food processor when making this dressing.

1. In a food processor, process the garlic until minced.

2. Add the ginger, water (starting with 3 tablespoons), peanut butter, lime juice, oil, low-sodium tamari, maple syrup, and sriracha. Process until smooth, adding up to a few teaspoons more water if the sauce is a bit thick (keep in mind that it will thicken as it sits). Taste, season with salt, and process briefly to combine. If you'd like the sauce a bit sweeter, you can add a touch more maple syrup. The sauce will have a thin, pourable consistency.

OSG House Sauce

Makes generous ¾ cup • **Active prep time** 5 minutes • **Total time** 5 minutes

6 tablespoons ketchup

6 tablespoons vegan mayo

1 tablespoon Dijon mustard

2 or 3 medium garlic cloves (8 to 12 g), minced

6 tablespoons finely chopped dill pickles or sweet pickles (optional)

Eric says this irresistible house sauce is worth buying this book for all on its own! I'd have to agree. With just four ingredients and a minute to whisk together, it brings any veggie burger or bite to the next level, such as my Smoky Black Bean and Brown Rice Veggie Burgers (page 131).

In a small bowl, whisk together the ketchup, mayo, Dijon, garlic, and pickles (if using) until combined. The sauce will have a slightly thin, spreadable consistency.

STORAGE

Store leftover sauce in an airtight container in the fridge for up to 4 days.

MAKE IT SOY-FREE

Use soy-free vegan mayo.

KITCHEN TOOLS
and APPLIANCES

These are the tools and appliances I use all the time in my kitchen, from basic $5 gadgets to investment appliances that make cooking so much easier.

KITCHEN TOOLS

Reusable glass, stainless-steel, or silicone straws

We have a small supply of wide glass, stainless-steel, and silicone straws. The kids love the silicone straws, especially the wide-mouth ones for smoothies. I use them all the time for my Mint, Ginger, and Lemon Sparkling Sipper (page 268); Immunity Glo Shot (page 263, if I'm drinking it in water, to keep my tooth enamel safe); and iced Solid Gold Pumpkin Pie Spice Coconut Latte (page 264). Bonus: Kids love using the mini straw-cleaning brushes . . . delegate whenever possible, I say!

Glass canning jars

I use glass for storage whenever possible, and mason jars are my favorite way to store things like dressings, pestos, and sauces. I also use them for storing nut milks, smoothies, leftovers (such as soups or grain salads), and dry ingredients. I love a variety of sizes, from 1/2 cup for leftover pestos, like my Pretty Parsley-Cilantro Pepita Pesto (page 275) or Perfect Basil Pesto (page 294), to 2 quarts for larger recipes, like Hunky Heartbeet Cabbage Soup (page 229) or Heavenly Chili-Spiced Jalapeño and Garlic Veggie Stew (page 223).

Chef's knife and paring knife

A good chef's knife and paring knife are essential in any kitchen—especially kitchens where lots of vegetables get sliced, diced, and chopped! One of my faves is my Wüsthof Gourmet 8-inch vegetable knife, and I use it every day. Be sure to invest in a knife sharpener so you can keep your knives sharp. Dull knives are more likely to slip while you're cutting your ingredients, which makes them more dangerous than sharp ones!

Microplane rasp grater

Microplane graters are wonderful for zesting citrus, grating fresh ginger or whole spices like nutmeg, or—my favorite use—grating chocolate directly onto a dessert! They're inexpensive and versatile, and they handle fine jobs with more finesse than box graters.

Mandoline

A mandoline is just the right time-saving tool for obtaining thin, uniform slices of hard and soft veggies and fruits. A mandoline allows me to easily slice 2 pounds of potatoes in just 2 minutes! My go-to mandoline is the OXO Steel Chef's Mandoline Slicer 2.0. Try this magic trick out for yourself when making my Ultimate Creamy Salt-and-Vinegar Scalloped Potatoes (page 147), or give it a whirl slicing onions for my Pretty Quick-Pickled Red Onions (page 302). Don't forget to use the food holder piece to protect your fingers from the sharp blade.

Reusable glass storage containers
I've tried a few brands over the years and I really love freezer-friendly Glasslock glass storage containers. I bought a set years ago in various sizes and they've been my go-to food storage containers ever since. The larger sizes are perfect for large-yield recipes like my Summery Chimichurri Chickpea Pasta Salad (page 185) or big batches of soup. Medium ones are ideal for freezing batches of my 6-Ingredient Chocolate Peanut Butter Oat Crumble Squares (page 252) or Fastest No-Bake Jammy Oat Crumble Squares (page 239) for speedy breakfasts, and the smallest ones are great for keeping my favorite sauces on hand, like my Creamy Cashew or Sunflower Aioli (page 293).

Large rimmed baking sheets
Rimmed baking sheets are perfect for roasting things like vegetables and chickpeas. The rimmed edge prevents spills and escapee chickpeas. I recommend getting the largest size baking sheet that will fit in your oven, so that you can maximize space. I have an extra-large (15 by 21-inch) rimmed baking sheet that gets tons of use!

Smaller baking pans and dishes
I use my 9 by 5-inch loaf pans and 8- and 9-inch square baking pans for so many baking recipes. The loaf pan is perfect for quick breads, such as my One-Bowl Vegan Banana Bread (page 255), and freezer treats, like my 6-Ingredient Chocolate Peanut Butter Oat Crumble Squares (page 252). My square baking pans are just right for making my Authentic-Tasting Vegan Feta Cheese (page 327). I love my 9-inch glass pie dish for frozen desserts, such as my O Canada! Spiced Maple Torte with Warm and Gooey Apple Pie Compote (page 233). I have a well-loved 9 by 13-inch glass casserole dish that bakes the perfect Cheesy Lentil Bolognese Casserole (page 59) and Ultimate Creamy Salt-and-Vinegar Scalloped Potatoes (page 147) every time!

Silicone muffin/mini-muffin mold or ice cube trays
I always have at least one of these in my freezer at all times, chilling individual servings of Cashew Sour Cream (page 321), Chia Seed Jam (page 279), or Tex-Mex Flavor Bombs (page 314). They are ideal for freezing small amounts of recipes before transferring them to an airtight container for longer freezing. I love having these single servings at the ready whenever I need them, and they are such a time- and effort-saver. When I don't have a silicone mold available, I line a regular muffin tin with If You Care paper liners, which never stick!

Ice pop molds
Not necessary, but dare I say a necessity with little kiddos in the house! I love making quick batches of ice pops for the kids, like my Brainchild Cherry-Lemon Coconut Cream Pops (page 241). I like Zoku brand mini pop molds—they're the perfect size for small hands—and I also have some standard-sized molds on hand for larger pops.

Metal potato masher
I use mine all the time for gently pressing potatoes, pureeing small amounts of soup or stew

right in the pot (whenever I need a bit of thickening action), and smashing chickpeas.

Silicone pastry brush
Such a simple kitchen item, but I use mine all the time! It's ideal for brushing oil onto potato rounds before baking or onto veggies before grilling. It's also handy for swirling a little oil over a skillet before cooking.

Citrus juicer
It's no secret that I'm obsessed with my OXO double-sided citrus juicer, and I've been using it for years. There's something satisfying about squeezing the heck out of my lemons, limes, oranges, and grapefruits and knowing that I got every last drop. This small, nonelectric device consists of a double-sided reamer that sits over a container, which collects the juice, and it extracts much more juice than simply squeezing citrus by hand. It's especially useful for recipes that call for a good amount of citrus juice, but really, I use it every time I need fresh citrus juice. Plus, it's dishwasher-friendly!

Kitchen scale
A kitchen scale will only set you back between 10 and 20 bucks, but it's worth its weight in gold. I use my scale for measuring flour (weighing flour really helps with the accuracy of baked goods), as well as vegetables and fruit, or whenever a recipe requires precision.

Enameled Dutch oven
Enameled Dutch ovens are not cheap, but dang it, they really last a lifetime, and they are so handy for making soups, stews, chili, and casseroles. The cast iron distributes heat evenly, while the lid keeps heat trapped within the pot as you cook. Since they last forever, you may be able to find one at a local garage sale or online. If not, Le Creuset and Staub brands can't be beat. I also have a large enameled Dutch oven from Costco (Kirkland brand) that, over the years, has proven to be durable and high-quality. Don't throw it in the dishwasher, though, as the detergents can etch and damage the enamel. I love using an enameled Dutch oven for making and serving my Mmm! Maple Baked Beans and Greens (page 81) and Italian One-Pot Buttery Tomato, White Beans, and Farro (page 96) for the coziest and prettiest presentation.

5- to 6-quart pot and steamer insert
I adore my 5.5-quart Zwilling pot and steamer insert. They've stood the test of time, and I use them at least a couple of times a week for steaming veggies and cooking pastas and soups. It's also handy for steaming the cauliflower when I'm making the stovetop version of The Mama Bear Bowl: Cauli-Power Savory Steel-Cut Oatmeal (page 108) and Cauliflower "Potato" Salad (page 203).

Cast-iron grill pan
A cast-iron grill pan is definitely not an essential, but I love it for year-round stovetop grilling when it's too cold to barbecue outdoors. Not to worry if you don't have one, though—you can get away with using a regular skillet (or a cast-iron one).

Nonstick skillet
I love my reliable 12-inch nonstick skillet for making pancakes like my Savory Herb and Veggie Chickpea Pancakes (page 116), or sautéing vegetables for recipes, like Fast Family Fajitas (page 53). GreenPan is a brand that I have used for many years with success.

Julienne peeler or vegetable spiralizer

Julienne peelers and vegetable spiralizers allow you to create fun ribbon- and spaghetti-shaped strands of fresh vegetables, including zucchini, carrots, beets, sweet potatoes, and more. I use a Kuhn Rikon julienne peeler and a World Cuisine vegetable spiralizer for quick-and-easy veggie "pasta" dishes. With the growth of the spiralizing trend over the years, there are many, many brands on the market you can check out. I use my spiralizer when making my 20-Minute Sweet Potato Noodle Bowl with Sesame, Cilantro, Lime, and Avocado (page 102) and Glow-rious Greek Pasta with Oregano, Basil, and Lemon Zest Parmesan (page 193).

Spring-release ice cream/cookie scoop

A spring-release ice cream/cookie scoop is my go-to for scooping even portions of batter into muffin tins and creating consistently sized cookies. I use it the traditional way, too, for scooping ice cream. I typically use a 2-tablespoon stainless-steel scoop, but I have a 1-tablespoon scoop on hand for smaller jobs.

Stainless-steel whisk

My trusty OXO 9-inch stainless-steel whisk is one of my most frequently used kitchen tools. I love using it to create smooth gravies, sauces, and dressings, and for whisking together dry ingredients when I bake.

Nut milk bag

I love creating creamy, homemade nut milks from scratch. A nut milk bag makes it easy to strain homemade nut milk, creating a perfectly silky texture. It's great for making fresh juices, too—simply blend your ingredients, then squeeze them through the nut milk bag into a wide-mouthed container. The recipes in this book call for store-bought nondairy milks for convenience, but you can absolutely make your own at home if you wish, and a nut milk bag will make the process easy peasy.

Fine-mesh stainless-steel sieve

It's handy for draining and rinsing beans and grains, and sifting flour, cocoa powder, or confectioners' sugar. I also use it to strain out the solids for my Immunity Glo Shot (page 263).

Measuring tape or ruler

This may seem a bit odd, but for recipes that require precise measurements (like my Rebellious Battered Broc-Cauli Burgers, page 113), I like to have a measuring tape handy to ensure accurate sizing.

APPLIANCES

Food processor

I have a beloved 14-cup (3.5 L) food processor that I use for making desserts like the Pecan-Oat Crust in my O Canada! Spiced Maple Cream Torte with Warm and Gooey Apple Pie Compote (page 233), energy balls, quickly chopped vegetables, nut butters, sauces, hummus (try my Rustic Roasted Carrot and Dill Hummus, page 179!), pesto, such as my Boom! Broccoli Pesto (page 276), and lentil balls, like my Festive Bread-Free Stuffing Balls (page 105). It is such a time- and effort-saver, and I love that I can throw the parts into the dishwasher.

Mini food processor

While I don't use mini food processors for heavy-duty jobs like hummus or nut butter, I think they're very useful (and quicker to clean than the full-sized version!) for quickly mincing a boatload of garlic, chopping onions (I love to use it for both these tasks when I make my Italian One-Pot Buttery Tomato, White Beans, and Farro, page 96!), or making quick sauces and dressings like 24/7 Avocado-Cilantro Sauce (page 286).

High-speed blender

If you get hooked on green smoothies and luxuriously creamy sauces and soups, then it's worth investing in a high-quality blender. I burned through three inexpensive blenders before finally taking the leap and buying a Vitamix, and I haven't looked back! I use mine to make perfectly smooth and velvety Vegan Cheese Sauce 2.0 (page 290) and Garlic Cashew Cheese Sauce (page 282), among other recipes. It's also great for making my Immunity Glo Shot (page 263) and Solid Gold Pumpkin Pie Spice Coconut Latte (page 264).

Immersion blender

An immersion blender is an inexpensive, handy tool for quickly and easily blending soups (right in the pot!) and making my 5-Ingredient Vegan Butter (page 318).

Handheld mixer

I use an inexpensive handheld mixer most of the time for convenience and easy cleanup (while my stand mixer tends to collect dust).

Ice cream maker

You can also file this one under "not a necessity, but really darn fun to have!" For years and years, I didn't think I would really use an ice cream maker. Then I fell in love with store-bought vegan ice cream, but not the expensive price, and I'm happy to say I've used my Cuisinart 2-quart (2 L) ice cream maker quite often since having kids. My Peppermint Crunch Ice Cream (page 246) is a must-try!

Instant Pot or other multicooker

Cooking beans, steel-cut oats, and other long-cooking ingredients without the stovetop pot-watching has definitely been handy! I pull out my Instant Pot frequently for making The Mama Bear Bowl: Cauli-Power Savory Steel-Cut Oatmeal (page 108) and Instant Pot Potato and Cauliflower Red Thai Curry (with Stovetop Option!) (page 65). If you have another brand of multicooker or pressure cooker, be sure to follow the manufacturer's instructions.

MY PANTRY STAPLES

Ah, my pantry—it's currently looking like a bomb went off inside it, with my kids' costume baskets and coloring supplies taking over. Someday I will get that organized pantry of my dreams, but that day is not today, my friends. As long as I'm stocked with my favorite ingredients, that's what's important and keeps us all fed!

Here are the pantry staples that I use frequently and like to keep on hand for creating new recipes, making favorites, and everyday cooking. These ingredients are all found in recipes in this book. I have shared my favorite brands, where applicable. (Please note that I'm not affiliated with these brands in any way, but readers tend to ask me for specific recommendations, and I love to help as much as I can!) Technically, fresh ingredients aren't considered "pantry" items, but I've included fresh herbs, jalapeños, and lemons/limes here as well, because I tend to always have at least one fresh herb and several lemons or limes on hand (especially during the summer, when my kids ask for my Brainchild Cherry-Lemon Coconut Cream Pops like it's their job—see page 241 for the recipe).

Grains and flours

- Rolled oats and oat flour
- Steel-cut oats
- Almond flour
- Light/white spelt flour
- Quinoa
- Rice: wild rice mix, brown short-grain, jasmine, and white basmati
- Arrowroot starch
- Chickpea flour
- Chickpea pasta (Banza, Maria's)
- Farro, quick-cooking (sometimes labeled "10-minute" or "Italian farro")
- Bread crumbs: panko-style and spelt

Beans and legumes

- Chickpeas
- Black beans
- French green lentils (du Puy)
- Red lentils
- Green or brown lentils
- Kidney beans
- Great northern beans
- Navy beans or cannellini beans

Nuts/seeds

- ○ Chia seeds, whole and ground
- ○ Sunflower seeds (hulled) and sunflower seed butter
- ○ Flaxseed, ground
- ○ Hemp hearts
- ○ Pepitas

  For convenience, I like to keep store-bought roasted pepitas on hand. If you use salted store-bought pepitas, you may need to reduce the salt called for in my recipes. To roast raw pepitas at home, spread them out over a small baking sheet and toss with 1 teaspoon olive oil. Roast at 325°F (160°C) for 10 to 13 minutes, until lightly golden.

- ○ Tahini (I love Soom!)
- ○ Cashews and cashew butter
- ○ Almonds
- ○ Walnuts
- ○ Peanuts and natural peanut butter
- ○ Pecans
- ○ Almond milk

Coconut

- ○ Canned coconut milk, full-fat and light
- ○ Unsweetened shredded coconut
- ○ Unsweetened large flake coconut
- ○ Coconut oil, virgin and refined
- ○ Coconut aminos (soy-free seasoning sauce)

Oils/fats

- ○ Cold-pressed extra-virgin olive oil
- ○ Grapeseed oil
- ○ Vegan butter, soy-free (see page 318 for my 5-Ingredient Vegan Butter)

Sweeteners

- ○ Pure maple syrup
- ○ Medjool dates
- ○ Coconut sugar

- ○ Organic cane sugar
- ○ Organic brown sugar
- ○ Blackstrap molasses
- ○ Brown rice syrup
- ○ Apple honey (I use Bee Free Honee apple-based honey substitute)

Salt

- ○ Fine sea salt
- ○ Herbamare (herbed salt)
- ○ Flaky sea salt

Herbs and spices

- ○ Black peppercorns
- ○ Smoked paprika
- ○ Paprika
- ○ Cayenne pepper
- ○ Chili powder
- ○ Chipotle chile powder (I use Simply Organic)
- ○ Cinnamon
- ○ Cumin
- ○ Dill
- ○ Garlic powder
- ○ Coriander
- ○ Ginger
- ○ Marjoram
- ○ Onion powder
- ○ Onion flakes (dried)
- ○ Oregano
- ○ Red pepper flakes
- ○ Rosemary
- ○ Sage
- ○ Thyme
- ○ Turmeric
- ○ Curry powder (I love Simply Organic)
- ○ Red curry paste (I love Thai Kitchen)
- ○ Pumpkin pie spice (see page 311 for my homemade version!)

- Apple pie spice (see page 308 for my homemade version!)
- Italian seasoning (see page 312 for my homemade version!)

Soy Products

- Tofu
- Low-sodium (lite) gluten-free tamari (I use San-J brand)
- Edamame

Chocolate

- Nondairy chocolate chips (I use Enjoy Life mini chocolate chips)
- Unsweetened natural cocoa powder
- Raw cacao powder
- Cacao nibs

Fresh Herbs

- Basil
- Cilantro
- Dill
- Mint
- Parsley
- Rosemary
- Thyme

Other

- Vegetable broth (store-bought) or vegetable bouillon powder
- Pure vanilla extract, vanilla beans, or vanilla bean powder
- Aluminum-free baking powder
- Vegan Worcestershire sauce (I use The Wizard's)
- Liquid smoke
- Vegan mayonnaise (Vegenaise makes a soy-free version)
- Baking soda

- Jarred roasted red peppers (I use Mediterranean Organic)
- Mustards: Dijon, whole-grain, coarse, old-fashioned
- Capers
- Canned diced tomatoes
- Canned fire-roasted diced tomatoes (I use Muir Glen)
- Tomato paste
- Sun-dried tomatoes (unsalted), oil-packed or rehydrated
- Marinara sauce (I love Victoria White Linen Collection, available at Costco)
- Jarred tomato sauce
- Sriracha (I use Simply Natural)
- Ginger, fresh
- Red chiles
- Garlic, raw (please note all garlic cloves used in this book are peeled unless otherwise instructed)
- Mild jalapeños

  Jalapeños are typically mild, but their heat level varies with age. The older the jalapeño is, the spicier it will be—you can tell if a jalapeño is older because it'll have raised white lines along the skin of the pepper. Younger jalapeños will have smooth skin and will be much milder. Also note that if you leave the inner white membranes in the jalapeños, they'll be spicier; if you remove them, they'll be milder.

Acids

- Apple cider vinegar
- Lemon juice and zest
- Lime juice and zest
- Balsamic vinegar
- Rice vinegar, unseasoned
- Red or white wine vinegar
- Sherry vinegar

HELPFUL RECIPE LISTS

Consider this your cheat sheet when you are looking for the meals, sides, small bites, and sweets in the book that are freezer-friendly, on the glow (great for travel and transporting!), one pot/bowl, kid-friendly, gluten-free, or nut-free! Please note that to keep this section as concise as possible, sauces and pantry staples are not included (please see the recipe itself for this information).

Gluten-Free and Gluten-Free Option

These recipes are gluten-free as written, or if they contain gluten, I'll provide a suggestion for how to make the recipe gluten-free. Be sure to check the labels of your ingredients, too.

GO-TO MAINS

102 • 20-Minute Sweet Potato Noodle Bowl with Sesame, Cilantro, Lime, and Avocado

49 • Bruschetta Veggie Burgers

59 • Cheesy Lentil Bolognese Casserole

67 • Creamy Buffalo Cauli Tacos

87 • Crispy Potato Stacks with Boom! Broccoli Pesto

127 • Dreamy Peanut Butter Crunch Veggie Noodle Bowls

53 • Fast Family Fajitas (*see Make it gluten-free*)

105 • Festive Bread-Free Stuffing Balls

55 • Glow Green 30-Minute Pesto Pasta

61 • Green Powerhouse Roasted Protein Bowl

122 • Humble Creamy Mushrooms and Toast

133 • Instant Marinated Chickpeas on Avocado Toast (*see Make it gluten-free*)

65 • Instant Pot Potato and Cauliflower Red Thai Curry (*with Stovetop Option!*)

72 • Italian Herb Parmesan–Crusted Portobellos with Sneaky Protein-Packed Mashed Potatoes

125 • Kitchen Sink Sheet Pan Buddha Bowl

119 • Mediterranean Smashed Chickpea Salad with Tzatziki Aioli

81 • Mmm! Maple Baked Beans and Greens

47 • Portobello Boats with Rosemary-Lentil Crumble and Balsamic-Apple Glaze

113 • Rebellious Battered Broc-Cauli Burgers with Sriracha Aioli

116 • Savory Herb and Veggie Chickpea Pancakes

78 • School Night Tofu Scramble with Roasted Red Pepper and Walnut Dip

90 • Sloppy Glows (*see Make it gluten-free*)

99 • Speedy 8-Ingredient Pantry Dal

71 • Spicy Potato Nacho Plate

108 • The Mama Bear Bowl: Cauli-Power Savory Steel-Cut Oatmeal

93 • Undercover Roasted Veggie Tomato Pasta

84 • Velvety Alfredo Mushroom-and-Chickpea Pot

75 • Weeknight Tex-Mex Quinoa with Cashew Sour Cream

SATISFYING SIDES AND SMALL BITES

141 • Apple Honey–Sriracha Roasted Rainbow Carrots with Cashew Cream

139 • Balsamic Roasted Root Vegetable Medley with Thyme and Cayenne

153 • Creamy Mushroom, Green Bean, and Wild Rice Casserole

151 • Crispy Brussels Sprouts in Garlic Oil

173 • Crispy Smashed Potatoes, Endless Ways

163 • Flavor Bomb Chimichurri Guacamole

176 • Game Night Crispy Potato Bruschetta

170 • Roasted Garlic Cauliflower Rice

157 • Romesco Roasted Potatoes and Green Beans

179 • Rustic Roasted Carrot and Dill Hummus

167 • Saucy Little Black Bean Skillet

159 • Seasoned Crispy Baked Potato Wedges

145 • Sizzling Maple-Sriracha Garlic Chickpeas

164 • Sneaky Protein-Packed Mashed Potatoes

147 • Ultimate Creamy Salt-and-Vinegar Scalloped Potatoes

One Pot/Bowl

Don't you love when a meal comes together using just one pot or bowl? I sure do. Here they are all together in one handy spot! Can we get a slow clap?

Freezer-Friendly

These recipes store well in the freezer. Be sure to see the recipe's Storage information for instructions on freezing the recipe.

On the Glow

These recipes transport well for work or school lunches, and they are great for travel, too! Be sure to see the recipe's Storage tip for freezing instructions.

122 • Humble Creamy Mushrooms and Toast

133 • Instant Marinated Chickpeas on Avocado Toast

65 • Instant Pot Potato and Cauliflower Red Thai Curry
(with Stovetop Option!)

72 • Italian Herb Parmesan–Crusted Portobellos with
Sneaky Protein-Packed Mashed Potatoes

96 • Italian One-Pot Buttery Tomato, White Beans,
and Farro

125 • Kitchen Sink Sheet Pan Buddha Bowl

119 • Mediterranean Smashed Chickpea Salad with
Tzatziki Aioli

81 • Mmm! Maple Baked Beans and Greens

47 • Portobello Boats with Rosemary-Lentil Crumble
and Balsamic-Apple Glaze

113 • Rebellious Battered Broc-Cauli Burgers with
Sriracha Aioli

116 • Savory Herb and Veggie Chickpea Pancakes

78 • School Night Tofu Scramble with Roasted Red
Pepper and Walnut Dip

90 • Sloppy Glows

131 • Smoky Black Bean and Brown Rice Veggie Burgers

99 • Speedy 8-Ingredient Pantry Dal

71 • Spicy Potato Nacho Plate

108 • The Mama Bear Bowl: Cauli-Power Savory
Steel-Cut Oatmeal

93 • Undercover Roasted Veggie Tomato Pasta

84 • Velvety Alfredo Mushroom-and-Chickpea Pot

75 • Weeknight Tex-Mex Quinoa with Cashew Sour Cream

SATISFYING SIDES AND SMALL BITES

141 • Apple Honey–Sriracha Roasted Rainbow Carrots
with Cashew Cream

139 • Balsamic Roasted Root Vegetable Medley with
Thyme and Cayenne

153 • Creamy Mushroom, Green Bean, and Wild Rice
Casserole

151 • Crispy Brussels Sprouts in Garlic Oil

173 • Crispy Smashed Potatoes, Endless Ways

163 • Flavor Bomb Chimichurri Guacamole

157 • Romesco Roasted Potatoes and Green Beans

179 • Rustic Roasted Carrot and Dill Hummus

167 • Saucy Little Black Bean Skillet

159 • Seasoned Crispy Baked Potato Wedges

164 • Sneaky Protein-Packed Mashed Potatoes

147 • Ultimate Creamy Salt-and-Vinegar Scalloped
Potatoes

MEAL-WORTHY SALADS

203 • Cauliflower "Potato" Salad

187 • Charred Broccoli Quinoa Salad with Apple Honey-
Dijon Dressing

207 • Cilantro-Speckled Green Rice and Avocado Stack

193 • Glow-rious Greek Pasta with Oregano, Basil, and
Lemon Zest Parmesan

204 • Mega Crunch Sun-Dried Tomato–Pepita Taco Salad

191 • Pumpkin Spice and Everything Nice Salad

185 • Summery Chimichurri Chickpea Pasta Salad

197 • Warm Roasted Asparagus and Baby Potato Salad
with French Green Lentils

199 • Zesty Lime and Cayenne Roasted Chickpea and
Sweet Potato Salad

HEARTY SOUPS AND STEWS

213 • Cold-Be-Gone Flavor Bomb Noodle Soup

215 • Cozy Butternut Squash, Sweet Potato, and
Red Lentil Stew

226 • Glowing Spiced Lentil Soup

219 • Green Goddess Gazpacho

223 • Heavenly Chili-Spiced Jalapeño and Garlic
Veggie Stew

229 • Hunky Heartbeet Cabbage Soup

220 • Immune-Boosting Hungarian Mushroom and
Wild Rice Stew

TREATS AND DRINKS

249 • Chewy Double-Chocolate Sunflower Cookies

263 • Immunity Glo Shot

268 • Mint, Ginger, and Lemon Sparkling Sipper

261 • Mint-Ginger Simple Syrup

255 • One-Bowl Vegan Banana Bread

264 • Solid Gold Pumpkin Pie Spice Coconut Latte

267 • Soothing Mint and Ginger Green Tea

235 • Warm and Gooey Apple Pie Compote

Kid-Friendly and Kid-Friendly Option

These recipes were approved by at least 60 percent of children who tried them. If a recipe isn't outright kid-friendly, we occasionally provide a tip on how to make it more kid-friendly.

Nut-Free and Nut-Free Option

These recipes do not contain nuts, or if they do, I have provided an easy tip for how to make the recipe nut-free. As explained in Tips for Cooking in the Oh She Glows Kitchen, I do not classify coconut as a nut product. Always check the ingredients and product labels if you have a nut allergy, and follow your physician's recommendations.

GO-TO MAINS

SATISFYING SIDES AND SMALL BITES

MEAL-WORTHY SALADS

HEARTY SOUPS AND STEWS

TREATS AND DRINKS

ACKNOWLEDGMENTS

There is no doubt that I would not be here living out my passions if it weren't for all the incredible people supporting my journey. Creating recipes, writing, and food photography are so personally rewarding, but the best part of this journey, by far, has been getting to know all the down-to-earth, kind, and encouraging people who've been brought into my life over these past twelve years. I wish you all could truly know how much you've impacted my life.

Being a mother of two has really shown me the huge sacrifices that parents make every single day, to give their best to their kids, juggle careers, and have seemingly no balance for years on end. I'm so grateful for my entire family's support throughout my life. My goal is to show Adriana and Arlo the same support, encouraging them to live out their passions and to do what makes them truly happy in life. To my mom, Lori, and siblings, Kristi, Kerrie, and Chris: I don't think anyone could ask for better OSG cheerleaders! You mean the world to me. A huge thank-you to my husband, Eric: Without your sacrifices and unwavering support, this book would not have been possible. I love you all more than words can say!

A huge thanks and high-fives to my dedicated and passionate group of recipe testers! I truly believe that I have the world's best group of recipe testers, and this cookbook benefited in countless ways thanks to their diligence and keen taste buds. A special thanks to Nicole White, my lead recipe tester, for spearheading our testing group and for pouring countless hours into testing these recipes. Over the past several years of working together, you've become a dear friend, and I truly don't know how I got so lucky to find someone as caring, hilarious, dedicated, and fun to work with as you. I'm also immensely grateful for Eric Liddon, Anna Gunn, Carin Crook (for your incredibly helpful editing and recipe testing!), Tana Gilberstad, Tammy Root, Laurie Ljubojevic, Caroline Dufresne, Danielle Pixley Wilkerson, Vanessa Gilic, Lynn Isted, Audrey Singaraju, Stephanie Downey, Anne Boyd, Kathy Hawkins, Stephanie Scilingo, Andrea Bloomfield, Beth Miller Erman, Katie Hay, Lindsay Mandry, Bridget Rosborough, Laura Beizer, Lindsay Vyvey, Erin Hansuld, Heather Bock, Suzanne Poldon, Adrienne Brown, Stephanie Muto, .Carolina Bertolucci, Kirsten Tomlin, Lori Thayn, Marina Selezeneva, and Kristen Klein for making up my rock-star recipe-testing group. Without a doubt, this book would not have been possible without all your eager help and thoughtful feedback!

To my editors, Lucia Watson and Andrea Magyar, thank you both for your excitement to continue creating cookbooks together. I pinch myself each time you tell me how much you'd love to work on a new book together . . . and I have to say, our cookbooks just keep getting better and better! All of my gratitude and high-fives to the teams from Avery, Penguin Random House, and Penguin Random House Canada for all your work on this book, including Ashley Tucker for the gorgeous design. It really takes a village.

Thank you to my talented glam squad (I've always wanted to say that) during our lifestyle photoshoot: Natasha Steip, my hairstylist, and Erin Winn, my makeup artist.

Sandy Nicholson and team, thank you for coming into our house and photographing the lifestyle photos of our family. Special thanks to Catherine Doherty for prop styling and Claudia Bianchi for food styling during our lifestyle photoshoot day. I'll quote a saying I learned from Sandy recently: Working together was "a stack of fun!"

I hope everyone who welcomes this cookbook into their home has a stack of fun, too—a delicious stack of fun!

INDEX

Note: Page numbers in *italics* indicate photos separate from recipes.

More praise for *Oh She Glows for Dinner*

"Oh my goodness, the recipes and information in this cookbook are exactly what I constantly hear people asking for: weeknight dinner ideas and meal plan/prep guides. The theme couldn't be more perfect for this day and age. Angela has absolutely nailed it . . . again! I literally salivated reading the index: Cheesy Lentil Bolognese Casserole, Dreamy Peanut Butter Crunch Veggie Noodle Bowls, and Ultimate Creamy Salt-and-Vinegar Scalloped Potatoes. Calling it now—this book will become a classic."

—ERIN IRELAND, founder of ItsToDieFor.ca and To Die For Fine Foods

"Years ago, when I began to discover I had some major food intolerances, the first cookbook I picked up was *Oh She Glows*, before I even knew what 'nutritional yeast' was. I loved the simplicity of the *OSG* recipes, which felt easy to follow along with and adapt as needed (like gluten-free!). A cookbook like Angela's helped me feel like my new dietary needs were not restricting but rather opening up new doors to delicious food I could make at home. With this book, I'm excited to have some new ideas, themed nights, and colorful dishes that serve up so much more than just a meal. Well done, Angela, *Oh She Glows* has done it again!"

—SARAH NICOLE LANDRY, creator of TheBirdsPapaya.com

"A few years ago, I was eating fish, poultry, cheese, dairy, and . . . well, you get where I'm coming from. And then it happened: I found Angela from *Oh She Glows* and she has been inspiring me to eat better, eat healthier, and have fun. What I love most about her new cookbook is that it's loaded with fun and FLAVOR. So many recipes are great for families—or, in my case, single people—and my plant-based 'cooking chops' just rose to a whole new level thanks to this beautiful recipe book."

—JANN ARDEN, singer/songwriter, actor, and bestselling author of *Feeding My Mother*